SCOTLAND

Christopher Harvie was born in then-industrial Motherwell in 1944 and was brought up in the Scottish Borders. He returned in 2007 partly to look after his near-centenarian parents. The author of fifteen books about the European, British, and Scottish past and contemporary affairs, he was a founder-historian at the Open University in 1969, and taught at the historic University of Tuebingen from 1980–2007. Associated with Gordon Brown in the frustrated devolution campaign of the 1970s, he served as an SNP member of the Scottish Parliament from 2007–11 and as adviser to Scottish First Minister Alex Salmond. The *Herald* newspaper voted him its 'Free Spirit of Parliament' in 2008, and the German government gave him its *Bundesverdienstkreuz* in 2012. The first edition of *Scotland: A Short History* was followed—and contextualized—by *A Floating Commonwealth* (also published by Oxford University Press, 2008) on Atlantic culture in the steam age, described as 'Harvie's extraordinary evocation of how Britain's nations are set around the inland sea' (*English Historical Review*).

Scotland

A SHORT HISTORY

Christopher Harvie

OXFORD
UNIVERSITY PRESS

OXFORD
UNIVERSITY PRESS

Great Clarendon Street, Oxford OX2 6DP,
United Kingdom

Oxford University Press is a department of the University of Oxford.
It furthers the University's objective of excellence in research, scholarship,
and education by publishing worldwide. Oxford is a registered trade mark of
Oxford University Press in the UK and in certain other countries.

First edition published 2002
This edition published 2014

Published in the United States of America by Oxford University Press
198 Madison Avenue, New York, NY 10016, United States of America

British Library Cataloguing in Publication Data

Data available

Library of Congress Control Number: 2014932548

ISBN 978-0-19-871488-0

Typeset in Minion by RefineCatch Limited, Bungay, Suffolk
Printed in Great Britain by Clays Ltd, St Ives plc

*In memory of my mother Isobel Harvie,
1917–2014, and in gratitude to my father George
and four friends: Paddy Bort, Christine Frasch,
Anne Laurence, and George Rosie.*

ACKNOWLEDGEMENTS

'I wanted to write you a short letter, but I hadn't the time, so I've written you a long letter.' That was Macaulay on the key problem. A history of under 80,000 words, written to be read consecutively, yet providing links with more complex discourses, is a devil to control—not least because its author has to keep himself in order. Particularly in somewhere like Scotland, where insights tend to come in extended lunchtimes and into the small hours, when hypotheses are set up and knocked down, reputations reviewed and buried. Balanced with the contributions of my German students, and others furth of Scotland—and their requirements when faced with Scotland's story—this has I hope, worked. At 57, one is trading on one's memory, published work and fact-files going back four decades, plus the huge bonus of information coming over the internet. The Scottish Parliament has already justified itself, if for no other reason than its transparency: the on-line availability of ministerial statements, press releases, inquiries, MSP's questions, and statistical sources.

But all of this can, unless controlled and discussed, drown rather than illuminate, so I am grateful for the information, criticism—varying from the scholarly to the downright but salutarily rude—of, *inter alia*, in Edinburgh, the much-missed John Brown, Angus Calder, and Bobby Campbell; Paul Addison, Robert Anderson, Paddy Bort, Henry Cowper, Cairns Craig, Owen Dudley Edwards, Michael Fry, Peter Jones of *The Economist*, George Kerevan of *The Scotsman*, Susanna Kerr of the National Portrait Gallery, Iain MacDougall, Douglas MacLeod of the BBC, Tom Nairn, Lindsay Paterson, Nicholas Phillipson, Tessa Ransford, George Rosie, Paul Henderson Scott, Iain Wood, in Glasgow, Richard Finlay, Douglas Gifford, Pat Kane, Isabel Lindsay, John Milne of the BBC, and James Mitchell; in St Andrews, Robert Crawford, Douglas Dunn, Rab Houston, Bill Knox, Bruce Lenman, Chris Smout, Iain Donnachie; in Aberdeen, Terry Brotherstone and Tom Devine; in Stirling, Iain Hutchison and Rory

Watson; in the Borders, the late Victor Kiernan, Allan Massie, Michael Russell MSP, David Steel MSP, and Judy Steel.

In Oxford, Geoffrey Best, Iain McLean, the late Colin Matthew, Kenneth O. Morgan, the late Raphael Samuel, and my editors at OUP, Shelley Cox, Catherine Humphries, Emma Simmons, and Mary Worthington; in Lancaster, Sandy Grant, John Mackenzie, and Jeff Richards. In Wales, Neil Evans, Ieuan Gwynedd Jones, Geraint Jenkins, Peter Lord, and Dai Smith. In London Ian Jack, Andrew O'Hagan, Chris Fyfe, Donald Munro, David Daniell, my agent Tony Peake, Alex Salmond, and Boyd Tonkin, David Walker of the *Guardian*. In Ireland, Gearoid ó Tuathaig, Joe Lee, Edna and Michael Longley. In Germany, Ruth Drost-Hüttl, the late Carola Ehrlich, Hans-Gustav Klaus, Roland Sturm, Wolfgang Sigloch. In France, Christian Civardi and the late Francois Bédarida. In Italy, Gioia Angeletti, and in Russia, Boris Proskurnin, in Taiwan, Ia-Fei Hsui; in the USA, Tony Judt, Martyn Thompson, G. Ross, Roy and Patrick Scott.

Dauvit Broun, Anne Laurence, and Roger Mason read over early drafts of Chapters 1–3, and my wife Virginia read through the lot at various stages, curbing a harvest of stylistic eccentricities. My debt to my parents, in the sixtieth year of their marriage, is marked by dedication. My aunt Jessie, my brother Stephen and sister Jane George helped sustain a peripatetic scholar, while Alison's cheery inquisitiveness—'Why, daddy, why?'—has kept us going from Maisie books to the hefty tomes on devolution in her Newcastle politics course. The usual disclaimer applies. None of these friends are in any way responsible for any mistakes, howlers, insults, etc., in what follows.

CONTENTS

LIST OF KEY PLACES

LIST OF ILLUSTRATIONS

LIST OF MAPS

INTRODUCTION

The first edition of this book came out in 2002. Its author was a professor in Germany which had, within thirteen years, incorporated nearly 17 million people from the communist German Democratic Republic. The expectation was that something similarly federative would happen in the UK. Yet in 2013 Scottish politics—fourteen years after self-government—revolved around the possible secession of Scotland from the Union, in a world where, so far from history 'ending' with the events of 1989–91, it seemed loose in the streets. Terrorists tried to blow up Glasgow Airport in July 2007; local youngsters were killed and wounded in Afghanistan and Iraq; a Scottish ministerial decision to release Abdelbaset Al-Megrahi caused an international furore. On 18 September 2014 the country could vote for independence. In autumn 2013 this looked unlikely, but would matters hold that stable for a year?

So there was a need for a book which could fit into a rucksack and be read in trains and planes, by the thousands of students, teachers, journalists, politicians, tourists, and business people who travelled to Scotland each year and might want to understand in short order the country and its way of life. Yes, there were histories, some of them huge, some excellent, and some both, but 'guid gear in sma' buik' was hard to find. The challenge was to provide a clear account, and to tackle attitudes filtered through stereotypes—romanticism, kilts-and-whisky, football—and (not least) fascination with a complex and astonishingly varied landscape which begs to be photographed.

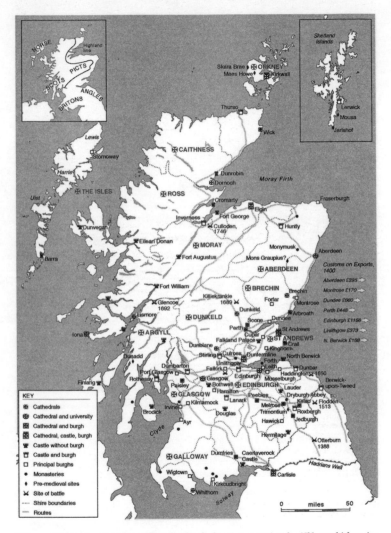

Map 1. *Medieval and early modern Scotland, showing counties/sheriffdoms, bishoprics, medieval burghs, important castles, the highland line*

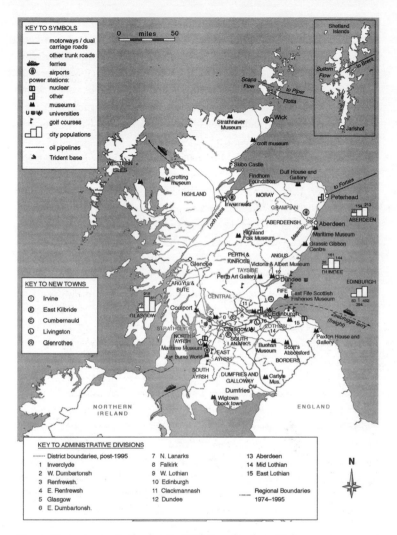

Map 2. *Contemporary Scotland, main North Sea oil and gas pipelines, motorways and power stations, local authorities, changes in urban population*

Prima facie, this required four things. To provide a narrative which, though correcting romantic-touristic assumptions and using recent research, wasn't dull; to present social, economic, intellectual, and political perspectives, enriching the 'story' without overwhelming it with names, dates, and statistics; to emphasize Scotland's changing links with Britain, Europe, and the world and, finally, to suggest the crucial turning points, the arguments over them, and where further information—visual, literary, geographic—could be obtained.

This begged questions about narrative, identity, and the slippery nature of 'hard fact', not least because the past was distorted by today's tourist 'Scottishness', with its string of the arbitrary and obvious: bagpipes, whisky, the Loch Ness Monster, and so on. To nail the critical facts, and account for the fiction—and the differing stresses that passing generations have put on both—meant that enthusing the reader went along with puncturing many Scots conceits. Not just the ethnic heroics of *Braveheart*, but often those dour dishtowels with screeds of inventors and explorers, not always as important as the Scots would like to think—penicillin owed as much to Florey and Chain as to Fleming, Logie Baird's mechanically based television was a dead duck.

———

This history was, and wasn't, about a small country. The boundaries of its, and its historians', concerns have been flexible, even protean. The number and influence of the latter—from George Buchanan via David Hume and Thomas Carlyle to Angus Calder—made for complex relationships. Understanding Scots history meant setting it in context, so that it often became more an instrument than a subject, a theme which led into, and then often was dwarfed by, a larger-than-national career, whether in Britain or in Europe: Robertson on Charles V, Carlyle on the French Revolution or Frederick the Great. This dual focus was enhanced when one held one's own breath and plunged into the *longue durée* of the country's history since human settlement began, and an endless range of questions.

Why was the place repeatedly so influential? The Romans recognized its unconquerability, an enigmatic refuge where the 'uncivilized' might also be more 'cultivated'. Was this quality borne out by the Scoti—a territorial-religious designation for that amalgam of Scots-Irish abbot-chieftains, tough travellers, scholar-missionaries, who conserved Christian learning and restored Greek, besides crafting an art in illustration and jewellery of rare complexity? Has their contribution any continuity with the contribution of the schoolmen of Scotland, Rome's 'special daughter', to the twelfth- and thirteenth-century European universities? How much did the heroes, historians, and poets of the independence struggle contribute to Europe's 'ballads of the nations'? And how did they relate to the fighting men the country exported, to France and furth of (beyond) there to Germany, Sweden, and Russia? Did they, more than the 'black Genevan ministers', the Reformers with their proto-republican 'federal Calvinism', build up a commercial civil society?

With John Knox and steamships more than half in mind, Karl Marx formulated 'scientific materialism'—paring away the superstructures of nation, religion, and culture to expose the bones and membranes of economic transactions. Max Weber advanced against him the counter-model of an 'ascetic capitalism' founded on religious doctrine. Yet such explorations were internalized by Europe seemingly without enquiry into their origins in a nation which had become subsumed into a mighty empire. The seventeenth century which started with Napier's logarithms would end with them being incorporated into the 'Newtonian revolution', just as Scotland was incorporated into the United Kingdom. The Enlightenment with its contributions to technology, sociology, and the scientific method was grossed up into a 'British' experience, not least by those who advanced its ideas into the confrontations of capitalism and 'scientific materialism'. What was lost in this?

In what frame had and has Scottish history to be studied? Earlier, I would have traced the 'relevant' past no further than the Reformation. Then, in trying to survey the medieval centuries, I became absorbed by the continuous and expanding influence of historical discourse and methodology, how it related to scientific advance, ecology, anthropology, sociology, and the comparative method. Scotland's lasting achievements moulded the intellect of the world, through the sociology of Adam Ferguson and the economics of Adam Smith, energy theory from Joseph Black and James

Watt to Lord Kelvin and Clerk Maxwell, and the social anthropology of Robertson Smith, J. G. Frazer, and Patrick Geddes. Not least because they were broadcast by the country's 'print-capitalism' of poetry, novels, journals, encyclopaedias. All of this was energized by a complex mental and cultural hinterland stretching back beyond written history. Hugh MacDiarmid, the driving force of the twentieth-century Scots intellect, put this brilliantly in one of his shortest lyrics:

> In the how-dum-deid o' the cauld hairst night
> > The warld, like an eemis stane,
> Wags i' the lift, an' my eerie memories fall
> > Like a yowdendrift
> Like a yowdendrift, so's I couldnae see
> > The words cut oot o' the stane
> Had history's hazelraw no yirdit them.

(In the cold silence of a harvest night I the world seems like a rocking stone I swinging in the sky, and my puzzled memories fall I on it like a huge snowdrift I so that I can't see what words are cut on the stone I because they're buried under the lichen that history has left.)

This poem has to be translated—so it's there for Scots in particular to decode—but what it says is universal. The rocking stone is eternal, but it's also been subject to human action: it could be engraved, obscured, overthrown, cast down. Clearing 'history's hazelraw' is where our younger medieval and environmental historians are at, and I owe a special debt to them.

I have attempted a chronologically based narrative of seven chapters, three of which deal with the early to eighteenth-century period, two with the industrial-imperial phase, and one with the twentieth century. I have cross-cut this with treatments of landscape and townscape, the artefacts preserved in museums, churches, and cottages and mansions, the country's literature and, in particular (because—see above—succinct and accessible), its poetry. My illustrations have tried to feature the range of visual evidence available, from archaeological sites to pamphlets, banknotes, and portraits. The best method of 'binding-in' the socio-economic dimension was to feature a number of communities which are either 'key' places in Scots history, or typical of a particular age/activity. Hence in the first chapter Skara Brae, Trimontium, and Iona provide ways into the Stone Age, Roman Scotland, and the early Christian period, while in the nineteenth-century chapter Glasgow highlights the importance of heavy industry and engineering, and Dundee stresses the imperial and capital-export dimension.

A 'short history' is by definition a dwarf. The debts of this particular dwarf to those on whose shoulders he's climbed will be found in the bibliographical essay. But from his vantage point he might have seen a few new views, and familiar things from a new angle. Or so I hope.

Tübingen/Aberystwyth/Melrose
December 2011/April 2014

1 | FROM FIREBALL TO THE UNIFIED KINGDOM, 10,000 BC–AD 1100

That is The Land out there, under the sleet, churned and pelted there in the dark, the long rigs upturning their clayey faces to the spear-onset of the sleet. That is The Land, a dim vision this night of laggard fences and long stretching rigs. And the voice of it—the true and unforgettable voice—the immemorial plaint of the peewit, flying lost.

(Lewis Grassic Gibbon, 1934)

THE LAND OUT THERE . . .

Confronted with the country's remote past, and those ranks of the *Proceedings of the Scottish Society of Antiquaries* which march into it, with their record of digs and finds and comparative studies, a twentieth-century historian has to be apprehensive. What is he doing *back there*? Yet most Scottish secondary schoolchildren know the standing stones which in Lewis Grassic Gibbon's *Scots Quair* (1932–4) mark the coming of the first farmers, and the end of the hunter-gatherers of the Golden Age. Gibbon's contemporaries in the 'Scottish Renaissance' invoked such symbols as a means of cutting through 'history's hazelraw' and religious dogma to a scientific comprehension of man and environment. Behind Gibbon were the likes of Darwin and Huxley, and Scots 'evolutionists' such as the anthropologist J. G. Frazer and the sociologist Patrick Geddes. *The Antiquary*, the title of the most contemporary of Walter Scott's *Waverley Novels*, which he wrote in 1816, came to mean something like a time-traveller in the Wellsian, science-fiction sense.

A materialist like MacDiarmid in 'On a Raised Beach' could make the land and its geology into a sort of anti-religious metaphysic:

> Do not argue with me. Argue with these stones.
> Truth has no trouble in knowing itself.
> This is it. The hard fact. The unoppugnable reality.
> Here is something for you to digest.
> Eat this and we'll see what appetite you have left
> For a world hereafter.
> I pledge you in the first and last crusta,
> The rocks rattling in the bead-proof seas.

The Scots watched the land they inhabited age enormously in the two centuries after Archbishop Ussher of Armagh dated creation to 4004 BC in 1651: something which was of economic as well as intellectual importance. Geologists identified the north-western mountains—among them Suilven, Canisp, Kintail—whose eerie shapes fascinate the tourist, as some of the world's oldest rocks, and called the oldest period of orogenesis—mountain-formation—the Caledonian. Its pre-Cambrian schists and quartzes, with outcrops of lavas and granites, were 2,500 million years old, Lewisian gneiss 500 million years older yet.

Scotland's history has always been a subject of controversy, even when dealing with the million-year calibrations of geology. The science itself was founded by the Edinburgh professor James Hutton in his *Theory of the Earth* (1785) where he proposed the 'Vulcanist' model of earth's origins as a fireball, against the 'Neptunism' of the German Abraham Werner, who held that all rocks were deposited from water. Not only did Scotland's complex geology bear Hutton out—of its great diagonal bands of strata, from south-west to north-east, some were volcanic, some sedimentary but all of immense age before being shaped by the glaciers of the ice age—but the land and its fossils provided, in Robert Chambers's *Vestiges of the Natural History of Creation* (1844), the first major statement of the evolutionary hypothesis.

We are currently going through a similar upheaval in studying the earliest history of man in the British Isles, through archaeological finds and the impact of new techniques. Human presence in what was then the rocky western rim of a plain stretching to what's now Denmark, once thought to date from the retreat of the ice cap, around 10,000 BC, is now being pushed back as far as 30,000 BC: analysis of remains in Leicestershire proved to be of hunters roaming the edge of glaciers somewhere around a line from Liverpool to Hull. There were centuries of warmth, and then the return of the ice. Recently, too, the investigation of DNA has suggested that most Europeans owe their genetic heredity to a tribe which migrated westwards from Central Asia through North Africa and into Spain, with a smaller later migration from the eastern Mediterranean. The latter seems to have coincided with the piling-up of alluvial deposits around the firths of Cromarty, Forth, and Tay, and the rise (of about 8 metres) in the sea level which came with the melting of the ice cap.

About a fifth of Scotland's 48,000 square kilometres (England: 93,000, Wales: 13,000) is under 60 metres above sea level; with islands and sea lochs its coastline is over 4,000 kilometres long, about the same as that of England and Wales, and about five times longer than that of Germany. Its east Atlantic position meant and means very heavy rainfall—about 700 cm per annum in the east, over 1,000 cm in the west—encouraging the spread of blanket peat bog, whose acidity, together with unremitting wind and salt-spray, rendered most of its islands treeless. Archaeologists have argued that a long, sheltered coastline was also particularly conducive to early human settlement, providing communications routes, driftwood for heat, and a reliable supply of food. In the Scottish case it was also a barrier to rapid and permanent invasion. Natural bottlenecks—the quicksands and marshes of the Solway, the point where the Lammermuirs shoulder their way into the North Sea, the marshes and meanders of the upper Forth—divided the land and gave an advantage to its defenders.

Who were they? The drafters of the Declaration of Arbroath (1320) had no doubts: 'This nation having come from Scythia the greater, through the Tuscan Sea and the Hercules Pillars, and having for many ages taken its residence in Spain in the midst of a most fierce people, and can never be brought into subjection by any people, how barbarous soever.' The notion of a travelled people contrasted with the English 'Brut' myth of a settled race, and there may be something behind it that correlates with the physical records. Records of the land mass date from the voyages of Pytheas of Marseilles around 300 BC, who circumnavigated the island. Silence fell until the Roman invaders came in AD 80–3. They made conjectures about its past which appeared in Tacitus' *Agricola* (AD 98), and (more reliably) about its physical shape. In Ptolemy of Alexandria's geography (*c.* AD 150 but drawing on earlier maps), it appears recognizable, but canted to the east. Such accounts were, initially, all scholars had to go on, to unravel the earliest years. Victorian Scotland's advances in geology and natural history helped, while as systematic research grew, the way that people organized their lives could be recovered from hard sandstones which, when worked or carved, endured, and peat and salt which preserved wood, leather, and bone. The 1850s, in particular, was a remarkable decade, with Daniel Wilson's *Archaeology and Pre-Historic Annals* of 1851, the uncovering of Skara Brae and Callanish, and in 1856–7 James Stuart's *The Sculptured Stones of Scotland* and the first edition of F. J. Child's *The Ancient Ballads of England and Scotland*.

The absence of a widespread, obscuring forest presented invaders with a partly man-made landscape which intrigued, but could also be despoiled. The result was enigmatic. Excavations subjected to such techniques as pollen analysis, dendrochronology (tree-ring dating), thermo-luminescence, and in particular after 1945 Willard Libby's radiocarbon-dating (drawing on nuclear research) and Crick and Watson's detection of DNA, have revolutionized our knowledge of the early inhabitants, replacing guesstimates which were often out by a couple of millennia. The exchange of information on contemporary developments from other parts of Europe and the projection back of discoveries from later periods will inevitably yield further information. Although Professor Geoffrey Barrow warned in 1962 that plotting early-medieval settlement patterns was like 'palaeontologists trying to reconstruct the whole body of an extinct form of life from a chance survival of imperfect fossils', things had progressed since the days before 1850, when the Scottish Society of Antiquaries labelled all non-Roman remains in its museum as 'Danish'! But it was from this period, particularly with the diversion of government funds from industrial subsidy to arts and culture, in the shape of the Scottish Museum, that the history of the remote past in Scotland was opened up. Still, the constant expansion of new knowledge creates new problems, since it subverts interpretations based on earlier, apparently reliable, written sources. Did St Ninian precede St Columba as a missionary? Was Pictish a Celtic language? Did Kenneth mac Alpin really unite Scotland? We know more about early Scotland than the Victorians did, but these 'landmarks'—often generalizations by later commentators with their own agenda—now seem far more indistinct.

HUNTER TO FARMER

The early settlement story came via two very recent episodes: the 1991 discovery of 'Oetzi', the Oetztal mummy from 3300 BC, and the post-1959 industrialization of the North Sea. Oetzi showed that prehistoric man, even in the Alps, was anything but primitive. Surveys and oil-drill cores revealed that the 'Britain' which emerged from the ice had been the westward rim of a low plain and a shallow sea. 'Doggerland', once plotted, had a topography like present-day Denmark: alluvial, fertile, and accessible by long sea inlets and rivers. Its existence ended around 6000 BC, in minutes. A huge undersea landslip in the trench between it and Norway released an eight-metre tsunami which swept over it, drowning most of its people. Those who escaped went west. Land—marshy and overgrown—could separate rather than join; water connected. But the evidence of boats made of wood and skin vanished so there was, so far, no nautical Oetzi. But the complex *kultstatte* at Ness of Brodgar, Orkney (3000 BC), excavated after 2003, suggested that Neolithic Britain progressed from north to south, and by sea.

This cut across the 'stadial' sequence of historical evolution that the Enlightenment—Adams Ferguson and Smith—had determined, derived from classical models. The actuality to be uncovered was more complex: hunter-gatherers who could live communally, governed by distinct, local rituals; the importance of burial and pilgrimage. This happened in a population which increased with the growth of agriculture, and around 3500 BC the keeping of cattle, sheep, pigs, and goats began, along with weaving of cloth and making of pottery; later on came the growing, drying by fire, and milling in querns of grain. The population density rose, perhaps, to about ten per 100 square kilometres in the habitable areas (only about a quarter of the whole) giving a total which may have fluctuated around 150,000 for centuries. A great timber longhouse, the centre of a well-established mixed farming community, was excavated in the early 1990s at Balbridie near Banchory and dated to 3800–3600 BC, and at the Knapp of Howar in Orkney the country's oldest known stone houses date back to 3500–3100 BC.

By then, more extensive settlement systems were developing. Originally marked by great religious sites—collectively built passage graves like Maes Howe in Orkney, c.2700 BC, and stone circles at Brodgar in Orkney and Callanish (c.2000 BC) in Lewis—these were highly sophisticated and labour-intensive in construction, and combined cultic functions with recording seasonal change. Barry Cunliffe, tracing similar techniques down the Atlantic's eastern shore, has argued that these were the monuments of territorial elites within a complex network, combining farming, fisheries, and trade by sea. Were the stone circles neolithic computers—as Alexander Thom argued—which enabled an accurate calendar to be maintained? This hypothesis remains to be proved, but such an advanced society seems to have used comparatively flimsy vessels of the curragh type, which required sophisticated navigational skills and deployment. Calculations would be vital in working out when storms might be expected and when fish would shoal.

SKARA BRAE

On Orkney, one of the oldest habitations long pre-dates any notion of 'Scotland'—to which Orkney only belonged after 1472. The warren-like settlements of Skara Brae, north-west of Stromness, date from around 3100 BC. They were buried for over 4,000 years under sand dunes, and only reappeared, as the result of a storm, in 1858. The absence of timber other than driftwood resulted in an ingenious use of stone to achieve almost the effect of a 'fitted kitchen' with sinks, cupboards, and (what still seems an innovation) a tank for live seafood. Built with stone slabs imported from Caithness, the

1. *Skara Brae, near Stromness, Orkney. The dwellings uncovered by a storm in 1858 formed one of the best-preserved prehistoric sites of the Scots Stone Age, not least because absence of wood made stone necessary for interior fittings. The result lasted for two millennia.*

remains also testify to a fairly sophisticated technology. The chambered dwellings then inland, surrounded by middens, show that the Skara Brae folk fished at sea, mainly ate shellfish, and probably roofed their houses with driftwood, whalebones, skins, and turf. Enough of the middens' content survives to give an idea of economy and society. The Skara Brae folk were close-knit, conservative, conformist—their doors could be barred from within. They had cattle and pigs, hunted deer, grew wheat and barley, made tools from bones and rope from heather. Things would not become much more sophisticated in the following millennia. Stone houses were exceptional in medieval Scottish towns, as were indoor toilets. But examination of skeletons has suggested a very short lifespan: no one was more than 30 years old.

In 1851, the archaeological pioneer Daniel Wilson was hypothesizing patterns of collaboration rather than culture clash: 'evidence not of a single breed but of one remarkable phase of the human mind!' But between about 2000 and 1500 BC stone was giving way to copper and tin (fused into bronze) and an enduring debate—did artefacts and techniques migrate, or people? The 'beaker people', described thus because of a type of ritual vase which accompanied them and was found containing cremated remains, were (by comparing bronze and pottery finds, mainly in eastern Scotland, with continental sites) thought to have come from Spain via the Low Countries, or via Ireland. Yet, because there was no overthrow of the existing order, but a coexistence with it, later theories have pointed to trade and cultural change, as well as limited migration. Despite further advances in technology, notably swords and daggers, bows and arrows, and jewellery in gold and jet, climate change seems to have put Bronze Age society under threat. Cooler and damper weather conditions meant a spread of peat, especially after 1400 BC, and a greater competition for cultivable land. There seems to have been an overpopulation crisis about 1000 BC. Struggles over land were settled by improved swords, metal shields, and the use of horses. Did this society between 1000 BC and about 300 BC incorporate further invaders, and reuse earlier sites? It is difficult to say, as the late Bronze Age seems to have been militarist, conservative, and lacking in innovatory building, at least of

...es. With the making of iron comes the debate about the
...riod language, religious ritual, and social organization
...how affinities with the tribes whose salt mines at Hallstatt
...) and hoards at La Tène (500 BC) in present-day Austria and
...d show evidence of the cultures which the Romans overcame in
the... ...orthward progress in the last century before Christ. Was this the
result of invasion, as was once thought, or—as in the explanation advanced
by Colin Renfrew—the continuing the spread of cultures along trade
routes, together with a limited degree of migration in response to war or
climate change?

Society had now become smaller-scale, family-farm-based, and
expressed a tribal (and probably hierarchical) identity, particularly between
100 BC and AD 400, through defensive fortresses—either stone and timber
enclosures or, in the north, hollow-walled brochs or towers. Lochs, and
Scotland has 30,000 of them, had defensive lake dwellings called crannogs,
founded on timber piles. (Estimates of the timber consumed by such
buildings—24 hectares for a smallish fort at Abernethy—may also help
explain the retreat of the forests). At the close of this epoch, by comparing
Roman documentation, such as that of Tacitus or Ptolemy, with archaeological evidence, we get the first sight of the tribes that would become the
Romans' enemies, allies, and tributary states in the north.

The tangible history of the north was by the invasion year of AD 43 rich
in tumuli (burial mounds), stone circles, 'souterrains' (underground grain
stores), and vitrified forts (ramparts whose rocks were fused by burning
timbers). These impressed both natives and invaders, and, given only slight
advance in material living standards, provoked for years comparisons with
'earlier ages', which did not seem at all remote. Tacitus recorded the Picts
using chariots at Mons Graupius in AD 81; the appearance of a coach in
Inverness in 1725 was greeted 'with the astonishment that would have
greeted an elephant'. The empty native *oppidum* on the Northern Eildon,
above the later Roman camp of Trimontium, had between 300 and 500
house platforms; Edinburgh had only 400 houses in 1400. Where else in
Europe do the traces of pre-classical life leave so much to be puzzled over by
antiquarians, anthropologists, historians, and psychologists? And where
else has the response to antiquity been so *alive*—whether this was Tacitus

on the Caledonii, the highlander-like 'ancient Greeks' who figure in Adam Ferguson's *History of Civil Society* (1767) or the neolithic farmers who spoke directly to the Mearns crofters in Grassic Gibbon's *Sunset Song* (1932)?

CALEDONIA

North-western, Celtic Europe was after 100 BC menaced by a Rome changing from urban republic to military empire. Julius Caesar pressed ruthlessly north through France, inflicting huge native casualties, and in 55–54 BC launched a punitive raid on Britain. In AD 43 the Romans replaced informal agreements with native south British rulers—notably Cunobelinus, king of the Catevellauni, Shakespeare's *Cymbeline*—with invasion under Claudius. Scots tribes were not targeted, though Claudius appears to have opened up negotiations with a king of Orkney. The securing of the island was not simple or complete. Twenty years after the suppression of the dangerous revolt of Boudicca in south-east England in AD 61, Roman forces under Gnaeus Julius Agricola penetrated into Scotland in a series of campaigns, built a head-quarters camp at Inchtuthill near Perth, and at Mons Graupius, probably on the edge of the Mounth, the eastern Cairngorms, met and devastatingly defeated an army of the Caledonii—according to Tacitus (Agricola's son-in-law) 10,000 of them died, against 360 Romans. Tacitus also recorded the Caledonian leader as Calgacus, 'the swordsman', the first name-bearing Scot known to history. Agricola circumnavigated the island, was ordered to Rome, and celebrated his triumph. The Inchtuthill camp was deserted by AD 86.

The Roman province of Britannia reached as far as Hadrian's Wall. A good economic proposition from the second to the fourth centuries, more stable than Gaul, it sustained a society of large estates and lavish villas and in the 'military zone' on its northern and western margins, productive lead, silver, and gold mines. It was worth having a major fortress at remote Segontium (Carnarfon) to supervise the mines and their slaves. Caledonia was much more problematic. Successive emperors found it easy to invade—usually in search of a definite frontier—but difficult to rule. Roman interest in Scotland wasn't colonial but defensive. Despite Rudyard Kipling's picture of the strong silent Romano-British keeping the Wall against the squabbling Picts to the north—

We gather behind them in hordes,
And plot to reconquer the Wall
With only our tongues for our swords.
We are the Little Folk—we!
Too little to love or to hate.
Leave us alone and you'll see
How we can drag down the State!

—the solid prosperity of Britannia was never securely extended north of the Humber, where the Cumbrian mountains and Pennine chain harboured disruptive local tribes. Walls, camps, and roads served more as fire breaks and observation posts than as barriers. Romanization got thinner, too: the frontier troops and their auxiliaries were often from the Mediterranean lands. Few 'went native' and the bleak Pennine country was effectively under a type of military rule. Protection was given to miners and local client Britons; peace was punctuated by regular punitive expeditions, but troops were always likely to be withdrawn when another imperial frontier came under attack.

In 121 Emperor Hadrian (117–38) halted his predecessor Trajan's policy of eastward expansion, and instead consolidated, not least in northern Britannia, where he built a wall between Tyne and Solway. This served to keep an eye on the Votadini of the eastern Lowlands and the tribes of the Selgovae to the west. These were usually loyal, but suffered raids from the less well disposed, making counter-attacks necessary, so Emperor Antonius Pius (138–61) had his commander in Britain Lollius Urbicus build in 142–3 a further wall, 7 metres high, with a 13-metre ditch facing north and forts every 4 kilometres, between Forth and Clyde, backed up by a northern extension of Ermine Street, called Dere Street (the modern A68) from Eboracum (York) to a port at Cramond, west of Edinburgh.

TRIMONTIUM

Eighty kilometres north of Hadrian's Wall Roman legionaries encountered the Eildon Hills, three-peaked, formerly volcanic, their 400-metre summits visible from transports off the mouth of the Tweed. This visibility—the Eildons had a signal station where the native oppidum had been—led to the

Ninth Legion building a camp in AD 80. It was strengthened in 86 and a vicus or native settlement grew up near it—stables, fast food joints, smiths, brothels, and locals (Votadini to the east, Selgovae to the west) coming to pay tribute or demand protection money. The Romans stayed only until 105. Trimontium was abandoned, raids into Scotland largely being carried out by sea. But between 120 and 140, just before the Antonine Wall was built, it was put back into commission as the hub of Roman Caledonia, with a road running west and water communication downstream to Berwick. A massive three-ditch rampart was constructed, topped by a two-metre-thick wall of red sandstone, probably brought by boat from Dryburgh. Inside were seventeen long barracks, space for 1,500 men, stables, granaries, and officers' quarters: for entertainment an amphitheatre, the most northerly in the empire. Perhaps it was this sense of being on the edge of their known world which made soldiers dig pits within the camp and bury treasured possessions—a helmet or a ring, or a piece of horse armour—as thank offerings or tokens of faith. In 185, following a native revolt and its defeat, the legions moved out. Though the ruins were probably occupied by further punitive expeditions, Trimontium slumbered until it was disturbed by the navvies of the Edinburgh and Hawick Railway in 1847, and partially excavated by a solicitor from nearby Melrose, James Curle, in 1905–10.

What sort of country would the Romans have seen? It was—when plotted roughly by Ptolemy—probably for the most part deforested: timber had been cut for construction, heating, and metalworking, accelerating the build-up of peat. For cultivable land, or tolerable grazing, only about a quarter was feasible: in the Lowlands what is now the Merse, north of the River Tweed, East Lothian, and the Dumfries and Ayrshire plains. Some of this was farmed for the Britannic market; there was even some colonization by Belgic tribes in the south-west. Apart from Strathmore and Buchan, the rest—and most of the central belt—was moorland, scrub, and marsh. Extrapolating from population density and habitable area, Caledonia might have sustained 200,000 people although the population of Britannia (perhaps four million?) was reckoned at twice its Domesday level. Yet its forts, graves, and megaliths must have impressed scouts and explorers with the 'otherness' of the place. When Tacitus reported the speech of Calgacus he gave him the repertoire of noble savagery, and something more:

Here at the end of the world, the last refuge of freedom, we have lived unmolested to this day, and that fame has kept us secure; for everything unknown is magnified. But now the furthermost parts of Britain are laid bare, there are no other people left, nothing but waves and rocks, and these more deadly Romans . . . raptors of the world, who, now that they have devastated all the earth, turn their attention even to the sea . . . Plunder, massacre, rape, they call these things empire: they make a desert and call it peace.

Antonius Pius, the wall-builder, came towards the end of a century of capable emperors maintaining Rome's economic foundations, a money economy running a system of long-distance trade. As this began to stumble, trouble broke out in Gaul and Britannia. Rome's other foundation, militarism, beckoned. In 208–11 the tough general Septimus Severus, blooded in Gaul, and his sadistic son Caracalla, again undertook the complete conquest of the island. Was this the age-old militarist strategy of provoking the sort of violence which made them indispensable? Such consequences would certainly plague Rome for several decades. But their offensive was neither sustained—Severus bought off the Caledonii and then died, Caracalla made for Rome—nor resumed. Indeed, with a colder climate phase setting in (it was to last for eight centuries) the minerally unproductive far north seemed even less inviting to the comfortable, increasingly rural-based society of the Romano-British. Perhaps in reaction to this and other conflicts between the Romans, their *Foederati* or allies, and 'barbarians' of one sort or another, the later Celtic bards would date great oral epics—Ireland's *Táin* and some of what would become *Ossian*—to this period.

THE HEROIC AGE

In 1298, having defeated William Wallace at Falkirk, Edward I of England celebrated with his commanders by hosting a Round Table. He saw himself as the successor to Arthur, king of Britain, and Falkirk was rich in helpful symbols. A local village was called Camelon, perhaps after Arthur's Camelot, and close to it stood a circular Roman temple which, until its demolition in the eighteenth century, was known as Arthur's Oo'n, or Oven. Arthur may have been a Romano-British warlord pitted against the Saxon invaders in the fifth century, around whom there accumulated the achievements of others. Certainly no more mythic than the average local saint incorporated into Catholic tradition, he raises the recurrent question: what matters more, explaining hard fact—what mattered at a particular time—or establishing what people believed had happened? In the Scottish case this involved explaining why the Arthur story—the British leader facing the new invaders—had emerged in two opposed accounts by Wallace's day. Edward's Arthur was powered by Anglo-French chivalry, the Scots' version by the evolution of their nation from a bundle of peoples who seemed, in their diversity and competitiveness, a miniature of 'the matter of Britain'.

Both led back to the final years of Britannia. Romano-British society had ridden out the upheavals which in the fourth century plunged Gaul into chaos and anti-emperors. But Britannia's rapid 'official' Christianization under Constantine, 314–24, didn't combat a general deterioration in imperial government in the west. A major Picto-British rising against Roman rule in AD 367–9, the 'Barbarian Conspiracy', was followed by increasingly frequent military putsches led by powerful frontier commanders. Old and new 'barbarians'—Scots ('pirates') from Ireland and Saxon settlers—fitted into such a frame, and were used by as well as against increasingly 'barbarized' Romans. In 367 Count Theodosius, sent from Rome, grafted loyal northern tribes onto the payroll, and stabilized the situation. In 388 his grandson Theodosius the Great tackled a Carnarfon-based commander, Magnus Maximus (a Spaniard: but the Welsh call him Macsen Wledig) who married into the *Foederati*, beat the Scots, invaded Gaul, and became emperor at Trier. Theodosius killed him in battle at Aquileia in August 388 and took the purple, but not before Magnus had permanently withdrawn the legions from Wales. A further revolt faced Theodosius' lieutenant, the Vandal-turned-Roman Flavius Stilicho, in 396–8, but the emperor's successors were now cutting their losses and regrouping in the Eastern Empire. Caught in the decrepit and unpredictable imperial network, the Romano-British fruitlessly pressed Emperor Honorius for assistance in 410, but then accepted the recall of the legions with some confidence that they could manage on their own. They did not realize how swiftly this departure would dissolve the bureaucracy, camps, armies, currency, and communications which kept Britannia together.

Britannia would not decline gently, not in an age of folk movements. It was fat booty for tribesmen evicted from their Baltic villages by poor weather and rising sea levels. Caledonia was not; so while it experienced migrations, there was no invasion on a southern scale. Welsh traditions claim a shift of the Christianized Votadini from the Borders to North Wales; as the 'Sons of Cunedda' they cleared invading Irish out. From this west-coast British milieu St Patrick (c.389–461, probably Cumbrian by birth) and his disciples made contact with scattered Romano-British congregations. About the same time, in 431, Pope Celestine sent Bishop Palladius 'to the Irish believing in Christ', and contact with the Scots followed. The latter remained in traditional conflict with the Picts of the central Highlands and the north-east, through the times, around 500, when Arthur might have lived. The British combined sufficiently to check the Saxons at Mount Badon, but thereafter their unity broke up, leaving Anglian principalities to the south-east, in Bernicia and Deira. The derelict Wall remained a significant post-imperial boundary, but though the monk Bede of Jarrow used the word 'English' in the title of his *Ecclesiastical History* (731) there was no sense of any 'national' confrontation.

Bede and the *Anglo-Saxon Chronicle* (c.900) were overstressed by Saxonist historians such as Edward Freeman and J. R. Green in Victoria's day, though Bede consulted the monk Gildas's *De Excidio et Conquestu Britanniae*, written in Strathclyde around 525. Later scholars used Irish lives which cast light on St Patrick, but other early Christians—Ninian, Thenew, and her son Kentigern or Mungo—were swamped by the miracles and cults that grew up around them. Bede wrote of the shadowy 'Nynia' as a near-contemporary of Patrick, building a stone church called Candida Casa south of the Mounth, and from there in the late fourth century converting the southern Picts. Probably the many sites of his cult between Whithorn and Aberdeen were later commemorations of itinerant preachers linking extant Christian communities and converts. The Solway was part of an extended water-connected community which also embraced Ulster, Man, North Wales, and Argyll. Whithorn is less than a day's sail from Ireland, and the people of this inland sea were probably using oar-and-sail skin-and-lath boats like Irish curraghs—gold models of fourteen-oared versions have been found in fifth-century Ulster graves. These were light, strong, fast, seaworthy, and could be portaged round falls or towed up rapids. This mobility sped them round the sheltered waters of the southern Hebrides, the lochs of Scotland and Ireland, and later along the rivers of Europe.

SCOTS, BRITISH, NORTHUMBRIANS, PICTS, SCOTS . . .

Scotia, the same as Hibernia, an island very near Britain, narrower in the extent of its lands but more fertile; this extends from Africa toward Boreas, and its fore parts are opposite to Hibernia and the Cantabrian Ocean. Whence it is also called Hibernia. But it is called Scotia because it is inhabited by tribes of the Scots. There are no snakes there, few birds, no bees; so that if any one scatters among beehives elsewhere dust or pebbles brought thence, the swarms desert the combs.

Isidore of Seville (c.560–636) was recently made patron saint of the Internet by Pope John Paul II. When he assembled his proto-encyclopaediac *Etymologies*, his Dark Age Scotland seemed very dark indeed. Isidore's 'Scotia' was in fact Ireland though, however confusedly, he brought out the sea-based nature of the region. Isidore wrote on the cusp of further migrations. In 632 the prophet Muhammad had died in Medina; under a century later, the militant, egalitarian faith of Islam would take Seville and almost reach Paris.

England was by now Saxon—ethnically and linguistically homogeneous—but the Scots were only one of five ethnic groups in the north. Their combination of faith, administrative competence, Latin, and effective sea transport—not to speak of accumulated 'best practice' in evangelizing within the *tuath* or tribe, and *fine*, or ruling family—saw their clergy become more enterprising, and in league with the Irish rulers carry the faith to the northern Picts. Columba of the Uí Néill (521–97), exiled from Ireland for turning a copyright dispute into a war (probably myth, but satisfactorily literary) settled on Iona, and in the course of over fifty missions with his scholar-disciples converted the Pictish ruler King Bridei at his court near Inverness in the 560s. The prince-turned-missionary, with his contemporary Columbanus (543–615) and his successor and biographer Adamnan (625–704), sent Scots-Irish clergy throughout Europe—to Würzburg, to St Gallen, to Bregenz and Bobbio. They could be energetic, resourceful hermits, or even married. They carried little in the way of property, but were marvellously skilled in illumination and metalwork, and untrammelled by episcopal control. Less elevated, but in the circumstances effective, was their skill in annexing the old gods' repertoire of magic and myth, which subsequent cults clothed them in: something which throve in the Dark Age micropolitics of the land the men of 900 would call Alba.

IONA

The small island off the south-west of Mull, only two by four kilometres, with ninety inhabitants, is as instantly recognizable as the basalt columns of the neighbouring Staffa, and has been a consistent presence in Scotland's history. From here, after Columba's arrival in 563, proceeded its Christianization, accompanied by some of the most complex and profound works of art ever produced—the reputed 360 high crosses and illuminated books. From here, too, missionaries sailed to Europe. Columba's life was written by Adamnan around 700, and is (for the time) thoughtful and quite accurate. Adamnan even counts as a pioneer of civil rights in his Law of the Innocents, *concerning the role of non-combatants in conflicts.*

Iona was a part of Dal Riata, the kingdom of the Scots—its fortresses and holy places connected not by land but by sea. Excavations have detected the structure of the Celtic monastery. Iona was then wooded, and a great enclosure of ditch and wall surrounded the wooden structures of cells, chapels, and workshops, punctuated by the high crosses. By 700 'learning of every sort', a Victorian commentator wrote, 'was hunted out of every part of Continental Europe, and concentrated its energies and its glories on the little arena of Iona . . . all the saints of unknown origins were reputed to be Scots or Irish'.

Iona's greatest age ended in 795–825 with several savage Viking raids. Sixty-eight died in the first. Abbot Cellach led survivors to a new community at Kells in Co. Meath, and only a few monks remained—though the abbot later rejoined them. A monk on a far-distant island, Reichenau on Lake

Constance, recorded that one of these, Blathmac, was ritually killed in 825— 'blood-eagled', his rib-cage torn open—a martyr who gained a European reputation, obviously of use in converting the Northmen. The graves of kings of Scotland, Ireland, and Norway were, following the uniting of the kingdom, joined by a romanesque Benedictine Abbey in 1166–1207. So nationalistic was the cult of Columba that Robert Bruce carried to Bannockburn a bone of the saint, in the breccbennach, or Monymusk Reliquary (c.800). At the Reformation, however, Calvinism had no use for tradition: the high crosses were reputedly thrown into the sea, and in 1609 James VI and I's Statutes of Iona were an ominous condemnation of Gaelic culture. The abbey was unroofed and abandoned to the elements. It was to be found again by the men of the Enlightenment in search of the picturesque—Staffa was only really 'discovered' at this time—and through the controversy over James Macpherson's Ossian after 1761. Dr Johnson was an Ossian-sceptic, but even he, visiting with James Boswell in 1771, believed 'That man is not to be envied . . . whose piety would not grow warmer among the ruins of Iona'.

The great Thomas Telford built a four-square kirk, to a standardized design, in 1816. The steamer brought Mendelssohn in 1829, Turner in 1831, Wordsworth in 1833, Victoria in 1847; in Kidnapped (1886) Robert Louis Stevenson, of the family which built most of the Scottish lighthouses, marooned David Balfour on nearby Earraid, and in 1899 the Whig intellectual duke of Argyll presented the abbey to the Kirk, which reroofed it. The island attracted the Scottish Colourists, post-impressionist painters such as Leslie Hunter and F. C. B. Cadell, rather as Brittany attracted Gauguin. From 1938 it became the centre of a Christian socialist revival in the Church of Scotland, headed by the Revd George MacLeod, a First World War hero turned pacifist and communitarian, in which the rebuilding of the Abbey was combined with social work with the Clydeside unemployed. Towards the end of his troubled life the psychiatrist R. D. Laing sought tranquillity here, and after his death in 1994 it was to the island cemetery that the body of Labour's leader John Smith, 'the architect of home rule', was brought.

In contrast to the progress of the new religion the politics of the land mass and islands was tumultuous, a struggle as much *within* the four racial

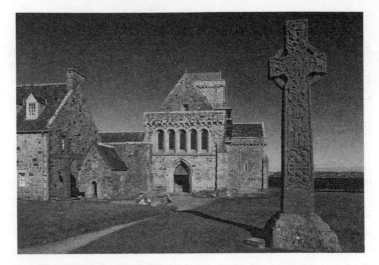

2. *High Cross and Abbey, Iona.*

'At last we came to Icolmkill, but found no convenience for landing. Our boat could not be forced very near to the dry ground, and our Highlanders carried us over the water.'

'We were now treading that illustrious island, which was once the illuminary of the Caledonian regions, whence savage clans and roving barbarians derived the benefits of knowledge, and the blessings of religion. . . That man is little to be envied whose patriotism would not gain force upon the plain of Marathon, or whose piety would not grow warm among the ruins of Iona.'

Samuel Johnson, *A Journey to the Westerrn Isands of Scotland,* 1773, p. 144

The 'high crosses' of Iona, 400 of which were erected when the monastery itself was a collection of wooden huts, combined Christian and Celtic motifs. The stone-built Benedictine Abbey followed in the 12ᵗʰ century, became a ruin after the Reformation, and was (like the other great West Highland attraction Eilean Donan Castle) completely rebuilt in the twentieth century.

groups which held territory (not to speak of smaller family groupings) as *between* them. Iona rose on the basis of the Scots of Argyll, who made up the realm of Dal Riata. Long believed to be the result of invasion from Ireland, recent archaeological finds suggest that it was in fact part of a loose Scot-ish realm connected by the firths and sea lochs. Its 'king' around 500, Fergus mac Erc, presided over a confederation of three family princedoms, Cénel Loairn, Cénel nOengusa, and Cénel nGabráin. Recent digs have shown that Dunadd, his timber-built capital on its outcrop commanding the isthmus of Crinan, had a trade, importing wine, glassware, and spices, which extended to south-west France and the Mediterranean. The Christian prince of Cénel nGabráin, Aedán, was ordained by Columba in 575. But Dal Riatan expansion was curbed by the Northumbrians at the battle of Degsastan in the Borders in 603; its rulers were put on the defensive by the 640s, and it was subsequently divided into smaller units. Thereafter the Picts—Columba's converts, but now centred on Strathtay—took over dominance.

The Picts remain enigmatic, partly because further from the grasp of monkish annalists. How many kingdoms did they form? Bede refers to a single ruler, Nechtan, in 710 but later accounts suggest several local kings on the Irish pattern, with matrilinear descent (though this is hotly debated). The obscurity about the major *ethnie* of Dark Age Scotland was more to do with the fact that the eloquence of their complex sculptured stones was not transliterated into Roman script. As 'the other' they were very useful to Bede's Northumbrians, even to contemporary Ulstermen, who see the *Cruithne* as their ancestors: Scottish, non-Celtic (and therefore Protestant?: 'a race of giant preachers who strode the cliffs of Antrim long before Christ' as the poet Tom Paulin put it, with Ian Paisley obviously in mind . . .).

The Picts left silence and pictures, while all the others—Scots, Britons, Northumbrians, Vikings—were commemorated in monasteries and saga-steads. The deciphering of Pictish Ogham inscriptions by Katherine Forsyth in the 1990s suggests a P-Celtic language similar to Welsh, but the near-demented Celtophobe John Pinkerton (1758–1826) claimed in 1787 that they were 'Gothic' or Teutonic, and even Kenneth Jackson in the 1940s, while claiming Pict as P-Celtic, observed traces of a non-Indo-European language. The name—painted or tattooed people—is from the Roman writer Eumenius and dates from 296, when Constantius Chlorus repaired Hadrian's Wall after their attack. The Romans identified two groups: the Caledonii around the Moray Firth and the Maeatae further south. 'Tribal, rural, hierarchical and familiar': D. A. Binchy's description of contemporary Irish kinglets could have applied to such a confederation of cattle-farming chiefs/princes. They had some arable land (with its harvest stored in *souterrains*), wove, worked bronze and lead, and oiled their economy by bribery and protection rackets before and after the Romans left. Around 670 the Christianized Picts in the neighbourhood of modern Perth extended their authority over the northern princes. This kingdom of Fortriu (as the Irish called it) was confronted to the south-west by the Scots in Dal Riata, and to the south-east by the Britons.

Pressed westward by the Saxons, and perhaps gaining unity through the southward migration of some of the Votadini, the Britons formed in the seventh century a chain of princedoms from Wales to the Forth (from south to north, Dyfed, Powys, Gwynedd, Elfed, Rheged, and Gododdin). Their great epic the *Gododdin* (the Welsh for the Votadini) was composed at this time by the bard Aneirin, near their capital Edinburgh. They were challenged by Northumbria, while the rise of Wessex put their southern rulers under pressure. Aneirin records a descent on Northumbria around 600 to try to take the old Roman fortress of Catraeth (Catterick), which led to a shattering defeat. Worse followed at the battle of Degsastan, and Elfed was lost in 617. Rheged passed to the Northumbrians, perhaps by marriage, in 635; Edinburgh fell three years later.

Northumbria represented the Saxon challenge. It played for dominance because it had taken command of the Christianizing process. The Christianity of the Scoti had also filtered south by sea to Europe. Columba's disciple Aidan took the gospel to King Oswald of Northumbria, and missionaries from Lindisfarne (founded 623) penetrated into Mercia. But the Roman rite began its process of conversion with the Benedictine monk Augustine's mission to southern England after 597, and at the Synod of Whitby in 663 Oswald's son Oswiu, who had curbed the Welsh and their Mercian allies, adopted Roman practices in tonsure, calculating Easter, and in Church government. Celtic ritual retreated, and before its own destruction Iona had accepted the new order. Northumbrian expansion, however, was challenged. When in 675 Oswiu confronted the Picts at Manau, probably near Falkirk, and beat them, this proved to be the Northumbrian high tide. Ten years later his successor Egfrith led a large invading army as far as Dunnichen (Nechtansmere) in Angus only to be wiped out. Later commentators (after the thirteenth-century appropriation of Andrew as patron saint of Scotland) created a legend where cloud-streaks in the sky are said to have formed the saltire (certainly a very early national flag), implying the nascent unity of Alba.

Who had dominance in eighth- and ninth-century Scotland? The traditional account had Pictish power consolidating during the long reign of Unnust Son of Uurgust 'Oengus mac Fergusa' (729–61), who successively took on Dal Riata, Northumbria, and Strathclyde between 741 and 744. Although defeated at Dumbarton in 756 (and shadowy thereafter owing to a dearth of records) his people became dominant in Scotland north of the Forth for the rest of the eighth century, and made Dal Riata a tributary. This relationship, however, started to change after the beginning—perhaps in the 780s, certainly in the 790s—of Viking raids. Perhaps through royal marriages, and Scots moving into Pictland to escape the Vikings, the initiative went back to Dal Riata. Constantine, son of Uurgust mac Fergus (reigned 807–20) was reckoned to be the last of the Pictish monarchs, but was also involved in Dal Riata, and shifted its religious centre from imperilled Iona to Dunkeld. Cinéad (Kenneth) I. mac Alpin (reigned 841–58), was claimed as the unifier of Alba, 36th king of the Scots, and dominator of the Picts. He established himself at Scone and Dunkeld, married his daughters into two Irish houses and one British, and absorbed his forebears into the ritual histories of the Scots kings. So, anyhow, said his grandson Domnall, son of Constantine (d. 900) and Constantine, son of Aed (d. 953), claiming a precedent for being the real founders of the kingdom of the Scots.

UNITING ALBA

'From the fury of the Northmen, Lord God deliver us!' In 793 raiders attacked the monastery of Lindisfarne, killed the monks, burned the library. An island gravestone of a howling, axe-brandishing mob still frightens. Vikings who had for centuries coexisted with Rome, and prospered, began to be driven from their Scandinavian fjords by colder temperatures and dwindling harvests. They descended on the Scottish coast, involving the land directly in the greatest early-medieval migration after Islam. Again, there was a technological drive: where Islam had its thoroughbred camels and horses, the Vikings as expert seamen had long-distance, timber-built, iron-nailed, oar-and-sail galleys. They were also traders—some have claimed that they 'recycled' the inert capital tied up in monastic religious ornament and injected it into business—but initially they were totally destructive, setting monasteries and villages to the torch, and celebrating voyaging, drinking, and slaughtering in their sagas. They destroyed much of the evidence of the austere but high level of Celtic civilization, vivid in the intricate workmanship of the mid-seventh-century *Book of Durrow*, and the late eighth-century *Book of Kells*, 'the wonder of the western world', both possibly written and illustrated in Iona.

Viking depredations—and later settlement—would be found particularly on the north and west coasts, leaving place-names (wick, dale, firth) and remains such as the Brough of Birsay in Orkney and Jarlshof in Shetland. Scotland was largely unrewarding territory—the east coast foggy and featureless, difficult to navigate—with few areas to cultivate and no one well enough off to bribe them to stay away; but it was a staging post en route to trading posts in Ireland—Dublin was settled in 840—colonies like Iceland, settled after 860, and Greenland and ultimately, albeit briefly, Vinland around 1000. Much war would subsequently be waged between Danish and Norwegian Vikings for control of the Hebrides and Northern Isles. Christianity didn't appreciably lessen the violence, but blended it with more positive elements: the practice of self-government (the Icelandic Parliament or Althing dates from 1000; the Manx Tynwald somewhat later) and the vivid, violent, but also political and stylistically disciplined literature of the sagas.

Northmen (adapting quickly both to Christianity and land power) and Arabs were both aspects of the forces which capsized the Carolingian empire after Charlemagne's death in 814. They would confront each other in the Mediterranean. As the European powers recovered, they also moved southward, while maintaining trading and religious linkages with the north, particularly through the growing towns of the Rhine delta and Brabant. The Viking influence meant that Scotland was both brought into the European picture, and united. The mac Alpin fusion of the Scots and Pict kingdoms wasn't a once-for-all act, but formally drew the balance in favour of the Scots. The eastward shift of the kingdom may have responded as much to Viking allies as to Viking attacks—their defeat of the Picts had eased the mac Alpin rise to power. Cinéad's successor, Constantine I, subordinated the remaining British kingdom of Dumbarton in 870, though he still had to negotiate with the Norse empire which extended to Iceland and the Isle of Man, and interdicted the traditional sea-links with Ireland. Attempting to break out of this, Constantine II was killed in 877, but by prising the Irish Vikings apart from the other Norse power, the Danes centred in Yorvik (York), the mac Alpins' drive towards the unity of Alba succeeded.

The result was to make Alba the minor of two great powers within the island of Britain, with various smaller regional monarchies between and to the north of them. The English, under Alfred (reigned 871–99) and Athelstan (reigned 924–39), rulers of great learning and administrative ability, gained the most but, at least in their handling of a multi-ethnic state, the Scottish monarchs were adroit. Greater national unity—the takeover of Strathclyde and Lothian—required greater cooperation with English rulers. Continuity was maintained from 960 to 1025 by drawing from the alternate 'segments' of the royal house, either from Atholl or from Moray, and devolving authority to Mormaers—the 'great stewards' or regional chiefs of Pictland. This meant that Alfred's sort of centralized, town-based personal government was unlikely, and that conflicts over succession were frequent, causing appeals outwith (outside) the kingdom.

'STANDS SCOTLAND WHERE IT DID?'

In 1050 the king of Scots arrived on pilgrimage at Rome. A competent, pious ruler, Macbeth had been enthroned at Scone following what had become the normal process of selecting a ruler: war. The battle for the succession after Malcolm II's death in 1034 is known only too well, though not accurately, through Shakespeare's 'Scottish Play' (1604), his welcome to England's new ruler, James VI and I. The events it was based on—drawn from Wyntoun via Holinshed—were far different from the politics of a Renaissance dynasty, but fairly common to England, Ireland, and Scandinavia in the eleventh century. Succession went not to the eldest son, but the eldest or most competent within the royal house: an invitation to selection by combat, and self-assertion on all sides.

Malcolm II (reigned 1005–34) had murdered Boedh, the other grand-son of Kenneth III. On Malcolm's death the throne passed to his grandson Duncan/Donncha (reigned 1034–40) the son of Crínán, secular abbot of Dunkeld, who had married Malcolm's daughter. But Boedh's daughter Gruoch was married to another candidate, Macbeth, Mormaer of Moray. In 1040 the two met in battle and Duncan was killed. Macbeth reigned until 1057, by all accounts well, and securely enough to make his visit to Rome during this period. He was killed in battle by Malcolm III Canmore, Duncan's son, in alliance with the Norse. If Macbeth had followed Irish practice, Sandy Grant argues, he might have been content to be 'king of Moray', and would never have made the Globe Theatre: the dream of unity made Scotland different and more advanced, if also more alarming. Malcolm was faced with quite a different problem in 1066.

William the Bastard, duke of Normandy, extinguished the old Anglo-Saxon order after a few years of hard campaigning, to which the battle of Hastings was overture. By 1070 only a few prominent English magnates survived. The Conqueror—backed by the pope—purged and Normanized the Church and imposed a systematic pyramid of feudal obligation, from Cornwall to the Tyne. Northumbria remained debatable land. The Scottish system of military tenure could not remain insulated from Norman dynamism—indeed no ambitious ruler, concerned to survive, would want to forgo a homeopathic dose of it. But the Normans weren't unique in their power-drive. Eleventh-century Europe—recovering from the invasions of Northmen, Saracens, and Hungarians—also saw the revival of the struggle between the papacy and the empire, and rapid development in finance and trade. The Hohenstaufen emperors encouraged clerical reform, only to find themselves under pressure from the ambitious Gregory VII, who humiliated Emperor Henry IV (1056–1106) at Canossa in 1077.

The result was disruptive and violent—Rome was sacked by a Saracen force in league with the emperor—but the papacy retained its power, encouraged legal and administrative reform, and the extension of monastic orders. Benedictines, Cistercians, Tironesians, Praemonstratensians were all out to colonize, and Scotland showed willing. In 1095–6 Pope Urban II set the seal on Rome's recovery by preaching the First Crusade, which was to focus Europe's attention on the Mediterranean for several generations, even beyond the final fall of Jerusalem to Saladin in 1287. Such factors meant that the evolution of social institutions in Scotland, whether abbeys or trade or learning, didn't simply—or even primarily—reflect local initiatives, but were the work of, or responses to, powerful European movements.

It was Scotland's good fortune, however, that it had, uniquely among the Celtic realms, a centripetal pattern of authority, and not competing kinglets. The years 1057–1153, moreover, were dominated by two formidable monarchs capable of negotiating this change: Malcolm III Canmore (reigned 1058–93) and his son David I (reigned 1124–53). Malcolm killed the last of his rivals, Lulach, in 1058; he secured through his first wife Ingibjorg, widow of Macbeth's ally Thorfinn the Mighty, an entente with the Viking north, and through his second, Margaret (sister of the pretender Edward Atheling of the Wessex line, though born in recently Christianized Hungary) with the Anglo-Saxon elite. He came to terms with the Normans in 1072. In return for an enforced submission and the presence as hostage in England of his eldest son, David, he got autonomy in Scotland and lands in England.

Norman influence, none too subtly exerted, would decisively alter the power of the Scottish king, still dependent on the sanction of the Mormaers. When Malcolm III fell in battle at Alnwick—one of several fortresses the Normans built in their far north—in 1093, the Scots nobility chose his brother Domnall Bán/Donalbane as his successor, the man who would keep the Normans out. The English king William Rufus supported Duncan II (Malcolm's son by Ingibjorg). When Duncan was killed in battle William cooperated to impose Edgar (Malcolm's son by Margaret), who ruled until 1107.

Effectively this ended the practice of the king being 'chosen'. The English then backed Margaret's youngest son, David, who had been taken south in 1093, and raised and schooled at the court of Henry I. David began by effectively ruling 'Cumbria' the southern part of the kingdom (but still north of the present border) while his older brother Alexander I ruled Scotland proper until 1124. David was able to take advantage of the English civil wars of Stephen (reigned 1135–54) and Matilda to invade Northumbria in 1149, a high tide of success in the south. Even more than Robert Bruce, his reign and its achievements would for centuries be a benchmark for the national estates: nobility, church, and burghers.

David I ruled about a quarter of a million people, a vague statistic that haunts the void where England had the obsessional Norman accounting of the Domesday Book (1088). The economy of the country was based on rearing cattle and, increasingly, sheep, and gradually extending (from waste or forest) the acreage under arable crops. This was aided by favourable economic conditions throughout the twelfth century, when the demands of the great Low Countries trading centres created enough of an export trade in hides, fish, and wool to supply funds for the Scots authorities to amass what would now be called 'social-overhead capital'. Just when some Norman and north European families—Hays, Bruces, Stewarts (Breton), Douglases (Fleming)—were interbreeding with the earlier Celtic elite, mixing up forms of kinship-based relationships with feudal superiorities, David's encouragement brought a flood of Normans and Flemings north, sometimes directly from Europe, sometimes from Yorkshire, the Midlands, and Sussex. 'Wisely taking thought for the future, he furnished his kingdom with castles and weaponry,' as a chronicler wrote around 1215: the incomers held the first and wielded the second. David, trying to modernize a military unchanged for four centuries, favoured them, particularly in the south-west, always an area of turbulence. This shows up if measured by the spread of characteristically Norman motte-and-bailey (mound and enclosure) castles—generally timber-built until the fourteenth century. There were more of them in the counties of Dumfries and Galloway than north of a line from Inveraray to Aberdeen.

David supplemented these with religion. Ailred of Rievaulx, his eulogist, credited him with taking the number of Scottish sees from three (St Andrews, Dunkeld, and Moray) to nine, adding Glasgow, Brechin, Dunblane, Caithness, Ross, and Aberdeen: though some of these were moves or reorganizations (Govan to Glasgow, Mortlach to Aberdeen). He also settled monastic institutions on crown land, notably the first of the great border abbeys. Finally, he established eighteen burghs, mainly in the south-east, mainly associated with royal fortresses, and mainly peopled by foreigners: English or Flemings. James I would later, with an eye on overmighty clergy and depleted royal resources, call him 'a sair sanct for the croon', but this gave him the lasting basis of effective administration.

SURVIVING

In 1736 an improving laird at Larbert near Falkirk demolished Arthur's O'on to yield materials for a mill dam, although it was known to be Roman. Countless such actions taken against sites from earlier times make the Dark Ages in Scotland even more obscure in the 'developed' parts of the country: like the Strathclyde capital that lies under the shipyards of Govan. This was paralleled by the displacement of earlier tradition by later, equally misleading, dogmas claiming to be rational: notably an anti-Gaelic 'Teutonism' in the nineteenth century, which some claimed had its roots in southern Scotland, and particularly Thomas Carlyle. In contrast with the straightforward ethnic and linguistic identity of the Anglo-Saxons—'a condition which readily breeds arrogant self-satisfaction', as Sir Geoffrey Elton foreboded— Scotland was not just ethnically complex, but wrapped in a mixture of legend, authentic accounts, and half-comprehended artefacts. It had also a supporting role within several great ethno-historical myths: the *Táin*, the Welsh epics, the lives of saints, the Viking sagas. The problem lay with the Pictish majority, so significant up to the ninth century, yet so obscure in its records. The Scottish monarchy was conscious of its Pictish past, and based its claims on the antiquity of the king-lists, and the people's supposed Scythian origins. This ritual history was probably as important in the Declaration of Arbroath of 1320 as any idea of demotic nationalism.

Belief in the 'constitutionality' of the king-lists would, however, be destroyed by the researches of the Catholic historian Father Thomas Innes, writing his *Ancient Inhabitants of Scotland* in 1729. Colin Kidd has claimed that this, and the ahistorical 'modernization' of the Whig historians, deprived the Scots of a weapon available to other European nationalisms. This is, perhaps, a rather one-dimensional view, underestimating Church and culture. The first was comprehensively Romanized under the Canmores, yet it retained one important institution in the *Céli Dé*, or Culdees. These were secular clerics living in a community under the rule of Tallaght, who later became Augustinians, but the belief persisted that they represented a localized collective ministry. The Church could co-opt at home the cults associated with earlier ruins or remains; abroad it could also claim a missionary role in European Christianity. If Macbeth was in Rome, it was probably to make this fact plain to the Holy Father: that Scotland was a 'special daughter', subject to no English prelate.

A distant and much later nation might provide a key to Scotland's unification: Canada. Asked to justify the existence of the place—huge land area, terrible weather, a great power on the southern frontier, a semi-Scots elite—intellectuals such as Northrop Frye, John Buchan, and George Grant suggested 'survival': through cooperation between Inuit, Scot, and Frenchman. Culture's survivals were random, yet when secular poetry comes with the *Gododdin* it is the record of a tragedy, not the blood-boltered glorying in sailing, slaughter, and drinking of the sagas. Tragedy is the consequence of ambition and conflict. Religious poetry reprises similar themes in visual and oral art: notions of eternity and salvation flashed together with the precise and local, with weather, emotion, food, and the character of a constantly changing landscape. The complex sculptured stones of the Picts and Scots, and the great illuminated volumes, suggest an oral tradition of 'praise poetry' directed at the land and emphasizing what people owed to it: chiefly solidarity.

Scotland's remoteness, ethnic pluralism, and sheer difficulty had consistently acted to make invaders think twice about total conquest, and settle for coexistence. The idea of *foedera*—treaty or covenant—was probably there long before the Romans bought off the Votadini, in the regionalism of prehistoric Scotland. Hence, perhaps, negotiating within Alba's continuing ethnic variety of Picts, Scots, Norse, Britons, and Angles, the Church became a national as well as international binding force, through the hagiographies of the saints and their travels, which, in Adamnan's editing and broadcasting of Arculfus's *The Holy Places* (c.690) moved from implausible marvels to anticipate the Crusades.

The Roman Church drew particularly on such emotions, and on the peoples on Europe's periphery, caught between the heathen and the imperial. Through this they acquired 'religious-national' loyalties while the nation-state was less developed. The impact of Viking aggression—itself a type of technological revolution, requiring high investment in shipping, trading posts, and months spent in voyaging with plunder as the pay-off—was particularly novel and terrifying for people whose remoteness had earlier insulated them. The Vikings may have been traders but the twentieth century has surely disabused us of trade being cognate with civilized behaviour. To see them off required the response from united Alba to be stiffened up by Northmen in their second modulation, into high-technology fighting men.

2 | THE COMMUNITY OF THE REALM, 1100–1560

Artibus his, totum fremerent cum bella per arbern,
Nullaque non leges tellus mularet avitas
Externa subjecta jago, gens una vestutis
Sedelus antiqua sub libertate resedit.
Subsistit hic Gothi furor, hic gravis impetus haesit
Saxonis, hic Cimber superato Saxone, et
Acri Perdomito Neuster Cimbro.

(GEORGE BUCHANAN, Epithalamium for Mary of Scotland
and Francis of France, 1558)

ANGLO-SCOTTISH AMITY

The stereotype vision of Scotland's past is notorious enough—
romantically clogged with the likes of Mary Queen of Scots and Charles
Edward Stewart. In 1996, with the Conservative government and the Union
under pressure, these were joined by William Wallace, 'Guardian of Scotland', as interpreted by the Hollywood-Australian actor Mel Gibson in
Braveheart. In 1997 50 per cent of Scottish schoolchildren could name him;
only a handful knew anything about the rulers of Scotland in the twentieth
century. Yet, so concerned was John Major, the prime minister, by the
prospect of Scottish ethnic nationalism that (under protest from the
queen) the Stone of Destiny was parted from the throne that Wallace's
executioner, Edward I, had built for it in Westminster Abbey, and returned
north after 700 years. If Scots frequently equated Mrs Thatcher with
Edward, Major seemed destined to emulate his luckless son. On 2 May 1997
not a single Scots Tory MP survived, and the road to self-government was
open. Something of this emotionalism marked 'The End of a Nightmare',
the documentary with which the Franco-German Arte channel greeted the
new parliament.

Gibson's film opened with the young Wallace returning to his house
to find his family butchered by the English, and wicked Edward setting
out to Anglicize the Scots by granting his barons the right to pleasure
Scots brides. Yet at the battle of Stirling Bridge the woad-covered leader
would be found exhorting his wavering troops in a speech in which
Shakespeare (and in particular *Henry V*) ended up ahead of such Scots
patriots as Burns, Blind Hary, and Archdeacon Barbour. The Scotland
into which Wallace was born, as the son of a small 'laird' in about 1270,
had been peaceable and unmarked by English invasion, enjoying the fruits
of a peace which—with some war scares in the 1240s—had lasted since
1217. The film's tone probably did capture the public mood of the country
between 'Malleus Scotorum's' invasion of 1296 (Edward I, 'Hammer of
the Scots') and the Reformation. The Scotland that its intellectual ambas-
sador George Buchanan, the greatest Latinist of the Renaissance, hymned
before the French court, was independent, historically conscious, and
proud of it:

> So was it when of old, each land
> A prey to every spoiler's hand
> Its ancient laws and rulers lost,
> The Scot alone could freedom boast!
> The Goth, the Saxon and the Dane
> Poured on the Scot their powers in vain;
> And the proud Norman met a foe
> Who gave him equal, blow for blow.

It was also less prosperous and secure, and more at the mercy of European power politics. Within a decade Buchanan himself would have turned against the queen and the Auld Alliance, and implicitly towards the greater kingdom to the south.

The country's first historians, John of Fordoun (*fl.* 1371–7), Andrew of Wyntoun (d. *c.*1420–4), and Walter Bower (*c.*1385–1449) compiled their accounts (Fordoun in Latin, Wyntoun between 1408 and 1422, and Bower in 1441–9) and based them largely on monastic chronicles, terse but for institutional and legal reasons fairly accurate. They wrote after what became known, much later, as the 'War of Independence', and were permeated by its spirit, something intensified by long-lived poetic epics on this theme such as Archdeacon Barbour's *The Brus* (*c.*1375) and Blind Hary's *The Wallace* (*c.*1476). The tone of *Braveheart* wasn't far adrift from that of Hary, which was composed as part of an aristocratic attempt to frustrate James III's schemes for an English alliance.

Written history, if remote from archival and material evidence, can be a dubious guide. Scotland—in the Anglo-Saxon historian James Campbell's words 'the worst-documented state in early-medieval Europe'—had until James III's reign (1460–88) nothing like the royal records which Victorian historians of the English constitution such as Bishop Stubbs quarried. Even experts admit an awkward gap between 1437 and 1482 in which 'confusion reigns'. The growth of most Scottish towns (Roxburgh, which vanished after 1460, was exceptional) also destroyed or obscured much of the material evidence for what Geoffrey Barrow has called 'a land of burghs rather than villages'. Edinburgh has scarcely a score of buildings which pre-date the Reformation of 1560.

THE GIANT TO THE SOUTH

The amity of the thirteenth century was a paradox. There were two expanding powers in the British Isles, Scotland and England, but the territorial ambitions of the first were regional: limited to the border counties (which took a long time, as Dauvit Broun points out, to regard themselves as Scots) and the northern and western Highlands. England was part of the Angevin realm. Extending from the Solway to the Pyrenees, and including half of modern France, thirteenth-century English monarchs ran an empire rivalling and in conflict with that of the Hohenstaufens: Frederick I Barbarossa (reigned 1152–90), the first Holy Roman Emperor, and Frederick II (reigned 1211–50). They coincided with the papacy at its zenith, under Innocent III (reigned 1198–1216) and Honorius III, and were made to feel the weight of Roman authority. To the north the kings of what the Declaration of Arbroath would later call 'this poor little Scotland' coped with their mighty neighbour by being pliable about their own power, tholing (tolerating under duress) the dual loyalties of many Scottish nobles, and exploiting Angevin over-extension. English kings were under pressure from European rivals, from a powerful baronage, and from the waning but still powerful distraction of the Crusades. Being small had its advantages.

David I and William I had tackled the traditional problem—how to keep the ruling family on top—by recruiting military force, administrative ability, and to a lesser extent the means of paying for both. Norman incomers were encouraged and were used to extend royal power. The future David I gave Annandale, for instance, to Robert de Brus (the family stemmed from Brix, near Cherbourg) around 1120. The great monastic orders were similarly co-opted to educate, administer, and farm. The dynamic centre of European trade, centred on the Rhine delta and in particular on Bruges, wanted Scottish products—fish, hides, wool, and markets at which to trade—and was catered for by David I's burghs, with their English, German, and Flemish merchants. But David's territorial gain of Northumbria was brief. His son Malcolm IV (reigned 1153–65) succeeded, as the first prince to do so without dispute, but faced attacks by Somerled, lord of Argyll, and by native noblemen in the south-west. In 1157 Northumbria reverted to the English.

Henry II (reigned 1154–89) behaved cannily. He took Angevin power to its zenith and made himself overlord of Ireland with a campaign in 1171, gaining the loyalty of important Irish rulers and establishing Normans as his lieges in Leinster. Otherwise he left the Welsh princes alone and spent most of his time managing his prosperous French domains and feuding with the Church. This culminated with the murder of Archbishop Thomas Becket at Canterbury in 1170. Murder in the cathedral didn't dent Henry's enormous power, but it diminished the papacy's desire to keep the Scottish bishops under the control of the archbishop of York. Pope Alexander III made Glasgow in 1175 a 'special daughter' of Rome, with direct access, and the rest of the country (save Galloway) followed in 1192. The Becket episode would later provide Scots constitutionalists with telling arguments both against absolute sovereignty and English claims.

With the Scots Henry was tactful but firm. William I 'the Lion' (reigned 1165–1214) continued—indeed accelerated—the Normanizing tendencies of his grandfather. He gave the great north-eastern lordship of the Garioch, centred on the new burgh of Inverurie, to his brother David, earl of Huntingdon. Moray, Gaelic and troublesome, went to Flemish settlers— provoking fury among such native nobles as remained. In 1174 William miscalculated. He tried to take advantage of Henry's religious imbroglio and retake Northumbria, but was captured at Alnwick and only got out of a dungeon in Norman Falaise by swearing fealty. On his return, he faced aggrieved Scots magnates irrupting in sporadic regional uprisings, in Galloway and the Highlands. They carried on doing this until his death.

Henry's sons gave the Scots kings more chances than trouble. Richard I Lionheart (reigned 1189–99) was preoccupied with the continent and the Crusades and sold William his suzerainty back for 10,000 merks in 1189. His brother John (reigned 1199–1216) showed the other face of the Angevins in the speed with which he extended his power in Ireland. This aggressive mentality, coupled with tactical hamfistedness after he became king, pro- voked the French, who threw him out of his domains north of the Loire in 1202–4. He returned to England, harried his subjects for cash, and launched himself on France once again in 1214—disastrously. Rebellion broke out in England and the Scots joined in and invaded repeatedly: Alexander II (reigned 1214–49) and his army—in fact substantially made up of northern

English—got as far as Dover in 1216, a year after John was forced to throw Magna Carta, the charter of their liberties, at the nobility in the hope of slowing them down. Baronial connections with Wales also helped Llywelyn I (reigned 1197–1240) to expand his princedom of Gwynedd to its maximum extent. In Scotland Alexander settled for a peace which would last for nearly eighty years.

This was partly because the English king Henry III was preoccupied throughout a long but insecure reign (1216–72) with fighting off the baronage and the French. He extended his feudal authority, first in Ireland and then in Wales. English castles rose in the Pale around Dublin, and on the Welsh marches. But while some Scots magnates took the anti-English side—the Galloway Comyns, Norman-French but with Gaelic connections, offered support to Llywelyn—on the Scots frontier peace reigned; even Carlisle Castle was allowed to fall into decay. Feudal tenures helped reinforce this settlement: they made up a sometimes remarkable patchwork which could extend from the Highlands to the Channel Islands. Over half the twenty-seven baronies in the English north were held by Scots, and over half Scotland's lordships were held by noblemen who also possessed properties in England.

The Scots kings turned their eyes north and west. Alexander II relinquished in 1237 his claim to the border counties in return for English estates and Henry's goodwill. He built castles in Argyll and the Inner Hebrides, encroaching on the Norse kingdom of Man. Though his son Alexander III (reigned 1249–86) succeeded as a minor, and his first years were marked by baronial turbulence, the amicable English connection—he married Henry II's daughter in 1251—helped when Scots–Norse relations came to a crisis in 1262. A Norwegian–Manx alliance was beaten back and the Norwegian King Haakon, whom the Scots defeated in a skirmish at Largs on 2 October 1263, died soon afterwards. With him died his cause. The Hebrides and Man were annexed to the Scots crown, and Norse rule was limited to Orkney and Shetland. Alexander reigned successfully for a further twenty-two years. He visited England in state in 1278 and did homage for his English estates, though later some English authorities would try to use this to broaden their king's claim.

PITMUNIE, ABERDEENSHIRE

*The township of 'Pict'munie, in the parish of Monymusk, about
48 kilometres north-east of Aberdeen, was a clutter of about eighteen
houses, built of clay and roofed with wattle and turf. Though surrounded
by unpromising moor and marsh, its folk tilled tracts of good loam; their
great eight-ox ploughs mainly broke the 'infield', of between 20 and
40 hectares, its long strips allocated to the husbandmen, and manured
almost as heavily as a garden, not least by the villagers themselves. The
size of the settlement was dictated by the technology of the plough, which
required the work of all the township's beasts, who also consumed much of
the fodder that was grown. The chief crops were oats and barley (wheat was
more common south of the Forth) and meat, fish, and poultry were
plentiful. The outfield, perhaps twice the size of the infield, if sheepfolds
and faughs (fallows) were included, was grazed by sheep, cattle, and pigs.
The husbandmen cultivated about 14 hectares of separate rigs (each rig
being 4–7 metres wide); there were also four 'croft' holdings, in which a
single farmer had his own land, and some 'cottars' who had less than
4 hectares. The township folk were Gaelic-speaking, and liable for service in
the 'common army', an obligation which lasted until the seventeenth
century. They paid rent in kind to the local laird—Gilchrist, earl of Mar in
1170—but in the thirteenth century his payments to his feudal superior
were increasingly being made in cash. The standard of Scottish country
dwellings earned little praise—animals mingling with the cottagers, smoke
blackening the interior and drifting out of the door, though this had the
advantage that an old cottage could simply be torn apart and used to
manure the infield. This is one reason why so little evidence of the medieval
Scottish village survives—though Monymusk, settled in the earliest times,
and then a Culdee monastery in the twelfth century, had a 'romanesque'
twelfth-century parish church. Robert Bruce came in 1308, before the battle
of Barra, in his hard-fought campaign to subjugate the north-east. The
monks of Monymusk Priory held the Breccbennach, or Monymusk
Reliquary, a tiny, finely chased Celtic casket fashioned about 750, within it
a bone of Columba. This accompanied Bruce to the field of Bannockburn,
and now rests in the National Museum in Edinburgh. Monymusk Priory*

was moribund well before the Reformation, when the Forbes family seized
its lands and built Monymusk Castle, a powerful tower-house safe against
all but the heaviest artillery. Pitmunie township became a 'muckle ferm'
through enclosure by the Grants, who bought the estate in 1712 and
radically 'improved' it, introducing turnips, rotations, long leases, and
planting a million trees. By 1800 two-thirds of the parish was under tillage,
and the village of Monymusk was totally rebuilt in 1840, thirty years before
the railway to Aberdeen was opened.

PEOPLE AND PRINCES

We know about Pitmunie because of the archaeological work of Henry
Hamilton in the 1930s, and records of leases and feus. What we know very
little about are the lives of over half the people who lived there: the women
and children. Women were important in the early history of Scotland,
producing two (otherwise rare) examples of saints who married and
brought up children: the shadowy Thenew, mother of the equally shadowy
St Mungo (*fl.* maybe *c.*540) and Margaret (*c.*1045–93), queen to Malcolm
Canmore, who played an important part in extending 'proper' Roman
Catholicism and monasticism, and was canonized in 1249 (her daughter
Maud, queen to Henry I, was no less energetic down south). Thenew, however, was regendered into St Enoch, which feminist historians have seen as
emblematic of unfriendly tendencies in Catholic thought associated with
Thomas Aquinas's rediscovery of Aristotle in the mid-thirteenth century.
Otherwise women's careers have to be inferred from the general practices
of peasant societies: they were responsible for children and household,
milking, tending farm animals and poultry, spinning (with the distaff or
rock until the fourteenth century, and the 'great wheel' after that), brewing,
and working in the fields at seed time and harvest. They seem to have had
more autonomy in coastal areas, where fishwives gutted, salted, and sold
their husbands' catch and managed the family finances, and in the burghs
woman innkeepers like William Dunbar's 'Kynd Kittock' brewed their
own ale.

Women were more put-upon in the Highlands, where visitors noted that they performed much of the severe manual labour while their menfolk exercised the time-honoured privilege of warriors and conserved their strength for clan conflicts by boasting about them and drinking a lot. Perhaps a quarter of countrywomen would, at some stage in their lives, work as servants, cooks, or children's maids in the houses of the clergy, merchants, and lairds; this proportion rose to 45 per cent in the burghs. Children would help on the farm as soon as they were able: herding, gleaning, or bird-scaring. Illiteracy was general. There was no Scottish education act at all until one in 1496 which tried to compel the better-off to have their sons taught, although in Pitmunie the nearness of the monks at Monymusk meant that there was some chance for a bright boy to learn his letters.

A twin to the Monymusk Reliquary ended up at Bologna, emphasizing how Scotland was increasingly part of European intellectual and cultural life. The pious went on pilgrimage to Rome or Compostella, or Amiens. The Scots Church levied taxes to support the Crusades, her traders, lawyers, and scholars participated in the 'twelfth-century renaissance': the recovery of Aristotle's philosophy, the codification of civil law, the absorption of the mathematics and philosophy of the Islamic world. 'Scotus Viator' in the church or university registers meant a travelling clerical savant from the 'nation' of Scots or Irish religious houses: they were amongst the first to attend the new universities at Bologna (1088) and Paris (1100). Michael Scot (c.1160–1235), maybe from Ettrick Forest, had European fame as Islamic scholar, translator of Aristotle, and intellectual at the Sicilian court of Frederick II. He was also a magician, fascinating writers from Dante and Boccaccio to James Hogg and John Buchan, and Borderers will tell you he split the Eildon Hills into three. Scotland also provided one of medieval philosophy's two central figures, John Duns Scotus, probably born in the Borders around 1270, and the rival to Aquinas. A scholastic 'realist'— meaning a thinker who distinguished strictly between natural phenoma and the subject matter of religious speculation—he was a defender of the doctrine of the Immaculate Conception, taught at Oxford and Paris, and died at Cologne in 1307. He would be remembered over five centuries later by a Victorian rediscoverer of Celticism and Catholicism, Gerard Manley Hopkins:

> Yet ah! this air I gather and I release
> He lived on; these weeds and waters, these walls are what
> He haunted who of all men most sways my spirits to peace;
>
> Of realty the rarest-veinèd unraveller; a not
> Rivalled insight, be rival Italy or Greece;
> Who fired France for Mary without spot.

One basic problem in envisaging medieval Scotland is population, and the demographic calculations that flow from it. David I's Scotland had, Lord Cooper guesstimated in 1947, 400,000 people against perhaps four million English, and this may have doubled by the mid-fourteenth century. Sandy Grant has more recently hypothesized an ambitious million, which I tend to doubt, as the 'lower end' of *English* projections is 2.5 million. No way did the Scots add up to nearly half the English: the problems that Edward I had in provisioning his invading armies, well documented by Fiona Watson, suggest that there was nothing like the food supply such a population would need. The country remained overwhelmingly rural, with Berwick its biggest town. Agriculture diversified, but there was a steady increase in sheep-rearing for the wool and hide trades. Archaeologists deduce from deposits of bones that if sheep had had parity with cattle in the later Celtic settlements, they were now ahead by a ratio of ten to one. Wool was Scotland's main export—some judged it coarse, but it got as far as north Italy, selling at three times its Scottish value—along with animal hides and cured fish, which were mainly traded at Boston in England or Bruges in Flanders. These exports paid for imports of the luxury goods increasingly found in lairds' houses, among burgh merchants, and in the various palaces of the royal household, not to speak of the considerable expenses of marriage among the nobility. Religion was also of economic importance. Wine, demanded by the barrel for the Catholic Mass—celebrated in around 850 parishes, with perhaps 200,000 communicants, on Sundays and feast-days came north; salted, dried, or smoked fish for Catholic fast-days went south.

Scotland had in the twelfth century a booming and monetized economy, with about £180,000 in circulation, against about £1,000,000 in England, within a common rate of exchange. Lord Cooper's friend and

Population, 1200–2013, in millions

									4.6	5.1	5.3
								2.90			
0.4 (e)	0.6 (e)	0.5 (e)	0.5 (e)	0.6 (e)	1.0 (e)	1.25	1.63				
1200	1300	1400	1500	1600	1700	1750	1800	1850	1900	1950	2013

3. *Scottish population from the earliest times to the present: estimates and figures.*

contemporary the socialist Tom Johnston, in his *History of the Working Classes in Scotland* (1922), saw feudal privilege exploiting those at the bottom, the husbandmen with their oxen, and nationality as no more than a chimera. Indeed the language, cash-relations, and mentality of the elite, clerical, noble, or commercial were supra-national; but as Marc Bloch, following the sociological tradition founded by Adam Ferguson, insisted, feudal society was dynamic, through the struggle between the 'community' of kinship groups and the 'system' of monarchy. In accord with this, the king of Scots was gaining both as a functional institution and a national symbol.

Malcolm IV was the first to succeed through primogeniture, but the Alexanders still emphasized the king's Celtic elements to distinguish him from the essentially feudal-imperial nature of his English counterpart and (as far as his English property was concerned) liege-lord. The king was revered as being in unbroken thirteenth-generation descent from Kenneth mac Alpin. Further back were Fergus mac Erc, and Gadelaus or Gaythelus (the Gael) who had led the Scots forth from Egypt. In the late thirteenth century he was credited with acquiring there the Stone of Scone, as a Norman-French ballad of 1307 told the English, who took it away:

> Gadelaus et Scota ceste piere menerount,
> Quant de la terre Egipte en Escoce passaeraunt
> Ne geres longus de Scone quant arriverant
> De la noun de Scota la Escoce terre numaunt.

(Gadelus and Scota brought this stone with them out of Egypt, and set it down in Scotland not far from Scone, and Scotland was named after Scota.)

Countering its kidnapping in 1301, Baldred Bisset claimed that Scots kings were enthroned on the stone brought by Scota, daughter of Pharoah. A recitation by the king's poet of the royal forebears testified to this, and helpfully sidestepped the fact that the pope wouldn't allow such a subordinate royal to be anointed and crowned.

The Scots monarchy pragmatically fused Celtic and Norman practice. The Celtic element lay in the thirteen Scots earls, successors of the Mormaers, responsible for mustering the army, whose consent was necessary for a secure kingship. The mac Malcolm dynasty accepted this, but also tried to overcome its implications. Its kings needed money and access to military power. They got it through a largely Norman machine, and increasingly a hereditary one. The Constable handled war. The Chamberlain brought in revenue, locally supported by the officials of royal burghs, and feudal barons. The Chancellor (a clergyman) acted as the monarch's secretary for government, the Steward administered the royal household, and the Justiciar administered law. This was either traditional law, Celtic in origin, which was known as the *Lex Terrae*, or law as enacted by Parliament, known to the English as Statute and to the Scots as the *Assisae*. These officials and the royal family met in the King's Council. This organized law enforcement and tax-raising, mainly through customs and feudal fees or cash commutations of service, and from within the king's own feudal possessions came food rents called *cain* and obligations to accommodate him and his servants on their itineraries, or *conveth*. The king depended on his own property for about two-thirds of his income. To supplement the royal household there came into being the General Council (or Parliament or Estates, embracing nobility and clergy) a fixture by Alexander III's reign. Local administration was in the hands of barons to whom the king granted the judicial power of Sheriff (from the Anglo-Saxon 'Shire-reeve'). Thirty sheriffdoms, corresponding to the modern counties, existed by 1296.

Patriotic Scots historians traditionally claimed that their society wasn't really feudal. There was certainly no Scottish equivalent to the English resentment of the 'Norman Yoke', which would nag away up to the nineteenth century. Yet David I's Norman noblemen were little different from their southern brethren. Nine of his thirteen earls held land in England in the early 1200s. This meant, however, that an English monarch up against a Scots Anglo-Norman elite had to tread far more warily than in

Wales or Ireland, where the traditional nation was firmly subordinate. David's other innovation, the burghs, had expanded to forty by 1210, including Dunfermline, Stirling, Perth, Edinburgh, and Inverness. Nearly all were guarded by a castle, and two of the most important, Berwick and Roxburgh, were right on the border with England. Their inhabitants tended to be settlers, often Flemings or Germans from the continent, privileged in handling trade, minting coins, and keeping up a limited welfare provision of almshouses and leper houses. Their constitutions were adapted from that of Newcastle, which in David's time was actually in Scottish hands, and Kirk and king claimed about 10 per cent apiece of their revenues.

Were monasteries—associated above all with David—his innovation, or would they have come anyway? They drew on a Celtic tradition of monastic evangelism, but they also paralleled religious developments in England after 970, encouraged by papal reforms refining the Benedictine rule, and creating Europe-wide networks out of the new orders which proliferated in the eleventh and twelfth centuries. David's foundations included the border abbeys of the Augustinians at Jedburgh (1138) and the Tironensians at Selkirk (1113). The Premonstratensians at Dryburgh (1150), like the Augustinians and Tironensians, who moved to Kelso (1128) were practically-minded, while Cistercian Melrose (1136), and ten other abbeys of that order, remained austerely contemplative. Followed by such houses as Sweetheart (1273), Pluscarden, Fortrose, and Dunkeld, the regular clergy came to hold around an eighth of Scottish land: the Kirk's income was by 1400 twenty times that of the king. It had its own legal concerns, governed by canon law and so by Rome: concerning morality, marriage, inheritance, its word counted among the ordinary parishioners. Yet it was also important in extending royal administration, educating clergy, lawyers, and gentry, and in re-establishing Scotland's intellectual presence in Europe. The cost was a dilution of royal power, but it secured a structure of government which could cope with royal minorities and maintain amicable (though not after 1192 subordinate) clerical relationships with England.

The reign of Alexander III seemed to subsequent generations a kind of golden age, something still visible in the red sandstone magnificence of St Mungo's cathedral in Glasgow, built by Bishops William de Malvoisin and George Wishart between 1200 and 1316 as one of the finest examples of pointed Gothic in north Europe. It was also a period when the 'Inglis' tongue began to push out 'Scots', which then meant Gaelic (but would eventually replace 'Inglis'). Alexander was commemorated in the earliest surviving poem to be written in the vernacular:

> When Alexander our king was dead
> Who Scotland led in law and le,*   [peace
> Away was sons* of ale and bread,   [abundance
> Of wine and wax, of gamyn* and of glee.   [amusement
> Our gold was changed into lead.
> Christ, born in Virginity,
> Succour Scotland and remeed,
> That is stayed in perplexity.

'GIF FREDOME FAIL . . .?'

This thirteenth-century balance was fortuitous: what Rees Davies calls 'English imperialism' had been increasing in ideological strength, but was checked by a weak monarchy in England and the pressure exerted on Plantagenet territory in France. After Magna Carta in 1215, the French confined the Angevins to Gascony, and then the English nobles, under Simon de Montfort, tried in the 1250s to force a baronial-parliamentary partnership on the monarchy, a situation which deteriorated into civil war in the 1260s. This power vacuum enabled the princes of Gwynedd to dominate Wales after 1216, having made the same sort of compromise with Norman feudalism as the Scots kings had done, and Henry III had repeatedly to concede to them. His son Edward, born in 1239, was a different proposition. Given the effective lordship of Ireland in 1254, he carried through administrative and judicial reforms which were successful: these presaged a logical, legalistic, energetic career. Having defended his father's cause in Aquitaine, 'this true treasure of Christ', as the Melrose chronicler called him, went crusading. He started pretty much as he would go on: 'Finding the Saracens, their wives and children in bed, he slew them all with the edge of the sword, for they were the enemies of the faith of Christ.' He was returning via Sicily when he succeeded in 1272.

Where the legalistic *amour propre* of the 'English Justinian' ended, and dynastic pride or a desire to consolidate English territory began, is hard to estimate in Edward's case, although in *The Making of Europe* (1993) Robert Bartlett ties this to the Christianizing, colonizing ethos of the period. He pursued his rights in Wales in 1276 against Prince Llywelyn, in campaigns which D. A. Carpenter has called 'absolutely breathtaking in their ruthless mastery and precision'. His forces took on Llewelyn, stripped him of his conquests and, after a last rebellion, killed him in 1282. Edward tried, hanged, and dismembered Llewelyn's brother Dafydd as a traitor, the first such death since 1075. He partitioned Wales with his more reliable supporters, and put it under the yoke of eighteen powerful castles. Built by French or Swiss engineers, Harlech, Beaumaris, Conwy, or Caerffili were 'state of the art': of an elaboration encountered otherwise only among the Crusaders' fortresses in the Holy Land. They cost the English exchequer over £80,000. In 1286–9 he campaigned in Gascony, but never returned there. Scotland beckoned, then obsessed him, conjuring up en route much of the paraphernalia of 'British' nationalism.

When Alexander III died, quite unexpectedly, thrown from a horse at Kinghorn in Fife in 1286, a personal union with England, on more or less equal terms, could have been in prospect. This would have meant a marriage between his granddaughter Margaret of Norway, and Edward's son, then 2 years of age (he would be invested as prince of Wales in 1301). In 1290, by the Treaty of Birgham, a small village on the Scottish bank of the Tweed, near Coldstream, the four 'Guardians of Scotland' agreed such a dual monarchy with Edward. The Scots would retain their own Church, Parliament, law, and administration. Unfortunately the little girl on whom this careful structure depended, the Maid of Norway, sickened on the voyage from Bergen and died in Orkney. Edward now saw the prospect of a settlement like the one his forebears had imposed on Ireland—a client king—when he was approached by the Guardians to adjudicate between two Anglo-Norman claimants—John Balliol and Robert Bruce, lord of Annandale. He then claimed sovereign rights, and produced another eleven candidates deliberately to confuse the process and enhance his power. At Norham Castle in 1291 the 'Great Cause' began between Balliol, Bruce, Florence of Holland, and John Hastings. In November 1292 Edward (who had had a year to make himself acquainted with Scotland) settled on Balliol, who with some reluctance swore fealty to him. The new King John was also, however, subject to energetic Scots Parliaments, and sided with them when Edward demanded service and subsidy in his French war. Four Scots ambassadors, two bishops and two nobles, sailed for France in July, and allied the country to Philip IV in October 1295. The army mustered on 11 March 1296 and the long peace was over.

DUNFERMLINE

> The King sits in Dunfermline town,
> Drinking the blude-red wine;
> 'Oh whare will I get a skeely skipper,
> To sail this new ship of mine?'—
>
> O up and spake an eldern knight,
> Sat at the King's right knee,—
> 'Sir Patrick Spens is the best sailor
> That ever sailed the sea.'—
>
> Our King has written a braid letter,
> And seal'd it with his hand,
> And sent it to Sir Patrick Spens,
> Was walking on the strand.
>
> 'To Noroway, to Noroway,
> To Noroway o'er the faem;
> The King's daughter of Noroway,
> 'Tis thou maun bring her hame.'

Patrick Spens did not want to go to Norway. His ship and its company perished. One of the greatest Scots ballads plainly reflects the tragic story of the Maid, whose death prefaced the Wars of Independence. Dunfermline, like Edinburgh, Roxburgh, Perth, Stirling, and Forfar was then a seat of the Scots kings. Lying along a ridge 115 metres above the Forth, it began life as a fortress built by Malcolm III Canmore. It was here in 1068 that he married Princess Margaret, and four years later founded the Abbey Church of the

Holy Trinity, which became a Benedictine abbey in 1128. Shortly after Malcolm's death, around 1100, a palace was built. It lasted as a royal residence for over 500 years; King Charles I was born here in 1600, and Charles II briefly held court, before his defeat by Cromwell at Worcester.

Dunfermline Abbey was one of the greatest in Scotland. It mined coal (only the third establishment in Britain to do this), and owned most of West Fife, parts of Lothian, and the town of Musselburgh. It had more than religious importance: it was a burial place of the Scottish royal family from 1107 to 1465. Blind Hary claimed that one of its monks, Arnold Blair, was chaplain to William Wallace, and Edward I burned it in 1304. Thereafter, elaborately rebuilt, it became an important place of pilgrimage—with three of Scotland's 112 hospices—to the tombs of Malcolm and Saint Margaret, David I, and Robert Bruce. In the fifteenth century the poet Robert Henryson taught at the abbey school, and his 'The Burges Mous and the Uponlandis Mous', a moral tale about the risks of the big city, anticipates Beatrix Potter's efforts by four centuries, though it's based on his own extensive European travels. Not that Dunfermline would face that sort of urban peril. Its houses were mainly fragile constructions of wood-frame, mud, and wattle, with small trades, as well as cattle- and poultry-keeping, carried on in their long 'backlands'. The abbey and its associated buildings were stone-built; arguably the town only became so when in 1560 the church was vandalized by the Reformers, and then unsentimentally quarried to bits. This may show Max Weber's 'ascetic Calvinism' prevailing over nationalism, but the town—badly damaged by fire in 1624—became a backwater with no more than 1,600 inhabitants.

It revived two centuries later as a centre of the linen industry, valued at £700,000 by the 1830s, and through local coal mines, connected by horse tramways to the Forth. Four kilometres away Broomhall, the neo-classical seat of the earls of Elgin, descendants of Robert Bruce, bore witness to another cultural coup; the seventh earl (1766–1841) shipped back to Britain in 1812 the Parthenon marbles, now in the British Museum. Scarcely less controversial was the town's other benefactor Andrew Carnegie (1837–1919), from a radical linen-weaving family, who emigrated to the USA in 1848, and became a steel boss. In 1901 he sold out to United Steel for 89 millions, in part by beating down the unions by using the private security firm of another Scots ex-radical,

Allan Pinkerton. In the 1890s Carnegie returned to Scotland and formed a trust to replan the town, now connected to Edinburgh by the Forth Bridge (1890). Under Patrick Geddes, this became the pioneering project of modern town planning, and nearby Rosyth became the first modern planned town in Scotland when it was built to house workers from the new naval base in 1915.

The short war of 1296 was dominated on both sides by nobility and cavalry: archaic on the Scots, overwhelming on the English side. Though nothing like—perhaps half of—the 60,000 once claimed, the English army was still massive (Edward would invest in his Scottish wars the unprecedented sum of £700,000 before the decade was out). Edward sacked Berwick on 30 March, and slaughtered its people (many of whom weren't Scots), crushed the Scots army at Dunbar in April, and by July had dispatched the Scottish records, hostages (including Balliol), and the Stone of Scone south. After securing the fealty of the Scots magnates, he dictated a colonial settlement to a Parliament at Berwick.

The Scots, however, were developing their own 'European policy'. The French alliance was accompanied in 1295 by a Norwegian alliance, part of France's way of avoiding encirclement. When Edward asserted his case in 1300 to the pope, his delegates would be met by émigré lawyers and clerics—such as Master Baldred Bisset, canon lawyer of Bologna, who led a three-man embassy to Rome in 1301—putting the Scots case, though their timing was unfortunate. In 1302 the death of Pope Boniface VIII (broadly sympathetic) and the Franco-English peace led to favour being shown to the English, albeit at a price.

Refining the Scots cause forged the fusion of history, myth, and ideology which would blaze out in the Declaration of Arbroath two decades later, but Edward's need in 1296 for Scots cash for his French wars had detonated an equally vivid practical patriotism. Within a year he was menaced by three separate Scottish revolts: Sir Andrew de Moray stirred up the north, and in the south-west a clutch of clergy and Norman magnates, including Robert, son of Bruce of Annandale, rose. Though the last group went back home, 'an unknown member of the lesser nobility with a dodgy reputation'—Fiona Watson's line—darted on the English, harrowing them in the Borders, besieging them in Dundee. On 11 September William Wallace linked with de Moray and faced the main English force at Stirling Bridge. An inept advance placed the van of the English army on the Scottish side of the bridge, and the Scots drove it into the river, killing—among many others—Edward's Treasurer Hugh Cressingham. The taxes Cressingham was to collect were an obvious mobilizer, but Wallace had also managed to create a tactic appropriate to the common army's *levée en masse*: close-packed infantry handling massive seven-metre pikes and massed in 'schiltrons' which could skewer (or deter) mounted knights. By the year's end the Scots armies controlled the country north and west of Edinburgh, and Wallace (de Moray died of wounds after Stirling Bridge) appealed to the Hanse at Hamburg and Lubeck for funds—almost the sole direct evidence which exists about him.

Edward could not immediately retaliate—his barons were making trouble about war taxation—but in July 1298 he got an army, questionable in its loyalty (many soldiers were Welsh) as far as Falkirk. Wallace then realized that the English had devised their riposte to the schiltrons. The bowmen who were later to prove so deadly in France broke the Scots ranks, the Scottish cavalry fled, and the Welsh, seeing this, joined in the slaughter. Edward celebrated with an Arthurian 'round table' banquet. The problem of holding Scotland, however, remained intractable, expensive, and to the English magnates, with an eye on fat France, unprofitable. Wallace turned guerrilla and ravaged northern England, while still swearing fealty to Balliol, then vanished in 1299 to Europe, to drum up support in France and maybe Rome. After a winter campaign that flopped, Edward's army was back in 1300; it reduced Caerlaverock Castle with mighty siege machines in thirty-six hours, but failed to find a Scots army to engage, and its campaign petered out, counter-marching in the south-west. By 1302, however, Edward was at peace with France and had his hands free. He invaded in strength in mid-1303, wintered, and after a series of successful sieges, took the last Scots stronghold, Stirling, on 24 July 1304. The Scots nobility had already come to terms on 9 February.

Edward exiled Balliol to his French fiefs, and imposed a peace which was more generous than 1296, at least to the magnates. One thorn in his flesh remained, but in 1305 Wallace, back in action, was betrayed and rushed south to trial for treason in London. Edward, following the precedent of Dafydd ap Gruffydd, had him butchered, appropriately enough at Smithfield. Were Wallace's limbs, on poles above Scottish gatehouses, meant as a sign to Edward's Scottish allies that they could deal likewise with uppity plebeians? If so, the gruesomeness did not deter. Centuries later, Robert Burns would write that 'the story of Wallace poured a tide of Scottish prejudice in my veins, which will boil along there till the floodgates of life shut in eternal rest', and a tide like this was in the making within the common army's ex-soldiers when one magnate, Robert Bruce, earl of Carrick, took his own road.

Bruce hadn't the most consistent of track records. Grandson of the claimant of 1291, he had backed Edward in 1296, switched to Wallace in 1297. Between 1298 and 1300 he was joint Guardian with Comyn and later Bishop Lamberton. In 1304 he surrendered to Edward, believing that Balliol would return. Seeing a chance of reviving his family's claim to the Scots throne, he tried to win over the de Burghs of Ulster and the Comyns, Edward's main opponents. Failing to do this, on 10 February 1305 he murdered John Comyn in Dumfries kirk. He then had the nerve to have himself speedily enthroned at Scone (few turned up) although this led to defeats at Methven and Dalry by English and Comyn troops. Bruce sought exile; his family were imprisoned or executed. Yet the popular mobilization started in Wallace's campaigns, coupled with the organizational skills he had learned from his ageing, increasingly demonic English opponent, enabled Bruce to turn a power struggle between Scots-Norman families into a national campaign. In Geoffrey Barrow's description 'a potentate in the immemorial mould of the western Gaidhealtachd, inured since youth to a rough country and to rough warfare by land and sea', he started winning back territory in the south-west in early 1307, his local, often rather plebeian, allies sapping the English and their noble allies by wrecking their castles. This retarding action didn't square with inter-family conflict, where possession of fortresses was the goal, but nonetheless it worked.

Edward's problems had only been deferred by the success of 1305. There was peace with the Scots and the French, but to keep the Scots detached from France, he had to conciliate them, while to pay for his invasions he had to either feed Scots land to English barons, or borrow from Italian bankers. (The Bardi and Peruzzi of Florence weren't complaining, and the dividends on their wealth would change the world's intellect and aesthetics.) He could not do both, and the pressure on him in France was steadily increasing, particularly since the pope was clamouring for further subsidies. In fact, the costs of war on two fronts—and the switching of expensive Cinque Ports shipping and victualling up and down the east coast—were to become in future penal for an English monarchy challenged in Parliament by a powerful baronage. At Whitsun 1307 Edward summoned his last invasion. He got as far as Burgh-by-Sands near Carlisle and then died. Froissart wrote that he commanded his body to be boiled down, and his bones to be carried before his army into his son's new domain: probably pure fiction, but somehow in character.

Edward II halted his troops and instead wooed the magnates—with some success. But Bruce and his brother Edward moved on Buchan with 3,000 men. They mobilized the smaller gentry and the commons against the traditional, hostile nobles, beat the Comyns at Inverurie, then wheeled south-westwards and beat John of Lorne at Brander in the autumn of 1308. Rival or pro-English nobles either submitted or cleared out. When Edward, brave but dim, invaded in 1310, Bruce confined him to the Roxburgh–Glasgow road, and captured his other strongholds; then when in 1314 he sped north to relieve his Stirling garrison, he forced him to fight at Bannockburn, 6 kilometres to the south. Bruce had taken advantage of the marshy terrain, pinned the English troops down, and made sure their cavalry was ineffective. After a day's desperate fighting, a knight fled from the English camp, saying morale had collapsed, and Bruce delivered, in the dawn of the next day, a shattering victory. Later patriotic estimates had 20,000 Scots vanquishing 100,000 English: the true figures were probably nearer 8,000 to 24,000—many of the latter being Welsh or Gascon. Bruce had triumphed, as Archie Duncan puts it, 'over the Scots', who now accepted him as king. Hostilities continued: Bruce ravaged northern England in 1314–19, bitter famine years, and Ireland in 1316–18. Edward was driven south and in 1323 came to a truce. In 1327 he would be dealt with by his noblemen almost as brutally as Wallace.

In the aftermath of this victory, the Scots nobles petitioned Pope John XXII to recognize their independence, in return for which they would go on crusade. In 1320 a declaration of the nobility, the Church, and 'the community of the realm' was transmitted to Rome. It ended with the remarkable passage:

We are bound to him [King Robert] for the maintaining of our freedom both by his right and his merits, as to him by whose salvation has been wrought unto our people, and by him, come what may, we mean to stand. Yet if he should give up what he has begun, seeking to make us or our kingdom subject to the king of England or the English, we would strive at once to drive him out as our enemy . . . For, as long as a hundred of us remain alive, we will never on any conditions be subjected to the lordship of the English. For we fight not for glory, or riches, or honour, but for freedom alone, which no good man gives up except with his life.

This splendid eloquence was promptly binned by the pope, and didn't reappear for three centuries, though the gist of it, derived from copies, figures in Fordoun, Bower, and Barbour's *Brus*. Historians then saw this distinctly qualified loyalty to Robert as a key document of popular nationalism, yet its language was not totally original, being derived from the Anglo-Norman dispute between King Henry II and the Church, which culminated in Becket's murder. Unsurprisingly, perhaps, for its drafter was the Abbot of St Thomas's Arbroath, dedicated to the 'turbulent priest'. Nor were Bruce's ambitions confined to Scotland. His brother Edward wanted to be king of Ireland and succeeded in 1316, repulsing the English sovereign lordship. For a few months the whole structure of power in the islands was put in play, as his army drove south towards Dublin, only to be halted by his death in battle at Faughart, near Dundalk in 1318. At Northampton in 1328, Edward III (or in reality Henry Mortimer, his father's killer) seemed to settle things. He recognized Scotland's independence, persuaded the pope to do likewise, and betrothed his sister Joan to Bruce's 4-year-old son David. Bruce himself, at 54, was at an end. Worn out, he retired to Cardross, his quiet, thatched, unfortified summer hall on the Clyde, and sailed and fished like the Celtic forebears he was careful to acknowledge. There in 1329, probably not of leprosy as legend has it, but of an aggravated scurvy, he died.

David II and Joan were married in 1328, when Edward III was also married to Philippa of France. But two years later Edward overthrew and executed Mortimer, and backed an invasion by John Balliol's son, Edward.

Hammered in two battles—Dupplin (1332) and Halidon Hill (1333)—fought on a Bannockburn scale, the Scots nobles sent the infant royals in 1334 to Philip VI in France, where they remained until 1341. Meanwhile, constant guerrilla attacks wore down the English—at war with France after 1337—and pretender Balliol. Independence was won here, not at Bannockburn, and by unknown men.

When David came back, he put himself at the head of resistance, but was captured after defeat at Neville's Cross, in 1346. What came to pass was the situation foreseen in the Arbroath Declaration. David was prepared to concede the succession to the English, but the Scots Parliament preferred to ransom him. In 1356 Edward and Balliol invaded again, and wasted the Lothians, but the former was now fully concentrated on France—he won the battle of Poitiers in that year—and had to cope with the impact of the Black Death. He released David against a ransom of 100,000 merks. In 1357 the Estates met and arranged taxation to accomplish this. In 1364 they had again to prevent David from conveying the crown to Edward, if he died childless; instead, they took over the ransom and extended the truce to twenty-five years. The English, under pressure in France, accepted. Unpopular and unfecund, David died in 1371.

By this time Scotland had become, through the French alliance, a counter in European affairs, and the feudal and economic linkages between the island kingdoms had been broken. Scots nobles lost their English fiefs; after 1380 the Scots pound floated (or rather sank) free of the English pound. The Black Death had not been, it seems, so severe in Scotland, something which fits with low, Cooper-scale population estimates. So there was no uprising of scarce, touchy labour like the Peasant's Revolt of 1381. While the Plantagenets fought in France, the French used the Scots alliance to check them. Scots expatriate academics, clergy, and troops underwrote the French line on the papacy, which shifted it to Avignon in 1309 under Clement V. In the Great Schism of 1378–1417 they would back the French Pope Clement VII and his successors.

OUR KINGS WERE POETS TOO THEMSELL, BAULD AND JOCOSE . . .'

Antonio Alati, bishop of Urbino, found himself papal legate in Scotland in 1437. His little city in the Italian Marches was just about to blossom under its benevolent ruler Federigo de Montefeltro into one of the great Renaissance centres, home to Raphael and Bramante and, seen in retrospect by Castiglione, the model of what a cultivated court should be. Alati was confronted with the corpse of James I, king of Scotland, murdered in the cellars of the Dominican friary at Perth. Southern cultivation faced again by northern barbarism? Not quite so simple. Duke Federigo made his money as a mercenary, while the late king was every bit as energetic a builder, as his great new palace of Linlithgow showed. He was a poet, too, whose 'Kingis Quhair', with its thoughts shifting from the late classicist Boethius' *Consolations of Philosophy* (translated by King Alfred, a suitable role model) to vivid descriptions of nature, would have passed muster in Urbino.

> And on the small grene twistis sat
>   The lytill swete nightingale, and song
> So loud and clere the ympnis* consecrat   [hymns
>   Of lufis use, now soft, now loud among,
> That all the gardyng and the wallis rong
> Right of their song, and on the copill next
> Off thair suete harmony, and lo the text:
>
> 'Worschippe, ye that loveris bene, this May,
>   For of your bliss the kalends are begonne,
> And sing with us, away, winter, away!
> Cum, somer, cum, the swete sesoun and sonne!'

But, however mindful, like Federigo, of the common weal in difficult times—'the key guards the castle and the thorn bush the cow'—James was less inspiriting. He was seen as 'passionate, greedy and vindictive' by another Italian, the Siennese roué Aneas Silvius Piccolomini (later Pope Pius II), who visited him in 1435. He modelled himself on Henry V, the battler of Agincourt, whom he saw close up as a prisoner-companion, yet he seems, in comparison, a king of a new and recognizably modern sort.

The Stewart dynasty lasted until 1714. It was never less than interesting (certainly when compared with the intellectual tundra of Hanover), hence its resilience and even—especially?—the veneration of its most dysfunctional members: Mary, Charles I, Charles Edward? It was also during its Scottish career chronically undercapitalized, and marked by violence, early deaths, and long minorities, dismaying to a judicious nationalist historian like James Halliday. When he ascended the throne James I was 11. James II would be 6, James III 9, James V only one, his daughter Mary under a week, and James VI thirteen months. Charles II, who was 19 when declared king of Scotland, was almost elderly. These kings—and their guardians—were faced with powerful noblemen, north and south, who regarded the Stewarts as just another ambitious family: the Clan Donald who boasted the title of Lords of the Isles after 1354, and the Douglases and their relations, whose lands marched with the Border. But the monarchy was still a nexus of Scots patriotism, and its income and power steadily increased, while England's internal turmoil and involvement in France were continuing factors of weakness. Only two Scots kings were actually murdered between 1300 and 1500: James I and III, compared with four—Edward II, Richard II, Henry VI, and Edward V—in England, which might indicate that as an institution the Scottish monarchy was regarded as essential even by the mightiest of territorial magnates. As such, it developed, and steadily accumulated resources, until it overshadowed them; in the early sixteenth century Gordon Donaldson describes it as playing 'a part in the international scene in almost ludicrous disproportion to the real importance of the country'.

The Stewarts' first phase was unpropitious, though minorities weren't the problem. David II was succeeded by the 55-year-old Robert II, son of Walter the Steward, who had married the Bruce's daughter Marjorie, and started the dynasty. Robert had been regent, 1338–41, and then the nominated heir, but he fell foul of his brother-in-law and after a rebellion was imprisoned in 1363. His reign turned out uneventful; the economy reached its medieval zenith; and the royal finances rose on this tide. Robert's problem remained that of becoming more than *primus inter pares* among the major magnates, who had done all too well out of the redistribution of lands held earlier by English noblemen. Whether he helped his line by siring twenty-one children is a moot point—he spent much time fighting them—but primacy became critical during the reign of his (legitimized) son Robert III, reigned 1390–1406. Robert had been injured in a riding accident two years before his accession in 1390, and his kingdom was effectively (ineffectively would be more accurate) ruled by his brother Robert Stewart, earl of Fife, who became duke of Albany in 1398. Albany captured Robert's scapegrace eldest son David, duke of Rothesay, and murdered him at Falkland in 1402. In semi-exile at Rothesay, Robert sent his surviving heir, James, to France in 1406. James was captured by the English—news of this was said to have caused his father's death—and held until ransomed in 1424.

By this time Scotland had become a factor in European affairs through the French alliance and its policy on the papacy. Charles VI of France had activated the alliance twice as part of his counter-attack on Richard II, who was embarrassed by the Peasants' Revolt (1381). This provoked English armies to invade in 1383 and 1385, wasting much of the south-east, despite the earl of Douglas's success at Otterburn in 1388. Dying before victory was achieved, he was immortalized in the ballads:

> But I hae dreamed a dreary dream
> Ayont the Isle of Skye.
> I saw a dead man win a fight
> And I knew that man was I.

Destruction was not on the scorched-earth scale that would be inflicted on Wales by the conflict of Owain Glyndwr and Henry IV (reigned 1399–1413), but French troops sent to Scotland could do little, and were liked less.

Although it was renewed in 1407–8, James's eighteen years at the English court weakened the Auld Alliance. Shakespeare's Captain Jamy fought for Henry V at Agincourt, because he would have been hanged as a traitor to Henry's royal hostage if caught fighting for the French. After Agincourt, English power in France reached its apogee, with the Treaty of Troyes giving Henry the reversion of the French throne, but even before James's release the Alliance was coming back into play, thanks to the contributions of impressive fighting men in the Garde Écossaise and Gens d'Ordonnance. At Baugé in 1421 the Scots soldiery tilted the balance against the English. This, and Henry's death the following year, opened the way for Jeanne d'Arc. In 1428 James I's daughter was betrothed to the dauphin, and Scots in the

French army helped enable the success of Jeanne, and the subsequent expulsion of the English, completed in 1453. The salience of Scots in France is enough, as with the Montefeltri in Italy, to suggest that fortunes that might have been made in trade were now being made on the battlefield or in the French professions.

James I's capture gave the great noblemen, notably the Stewart dukes of Albany, a reprieve, though it and the terms of his ransom also kept several out of harm's way as hostages in England. From 1424, however, he could demonstrate the Stewart characteristics of energy, intellect, and impulsiveness. He arrested and executed Albany and his allies, summoned Parliaments, and extended taxation, backed the burghs and gentry against the great nobility, and (though with little success) tried to extend his rule into the Highlands. His symbol was Linlithgow Palace, with its accent on opulence rather than defence, the home of a Renaissance monarch. A palace conspiracy led to his assassination by Sir Robert Stewart, Royal Chamberlain, in 1437. His widow, aided by Bishop Alati, had the killers tortured (peculiarly brutally) and executed, but another twelve years of minority rule weakened the monarchy.

T. C. Smout famously wrote of Scotland at this time: 'Highland society was based on kinship modified by feudalism, lowland society on feudalism tempered by kinship. Both systems were aristocratic, unconscious of class, designed for war.' Re-examination of concepts and environments has shown more complex variations. At its anarchic worst this could break down into the sort of mayhem in which getting blood-feuds sorted out according to rules created a system of sorts: not unlike Albania today. But a system of alliances which ran from legal dependence to protection racket was developing from the mid-fifteenth century in the 'bond of manrent'. Lairds paid homage to superiors among the great magnates by legal covenants. The latter in turn disposed of extensive 'heritable jurisdictions' in which they exerted wide authority, most notably the MacDonald Lords of the Isles, whose power was pushed eastwards to Inverness, and who conducted themselves in the fifteenth century almost as sovereigns.

In the south-west the Douglases, descendants of Bruce's ally, were similarly unchallenged. By the time, James II took up personal rule in 1449, they had forged an ambitious alliance with the courtier Livingstones. As the

English court of Henry VI was weak, and about to lose Gascony, it could not throw its influence one way or another in Scotland. James had to undertake the reduction of the Douglases on his own. This he did with diplomatic skill—building allies among other magnates—and total ruthlessness: notably the straightforward murder of the eighth earl of Douglas at Stirling in 1452. Gunpowder helped: in 1457 James got 'Mons Meg', the huge bombard now in Edinburgh Castle, as a present from the duke of Burgundy, though other guns were used to raze the chief Douglas strongholds. By 1455, at the battle of Arkinholm, he had destroyed the family and annexed their lands, a valuable financial strengthening of the monarchy. Again a speculative attack on England followed, triggered by the overthrow of Henry VI, but at Roxburgh in 1460, besieging an English garrison, James was killed when one of his guns exploded. That Berwick was retaken in the following year did not compensate much.

James III, then 8, did not rule personally for nine years. Queen Mary and Bishop Kennedy disputed control, and into the vacuum came the ambitious Boyd family, until their overthrow in 1469. The Scots crown was now embroiled in the Wars of the Roses, the internal English power struggle which followed defeat in France. James favoured the Lancastrian side, which had the hapless Henry VI in its power, while the Yorkist king Edward IV backed the highland nobles, and particularly the Lords of the Isles, against him. A useful dynastic alliance with Norway—James's marriage to Margaret, daughter of Christian I of Denmark and Norway—was carried through in 1469. In default of a dowry, Orkney and Shetland formally became Scots in 1472. Devious and unpopular, James pressed for an English alliance (Blind Hary's *Wallace* was a riposte to this by the southern nobles). He sent a detachment to fight against Richard III at Bosworth, but soon after was opposed by his son. James III dispersed the rebels at the battle of Sauchieburn (near Bannockburn) in 1488, but fell from his horse and was mysteriously murdered in its aftermath.

Independence made for pride—'Fier comme un Écossais' the French would remark—but it meant that the prosperity of the thirteenth century, largely sustained by the export of wool and cattle to England, was over. Wool exports fell after 1390. Comparing 1320 and 1475, they were down by almost three-quarters, and exports of hides were down by half. Trade

4. The elaborate crown spires of late medieval Scotland (left) were to be found at Glasgow Tolbooth, Aberdeen King's College, Linlithgow Kirk, and here at St Giles Edinburgh. They made concrete the boast of the Scottish monarch to have 'crown imperiall' ambitions, the equal of any European monarch, so the crown resembled that of Charlemagne. This appealed to Henry IV (right) whose father got full monarchic access to church patronage status from the Pope in 1487.

remained depressed until the 1570s. Why was this? South of the Forth the waters were hostile, where they had once been friendly: continental traders noticed the sheer size of Scottish merchantmen, and put it down to their heavy armament. The effects of export decline were felt in the towns, where trade stagnated where it didn't decrease, and the merchant guilds became deeply defensive of its privileges, provoking counter-organization by the craftsmen. Scots urban backwardness was shown by the fact that Norwich, with about 10,000 people, England's second-largest city in 1500, had four times more trades than Edinburgh, Scotland's largest. The negative trade balance was reflected in the state of the coinage: by 1400 its silver content fell to only 30 per cent of its 1296 level, and halved again by 1470. Besides remote allies and perilous seas, there was also the factor of the plague. First attacking Scotland in 1349, and then a further seven times in the next century, even its first visitation was reckoned by Wyntoun (still the main authority) to have cut the population by a third, though more recent estimates suggest that the long-term decline was probably by a fifth. Although less devastating than in England, only in the late fifteenth century did the population start to rise again.

Despite violence and minorities, attempts at the assertion of royal authority seem to have been credible. James I's killers were punished, the Douglases broken; James III, murdered indeed, was smoothly succeeded by his son. In fact, in contrast to England, the Stewarts preserved the institution of the crown at the centre of the institutions of the realm. Parliaments were regularly summoned; including a peerage; law reform carried through; the foundations of the High Court and Court of Session (established 1532) were laid; and a type of parliamentary agenda committee was set up which eventually attained permanence as 'The Committee (or "Lords") of the Articles'. As well as the nobles' jurisdictions, there was also a practical devolution of authority to the great institutions of the nation. The Church, endowed by king after king, and marked by the many rich monastic foundations, had twenty times the income of the crown. After 1411 the country gained its first university, at St Andrews. Glasgow followed in 1451 and Aberdeen's King's College in 1495. The larger burghs expanded in trade and influence: notably Edinburgh, now de facto capital. Of the 243 acts approved by James I, 190 were issued from there. Burghs under royal patronage were now supplemented by the 'burghs of barony' established by the nobility or Church, ninety of which were chartered 1450–1540. The burghs were given a greater role in Parliament, contributed about a fifth to national taxation, and around 1550 would constitute their own chamber, the Convention of Royal Burghs, effectively a specialized Parliament which met far more frequently. Altered in 1973, it continues as COSLA, the Convention of Scottish Local Authorities.

ST ANDREWS

Legendarily, a monk of Patras (where the Apostle Andrew, brother of Peter, was martyred) called Regulus (Saint Rule) arrived in AD 365 at Mucross, a headland on the northern coast of Fife, bearing relics of the Apostle, and converted the local Picts. The place became known as Kilrymont, a Culdee centre and, after the Scots took over Pictland in the ninth century, the name of its church was attached to the surrounding town, which was also a seat of the royal court and a bishopric which (according to Walter Bower) moved from Abernethy. In 1140 David I created the royal burgh of St Andrews, an Augustinian monastery followed, and between 1159 and 1318 St Andrews Castle and the huge cathedral of Saint Andrew were built—despite a stormy history involving sack by Edward I in 1298 and Robert Bruce's first Parliament in 1309. The Augustinian cathedral monastery was supplemented by Dominican and Augustinian convents.

It was from such places that Scots scholars travelled first to Oxford and Cambridge, and after the fourteenth century to Europe. In 1411 Bishop Wardlaw, fearing the contagion of foreign heresies, founded the university and its three colleges followed—St Salvator's in 1455, St Leonard's in 1512, and St Mary's in 1537. The see became politically important under Bishop James Kennedy during the minority of James III, and Rome made it an archbishopric in 1471. A university which was also an important port, however, became the stepping-stone of the Reformation in Scotland. The martyrdom of several reformers at the hands of Cardinal Beaton provoked his assassination in 1546 and the capture of the castle by a Protestant faction, including John Knox, who held out until 1547. Twelve years later, after exile in Geneva, England, and France, Knox's preaching brought about the

5. *St Andrews, engraving by John Slezer in* Theatrum Scotiae, *1693. The Reformation had already claimed St Andrew's Cathedral and Cromwell destroyed the castle, but the collegiate church of St Salvator and the colleges of Scotland's first university (1411) survived. Golf was almost certainly already being played on the links.*

desecration of the cathedral, which in the next century was quarried to vanishing point, to extend the town. St Mary's College, the project of Andrew Melville, became the chief seminary of the new Calvinist ministry, and under the Kirk session drunks and fornicators had a hard time.

The archbishops, insisted on by the Stewarts, survived thanks to the dynasty until 1688—one of the last, James Sharp, was assassinated in 1679—but by 1656 the town was being called 'a petty, neat thing, which formerly hath been bigger'. By the late eighteenth century the university had fallen to less than 300 students. It had once provided over a third of the Scottish clergy, now it could only manage 12 per cent. It was only to be the nurture of the town and university by the Playfair family, the marketing of golf (the Royal and Ancient Clubhouse, temple of the game, dates from 1853), and the settlement in it of many wealthy Dundee traders and colonial magnates, which restored its fortunes.

A small and far from opulent country, Scotland remained a middle-ranking European power. It was on the major European commerce routes. Its herring fishery provided the approved foodstuff for Catholic Fridays: the shoals were intercepted round the country's coasts by small inshore boats and the fish, gutted and salted onshore, were dispatched to Europe in 'busses'—bluff-bowed cargo vessels, owned by the Dutch. This trade and the export of wool kept the Scots in contact with the Rhine delta, where after 1540 they would have their Staple at Veere. The Scots migration to Europe was ambitious, if not always honourable. From the close involvement of Scots academics and clergy with European intellectual currents—which continued after the country had its own universities: 800 Scots studied in Paris, 1492–1633—came much of the country's reforming fervour. A rich land and promotion prospects often led to permanent settlement, something which Bishop Leslie in the 1570s attributed to primogeniture, and the need of younger sons to make good: 'Of this comes, that so many of our countrymen, having such good success among strange Nations, some in the Wars, some in professing Sciences, and some in Merchandise.'

'FIER COMME UN ÉCOSSAIS?'

As 'imperium'—the European power of the Holy Roman Empire and papacy—ebbed, the nation-state gathered momentum. Scots kings pretended to the 'closed' imperial crown, and built it in stone to cap the towers of St Giles and Linlithgow churches and King's College, Aberdeen. Defining 'power' became important. Did states need a break-even point in terms of population and resources, the ability to wage capital-intensive war—castles, heavy cavalry, efficient logistics—and thus to sustain foreign embassies, credit with Italian or Flemish bankers, and marriage alliances of credible weight? England and France were 'proper' powers, though with the loss of its French territories, the former was now down to about 5 million and the latter up to maybe 16 million. The empire was theoretically much larger than either, but limited by its complicated quasi-federal structure.

A small state wouldn't think of itself as a 'power' unless it was a compact city state or trading federation. It would tend towards internal divisions, with its elites also aiming for success in (*a*) bigger nations, (*b*) the international Church, or (c) trade. Scotland was like Sweden and the Italian states, a tangential player which could prosper through the stasis of greater powers. But the Auld Alliance was not an exclusive factor in a decentralized polity; the nobility and the burgesses could always play English interests against it.

What were the dynamics of late-medieval Scotland between 1300 and 1500? By 1400 the serfs had vanished (though not for good) but cash rents were high. Paid in grain or equivalent, these—along with the inland fisheries and animal products—built up commerce to Scandinavia and east Europe, though this was always marked by weather instabilities. There were also, until the late seventeenth century, the continuing internal effects of family confrontations and religious conflicts. The French sociologist Emanuel Todd (part-Scots by ancestry) has found in family organization a quasi-ethnic Scots identity: the 'authoritarian family'. This didn't (necessarily) mean children quailing under some terrifying father-figure, but a family which functioned as a political unit, as distinct from the English 'nuclear' family, which was smaller and more intimate.

The authoritarian family wasn't limited to blood relations, and was adaptive: to military activity, to intellectual life, to trade. In the European politics of the time and given a country with a taste for classy imports but little to export but manpower, this sort of institution was a potential utility: factoring remittances, furthering careers. It also leaves questions: in particular how quantifiable or economically important *was* Scots militarism? How many Scots were involved in the Hundred Years War on the French side (given divisions *within* Scotland, soldiers would inevitably be found on the English/Burgundian side as well)? And what was the pay-off? The Scots seem to have been—and stayed—remitting men, unlike other military castes who attached themselves permanently to their employers like the Croats or the Welsh. The laws of chivalry and truce, too, seem to have allowed them passage through England, gaining the best of both worlds. Did this military commerce contribute to their patriotic ideology—not so much for home consumption as to foster a 'Scottish' loyalty among the exiles, and maintain the independence of the great families?

Men, as well as goods, require transport: the Scots provided soldiers and pilgrims, slotting their movements into trade. The major trade routes were sea lanes *round* England. They carried Scottish hides, preserved fish and raw wool/rough cloth, to the complex of towns in the Rhine delta where they could be trans-shipped. This created capacity for return cargoes: spices (necessary for preserving), salt, glass, wine, pottery, steel products (knives, armour), luxury items (high-grade woollens, furs, hose). Probably, this further differentiated Scots society, as only the well-off would be able to afford such goods: an alliance therefore developed between the gentry and the burgh merchants to supply these. Castles near the cities were elaborated, like Crichton or Craigmillar, with halls, courts, and gardens, and the burgesses tried to emulate these with Provost Skene's house in Aberdeen, Provand's Lordship in Glasgow, and Culross Palace.

The statistics we have for trade are limited, but how accurate are these? Later, in the seventeenth century, officials would calculate that perhaps a third of Scottish trade was in smuggled goods. Can we rule out equivalent dealings earlier on? The cog loading or unloading off the small Fife port, the herring buss bartering material while provisioning on the east coast? Particularly if Scots administration was as creaky and disorganized as all accounts suggest. If we add pilgrims/churchmen/soldiers to the conventional trade we have a more dynamic economy, if also a more unequal one.

Scotland mattered: in the early fourteenth century it pinned down enough English troops and cash to maim Edward I's policy in France, increase his debt to Italian bankers, and his dependence on the English baronage and Parliament. Through this came the germ of an English constitutional state, and maybe the cash that mobilized the Florentine Renaissance. After Agincourt, did the Scots troops in France give enough sustenance to the national cause to break the power of the Plantagenets, and energize on behalf of the devious Dauphin, betrothed to James I's daughter, the patriotism that flamed from Jeanne d'Arc?

LAMENT FOR THE MAKARS

> Sire, ye have many servitors
> And officers of divers cures:
> Kirkmen, courtmen and craftsmen fine,
> Doctors in law and medicine,
> Divines, rhetorics and philosophers,
> Astrologers, artists and orators,
> Men of arms and valiant knights
> And many other goodly wights,
> Musicians, minstrels and merry singers
>
> .   .   .   .   .   .
>
> Masons laying on the land
> And shipwrights hewing upon the strand,
> Glazing wrights, goldsmiths and lapidars,
> Printers, painters and pottingers;
>
> .   .   .   .   .   .
>
> And right convenient for to be
> Of your high regal majesty,
> Deserving of your grace most ding
> Both thank, reward and cherishing.

Snuggling up to James IV was William Dunbar: cleric, mystic, pornographer, satirist, envier of the English, slanderer of the Gaels, out for patronage. While England was recovering from the Wars of the Roses (1453–85) the later fifteenth century was, intellectually, a Scottish golden age. On the face of it, such mastery was unexpected, as the country was linguistically so various. Three languages were in regular use: Latin in the Church, Gaelic in the west and the Highlands, and at the court (displacing Norman French) and along the eastern coast 'Scots', which had ousted 'Inglis' as the name for Lallans. In the recently acquired Orkney and Shetland islands there was a fourth, Norn, a dialect of Norwegian. While no English monarch between Alfred and Henry VIII could write to save himself, James I, and later on James V, Queen Mary, Henry Darnley, and James VI were poets of skill, and the reign of James IV produced a particular efflorescence.

James had as a 15-year-old in 1488 helped overthrow his father. He set up his bastards in Kirk positions, but he was a monarch of the Renaissance type, building up his own power, tapping (at last) the wealth of the Church by putting much of its property under royally appointed 'Commendators', and keeping the nobility at arm's length by summoning fewer Parliaments. In 1493 he took over the Lordship of the Isles, the bane of earlier Stewarts' existence (though this did not subordinate Gaelic Scotland), and played on the regional problems of Henry VII to get concessions out of him before marrying his daughter Margaret.

The richness of his buildings—the palaces of Stirling and Holyroodhouse—showed his desire to keep up with England and Europe. The opulence of such clergy as were close to the court expressed itself in the overripe late Gothic of the great collegiate churches at Stirling, Linlithgow, Rosslyn, and Perth. As farm buildings and parish churches remained primitive in the extreme, and rural industry, unlike in England, stagnated—there are no farmhouses comparable to those of Norfolk or Leicester—the few (a laird/yeoman class estimated in 1600 at about 8,000) seem to have got affluent at the expense of the many. Scots husbandmen might have used the Wars of Independence and the Black Death to shuffle off the status of serfdom, but the depreciation of the currency penalized them in an increasingly monetarized economy, something accelerated by the widespread practice of 'feuing' land—effectively a sale of property which still maintained the 'superior's' rights, traces of which lasted to the late twentieth century. When the common people at last speak, in David Lindsay's *The Three Estates* (1544) their judgement is sharp:

Rex Humanitas: What is the cause the Commonweal is crooked?
John the Common-weill: Because the commons' weal has been overlooked.
Rex: What makes you look so, with a dreary heart?
John: Because the Three Estates go all backward.

Noblemen, who had arrogated jurisdictions—powers of pit (prison) and gallows—to themselves, and probably earned a bit by fighting abroad as well, tried to keep up with Europe, and incorporated Renaissance details into their (still defensive) country houses, like the Italianate work at Cardoness and later Crichton Castle in Midlothian. These had a certain parvenu quality: compared with contemporary work in Italy and the Low Countries, Scots sculpture and pattern were crude. This did not apply to the 'functional' architecture of the tower-houses, or to poetry, where the vernacular style had rare force and cogency. Dunbar (c.1460–1514) and Henryson (c.1430–c.1500) were published in the first printed Scots book, by Chepman and Myllar, 1508. Bishop Gavin Douglas's (c.1475–1522) translation of the *Aeneid* into Scots appeared on the eve of Flodden, while Sir David Lindsay bridged Renaissance concerns and those of the Reformation. This poetic output, at a time when post-Chaucerian England was fallow, was a combination of classic grace, religious fervour, eroticism, and bawdry which was almost hypnotic. 'Not Burns, Dunbar!' was MacDiarmid's prescription for the Scottish Renaissance of the twentieth century:

> Done is a battle on the dragon black,
> Our champion Christ confounded has his force;
> The yetts of hell are broken wi' a crack,
> The sign triumphal raised is of the cross;
> The devils tremble with hideous voice,
> The souls are borrowed and to their bliss can go,
> Christ with his blood our ransomes does induce:
> *Surrexit Dominus de sepulcro.*

James IV married in 1503 Margaret Tudor, whose dynasty had been on the throne for less then twenty years. Henry VII and his son were thoroughly renewing the administration of the English state in what Sir Geoffrey Elton called 'the Tudor revolution in government'. They added to its trading and industrial wealth a concentrated power it had lacked since Edward III's time. A Treaty of Perpetual Peace—the Union of Hearts—was signed, and a dynastic union could have been timely: this goal would be commended by the Scots academic John Mair (or Major, 1470–1550), in his *Historia Maioris Britanniae* (1521). But tensions remained. James IV tried to expand the tiny Scottish navy, and became involved in an arms race with England. Henry VIII's European designs, and his pro-Spanish and pro-imperial line led to a steady deterioration in his relations with France and caused the Auld Alliance to come into play.

In 1513 James attacked northern England to back up Louis XII—a large-scale business, involving a major siege at Norham, but undertaken more as a raid than a proper campaign. After a series of tactical blunders he ran into the smaller English force four miles south of the Tweed. Their guns were light and accurate, their 'bills' (spear-axes) beat Scots pikes. James, along with much of the Scots elite, was killed. Flodden showed the imbalance which now existed between the strengths of the two countries, though the English found it no easier than before to stay in Scotland. They were hated for their depredations—the Borderers still celebrate their resistance at the 'Common Ridings' of Jedburgh, Hawick, and Selkirk, and in their ballads—but Scotland's diplomatic options were narrowing, and her dependence on France was beginning to be a constriction, not an opportunity.

Could a subtler policy from Henry VIII (not a man noted for this sort of thing) have regained the initiative for a union? Perhaps, but his courtship of France after 1513, potentially dangerous to the Scots, was inept. The duke of Albany, regent for the infant James V, was able to wriggle free, though not to counter-attack. In the 1520s Henry became preoccupied with his struggle with the emperor and pope, and his attempt to divorce Katherine of Aragon, which eventually led to the English Reformation (1529–36). James V ruled personally from 1528. He began to tackle Church abuses (though siring numerous bastards) and put the royal finances and the justice system back into order. He became legendary as the 'gaberlunzie king' or 'gudeman o' Ballengeich' who went about as a beggar or at any rate peasant and detected maladministration that way, and, in a campaign of great energy and ferocity, he began the pacification of the Borders in 1529–30. He condemned the leader of the Armstrong clan, while under safe-conduct. The balladists had Johnnie Armstrong complain:

> I have asked for grace from a graceless face
> But there is nane for my men and me.

before he was strung up. James moved towards France. In 1537 he married Madeleine, the daughter of Francis I, and on her precipitate death wed within the year Mary of Guise-Lorraine, of a powerful French family. This testified to Scotland's diplomatic importance ... rather awkwardly, as Flodden had shown what a poor hand the Scots actually had in the event of a war. Besides, the Guises' identification with the Counter-Reformation made them even more suspect in Scotland. This alliance led again to another attack on England in 1542, and a further Flodden-like defeat at Solway Moss. James missed the battle but died soon afterwards at Linlithgow, supposedly remarking of his dynasty, anent his baby daughter, 'It cam' wi' a lass, an it'll gang wi' a lass'.

3 | REFORMATION AND DUAL MONARCHY, 1560–1707

that the word be truly preached, the sacraments rightly administered, common prayers publicly made; that the children and rude persons be instructed in the chief points of religion, and that offences be corrected and punished. These things, we say, be so necessary, that without the same there is no face of a visible kirk.

(*The First Book of Discipline,* 1560)

The Solemn League and Covenant,
Now brings a smile, now brings a tear;
But sacred freedom too was theirs,
If thou'rt a slave, indulge your sneer.

(ROBERT BURNS)

'OUT OF THAT DESOLATION WE WERE BORN?'

Thomas Carlyle claimed 'Gunpowder, Protestantism and Printing' as the impelling forces of modernization. Others might have, more quietly, added price inflation, the scientific method, and sovereign power. All save the last were transnational. Gunpowder had been in Scotland since the early fifteenth century—killing James II at Roxburgh in 1460. Chepman and Myllar set up a pioneering press in Edinburgh in 1508 (thirty years after Caxton in London) and broadcast the works of Dunbar and Henryson, though Scots publishing was only a trickle in the torrent of European print. Protestantism, too, came late. Only in 1560, forty-one years after Luther's theses and twenty-five years after Henry VIII, did the Scots break with Rome. Their Reformation irrupted in a continent in which the power of monarchy had recently strengthened, not least vis-à-vis the Church, in claiming the right to prescribe subjects' religious beliefs. This was an early stage in its long struggle with old nobility and new socio-economic forces—twentieth-century Marxists would call it a 'general crisis'—which impelled conflicts throughout Europe, and ultimately a counter-movement. Max Weber christened the last 'ascetic capitalism', an attempt to turn 'proto-industrialization' and the fight with inflation—the result of silver flooding in after 1545 from the New World—into an urban entrepreneurialism: bourgeois, dissenting, if not rationalistic.

This process was recorded. Printing provoked writing and archiving. On all sides there's no lack of evidence—letters, diaries, minutes, double-entries in ledgers—but less of it was in Scots, and more in the 'common tongue'. The new bourgeois ideology would be embodied by—more than anyone else—John Milton, John Bunyan, John Locke, and Daniel Defoe, four very English writers who gained an importance in Scotland that Shakespeare or Hobbes never enjoyed. Milton was the paradigm of the intellectual visionary and reformer; his greatest biographer, in six volumes between 1859 and 1880, would be David Masson of Edinburgh University, Carlyle's disciple. A copy of Bunyan's *Pilgrim's Progress* (1678, and published in Edinburgh within two years) was found, alongside the Bible, Blind Hary's *Wallace*, and Burns, 'in every pious household', according to Robert

Chambers. Locke's principles of toleration and experimentation underpinned the eighteenth-century Enlightenment. In 1719 Defoe, fascinated by engineering and technology, with a past as a pro-Union agent in 1706 Edinburgh, created Robinson Crusoe—the ultimate capitalist individualist—out of the tale of a thrawn (aggravating) Scots mariner Alexander Selkirk.

Scotland's modernity was born out of this crisis, but it broke the national frame. Burns's passionate verse *in English* praised not the National Covenant of 1638, but the pro-Presbyterian alliance of 1643 with the English Parliament. This was a 'Great British' declaration; and though Britain was often challenged by specifically Scottish politics and ideas, it was something that Burns's compatriots accepted (as it didn't imply the precedence of England over Scotland) and the English did not.

A later poet, Edwin Muir, expressive of so many modern Scottish writers, saw the religious-radical outcome as smothering humanism as well as Scottish identity:

> We were a tribe, a family, a people.
> Wallace and Bruce guard now a painted field.
> And all may read the folio of our fable,
> Peruse the sword, the sceptre and the shield
> A simple sky roofed in that rustic day,
> The busy corn-fields and the haunted holms,
> The green road winding up the ferny brae,
> But Knox and Melville clapped their preaching palms,
> And bundled all the harvesters away.
> Hoodicrow Peden in the blighted corn
> Hacked with his rusty beak the starving haulms.
> Out of that desolation we were born.

Reformers and covenanters alike were seen as crows: scavengers, not cultivators. Muir wasn't alone in returning to the subconsciousness power of religion to warp human action. The seventeenth-century specialist Wallace Notestein, American-Scottish-Jewish, detected a similar over-strenuousness in *The Scot in History* (1946). Behind both rationalizations, perhaps, was the great psychologist of religion William James, himself of Ulster-Scots descent, who argued in 1897 for the religious instinct as a force for social and personal coherence, even when the truth of its propositions was questioned. Carlyle wrote that 'A country where the entire people is, or even once has been, laid hold of, filled to the heart with an infinite religious idea, has "made a step from which it cannot retrograde". Thought, conscience, the sense that man is a denizen of a Universe, creature of an Eternity, has penetrated to the remotest cottage, to the simplest heart.' This religious nationalism was so internalized that it displaced political Scotland. The same Carlyle coined 'the Condition of England Question'.

MONARCHS, RELIGION, PEOPLE

Whatever it did to people, the Reformation was rooted both in internal Scots politics and in the nation's relevance to the contests of European states. The Enlightenment savant William Robertson implicitly admitted this when he followed his *History of Scotland* (1759) with, a decade later, his *History of the Reign of Charles V*. There were perhaps 500,000 Scots among the 5 million inhabitants of the British Isles in 1500: there were 16 million subjects of the king of France and over 20 million subjects—in Spain and Germany—of Charles V. Was Scotland marginal? For anyone on the small archipelago, the space between independence and absorption was thin enough to make every thousand count.

The emperor was preoccupied with the challenge of Luther. The French tried to take advantage of this and swoop on Italy. On 24 February 1525, their army collided at Pavia with Charles's forces. They ought, roughly, to have been well matched but, using new cannon and new tactics, Charles devastated the French and captured King Francis I. It was a 'turning-point' battle of the sort Victorian military historians loved. Charles was now powerful enough to stop Henry VIII divorcing his own sister. Henry was determined; he needed a male heir to front the powerful Tudor monarchy, and Katharine of Aragon was unable to give him one. Charles could, and did, prevent the pope from authorizing a divorce, so Henry split with Rome. No Lutheran, he still dissolved the monasteries—the climax of an age of plunder—to bribe the nobility to support him, at the cost of serious regional revolts. He was also aware that, abroad, he could only count on some small, though sometimes wealthy, Protestant states. The two great

Catholic powers wouldn't always be at one another's throats, and in Scotland they had an ally on his doorstep.

How Catholic *was* Scotland? Another dynastic *fait accompli* had nourished a lively clutch of grievances; this didn't involve resentment of Roman dominance, but the malign effects of a sort of religious home rule. The Stewarts had got this by exploiting the longer-term effects of the Rome–Avignon breach and its resolution. In 1487, eager to appease France, Pope Innocent VIII granted James III an 'indult', giving him the right to prefer to Scottish livings and higher Church posts. Although St Andrews and then Glasgow were raised to archbishoprics, an ambitious and increasingly secular elite, in the burghs and the universities, in the court and diplomacy, battened on the Church's resources, appropriating as 'Commendators' 86 per cent of parochial church revenues. The monasteries had become backwaters (about to be robbed by the Scots and wrecked by the English in the 1540s) but this was balanced by some internal reform, notably by Bishop Elphinstone of Aberdeen, and an enthusiastic uptake of European devotional innovations—new orders of friars, processions, pilgrimages, and the veneration of eighty-odd local saints. Elaborate 'collegiate' churches were founded in such prosperous burghs as Dundee and Stirling: teams of priests providing customized piety for the well-off. By 1500 there were twelve in Lothian alone.

The main problem was the increasing misery of rural priests. Many of the more remote areas (and a third of the folk lived north and west of Strathmore) had no parochial organization even *after* the Reformation and where there were priests, some received only 10 Scots marks a year, scarcely a thirtieth of their deserts, if the wealth of the Kirk were divided by the number of its clergy. This poverty was glaringly obvious in rural churches, which were no better than byres, and christening, marriage, and burial dues, which were deeply resented. Sir David Lindsay (1486–1555) had his eye on it, in his powerful morality *The Three Estates*, performed before the court in 1540, and repeated in 1552 and 1554. He gave John the Commonweal the insubordinate lines:

> As for our reverend fathers of Spiritualitie
> They are led by covetousness and careless Sensualitie.

And, as ye see, Temporalitie has need of Correctioun,
Which has long been led by public oppressioun:
Look! Where the loun lies lurking at his back –
Get up, I think to see thy craw in a rope crack!

As a diplomat when Scotland was strutting her stuff, as well as a political reformer and poet, Lindsay was well aware of the troubles of Church and State in Europe. Scotland might be small, poor, and remote, but the balance of forces was delicate enough for it to count.

Lollardry had persisted in the fifteenth century, and after the 1530s Lutheran and, even more, Calvinist ideas from Holland, Switzerland, south-west Germany, and France arrived through England and the seaports. These did not, however, dominate a clergy which tended to be undogmatically conservative in its desire to return to older and more austere values. On this discontent, the noble factions superimposed their own policies. The Hamiltons, who had a claim on the throne through Lord Hamilton's marriage to Mary, daughter of James I, leant to the reform side, but the Guises in France and in Scotland were not to be budged from the old faith. Their connections in 1537 helped James V get the strong man of the Catholic Church, David Beaton (1494–1546), archbishop of St Andrews and Chancellor of Scotland, named as the country's first cardinal. Pope Clement VII, who had just seen the last vestiges of his authority vanish from England, required little prompting.

James V's death in 1542 might have welded Scots religious dissent to the idea of a renewed alliance with England. The Treaty of Greenwich in July–August 1543, which betrothed the infant Queen Mary to Prince Edward, aged 6, was supposed to do this. But the governor of Scotland, James Hamilton, earl of Arran (who had his own ideas about her future: marriage to his son) prevaricated and resisted further demands from London. The French alliance came into play again and Bluff King Hal ordered the earl of Hertford to 'beate downe and overthrowe the Castle, sack Holyroodhouse and as many towns and villages about Edinburgh as ye may conveniently do . . . Lyte and burn and subverte it and all the reste, putting man, woman and childe to fire and sword without exception where any resistance shall be made against you.' Compared with this psychopath stuff—executed by an army of 12,000 in 1544–5—Edward I had been subtle and persuasive. Enthusiasm for the English evaporated, while Arran came to an entente with the French, represented by James's widow, Mary of Guise-Lorraine, who ultimately became queen regent in 1554. This link, however, was put under pressure by growing religious polarization in Europe. In 1545 Pope Pius IV convened Catholic reformers at Trent in north Italy: one of his leading advisers was the Englishman Reginald Pole, another the Scot Robert Wauchope, archbishop of Armagh, friend of Erasmus and humanist. Such moderates would soon be faced with the death of Henry of England and, under his weakly son Edward VI (reigned 1547–53), a more explicitly Calvinist order.

Beaton was no reformer of the Wauchope sort but a worldly politician, who had pressed the French alliance on Arran, firmed it up, taxed the Church in the interest of the state (his version of Henry VIII's confiscations), and—though he also allowed the use of the Tyndale Bible—burned a few reformers as heretics between 1543 and 1546. This didn't make him popular, but his fall in May 1546—he was stormed in St Andrews Castle by local gentry and hacked to death—stemmed largely from English intrigues. The premature Protestant rebels held the castle for a year, expecting—but not getting—English help. They were visited by the elderly Sir David Lindsay, and joined by an enthusiast: John Knox (1512–72) of Haddington, teacher and polemicist, a former student of John Major. When the castle surrendered in July 1547 Knox was sent to the galleys in France until 1549. He reached England during Edward VI's reign.

Hertford, now duke of Somerset, was running things, but hadn't acquired patience and tact from his 1544 experiences. He revived the marriage plan by invading with another powerful and costly force, thrashing the Scots at Pinkie, near Musselburgh, in September 1547, and then fortifying the parts of the country that he held. This would make later invasions easier, but pushed Scotland deep into the Auld Alliance. The French reinforced their army and bribed Arran with the duchy of Châtelherault. They had got custody of the little queen, who was now taken to France and betrothed to the dauphin. Under patronage of the Guises—Cardinal Guise, the queen dowager's brother, was a leading force at Trent—Catholic reform was promoted in Scotland by Archbishop Hamilton, Châtelherault's half-brother, and formed the basis of a Scottish Church Council in 1549. In that year the English ousted Somerset as too expensive, and made peace in 1550–1, realizing that the Auld Alliance had—at exactly the wrong time for England—been strengthened.

The situation was a tangle of dynastic interest, diplomatic *realpolitik*, and religious discontent. For the 'new monarchs' their own powers were important—'Paris is worth a mass' as Henry IV would later put it—but did not always outdo religious conviction. The French kings, under threat from the empire and internally from a powerful Protestant faction, could use Scotland to keep England in check, whatever the religion of the English monarch. Should the Tudor line die out, there would be a Stewart heir to the English throne. But any European diplomat, glancing at Scots history (now in print in some quantity) would quickly learn that in the north, dynasticism had lots of opponents.

Edward VI died in November 1553. Dynastic momentum—which no amount of Protestant intrigue could check—meant that Henry's Catholic daughter Mary took the English throne and slammed the Reformation into reverse. In July 1554 she married Philip of Spain, son of Charles V. Almost simultaneously Mary of Guise became regent of Scotland, and by April 1558 had carried through the marriage of her daughter, now 16. There was religious congruence throughout Britain, but for a few months in that year, when the consorts of both kingdoms were European Catholics, the shadow of France lay over the north, and of Spain over the south. Scots Catholic humanists like Wauchope contemplated, nervously, a British return to a purified Church, while worrying about the rise of the counter-reforming Jesuits. Knox, safe in Frankfurt with the 'Marian exiles', lashed *The Monstrous Regiment [rule] of Women* (1555) and hymned the martyrs to Mary Tudor's fanaticism. In Scotland the queen regent had to tax, in order to hold on to her troops. This irked the lairds, and her favouring of the merchants irked the urban craftsmen; the reformed faith made steady progress among both. Mary of England's death in November 1558 meant that European affairs would trigger a Scottish religious crisis.

TWO MARYS, ONE KNOX

Elizabeth, Henry VIII's surviving child, was a 25-year-old whom the Scots or French could regard as illegitimate. Understandably, she almost instantly authorized work on a bulwark against both: Berwick-upon-Tweed, one of Europe's most massive and modern fortresses. In 1559 the Treaty of Câteau Cambrésis—formally a European peace *with* England—promised to set up a Franco-Spanish Catholic alliance. In Elizabeth's entourage Mary's marriage to the dauphin aggravated the sense of being encircled. Both factors prompted her astute secretary, William Cecil, to appraise the Scots reformers (who wanted a more radical sort of Reformation than Henry VIII's) and the Scots nobility (who wanted a weak monarchy). Squaring both of these would curb the threat of regional risings in northern England, and get rid of the French.

Reversing the policy of over two hundred years, reform-minded Scots nobility and clergy, who had been entering into a network of religious 'bands' or internal alliances, began to look to the English as allies against the queen regent. Mary of Guise, in her mid-forties, had much of the acumen of Elizabeth and masked her inclination to the Counter-Reformation with apparent toleration for Protestants and Church reform: another Provincial Council sat in 1559. Yet to taxation, and the burning of Walter Myln for heresy, was added the suspicion that she wanted to see Scotland annexed to the French crown, like Brittany. At least 400 well-armed French troops remained. In 1558 she 'began to spew forth and disclose the latent venom of her double heart'.

According to Knox, at any rate. A redoubtable pamphleteer in Germany among the 800 or so exiled clergy, mainly English, he had stoked up resistance among the Scots nobility on a visit in 1555, and returned in the spring of 1559. He drew within days on artisan discontent, aristocratic worry about the French, and nationalism, to launch in Perth (a town already notorious for craftsman–merchant conflict) an attack on the old faith. A riot erupted, images were smashed, and churches and friaries looted. This spurred the nobility into mobilizing as the Lords of the Congregation, 'purging' the lowland towns. Mary of Guise was departing, true: she lay mortally ill of dropsy in Edinburgh. What no one could expect was the death, in July, of Henry II of France in an accident at a tournament. This made her daughter queen of France and Scotland. Elizabeth was activated by the fact of encirclement, and the Lords of the Congregation acquired not only the ever-pliable Châtelherault at their head, but his son the earl of Arran who, escaping from French captivity, negotiated for support in London.

The Congregation's forces made little progress against the French troops. They had to appeal to—and after the Treaty of Berwick in February 1560, be joined by—an English army. With an English fleet blockading the Forth, the balance shifted and the new allies (or rather, the English: the Scots sat on their hands) dislodged the French from their citadel at Leith. Within sight of the siege, the queen regent died in Edinburgh Castle on 11 June; less than a month later, on 6 July, the Treaty of Edinburgh brought peace between England and France, and the withdrawal of both armies.

In August, under the governorship of the now openly Protestant Châtelherault, the Scottish Parliament met. A Protestant party of lairds and burgesses gave it a radical tone, though whether they had any right to be there was unclear. It broke with Rome and gave the Scots Kirk a reformed constitution, the Confession of Faith, which generally followed the *First Book of Discipline* Knox had issued earlier in the year. This outlined a federally organized Church, with courts rising from the kirk session in the parish through the synod and presbytery to the General Assembly meeting annually, and a programme for national education: a challenge to royal authority which would be reinforced by Andrew Melville's *Second Book of Discipline* in 1578. The Scots Reformers were, compared with Henry VIII's executions and the slaughter which followed the Pilgrimage of Grace (1536), very mild. Catholic martyrs were few, but destruction was great. In part for mercenary motives—recycling building material and precious metal—the burgesses smashed the 'images' of medieval Catholicism in their thousands: not just the great cathedral of St Andrews but the royal mausoleum at Dunfermline, a national rather than a Catholic shrine, and the religious houses. Of pre-Reformation Scots stained glass, only one window (in the Hammermen's Chapel, Edinburgh) remains.

Another shock came from France: in December 1560 Mary's consort, King Francis II, died quite unexpectedly, after scarcely sixteen months on the throne. His widow returned to Holyrood in August 1561. The transition from the *politesse* of the Loire chateaux to the dark fanaticism of the north still makes novelists' and film directors' fingers itch, but courtly life in the Garden of France was exceptional: most of that huge country was as, if not more, primitive than Scotland. Mary inherited a difficult task from her mother but she also stood to inherit the English crown from Elizabeth, provided she played her cards right. Further, she had additional income prised from the Church as well as her inheritance as queen dowager of France. Should she be religiously neutral among her awkward new subjects—biding her time until she could succeed Elizabeth? Or prepare for the European Catholic powers transforming their vastly greater population into military power?

Mary was not as committedly Catholic as her mother. Tall, accomplished, athletic—whatever their defects, the Stewarts were a virile lot in comparison with their English or French royal contemporaries—she enjoyed an initial period of acceptance, when her progresses carried her over much of the country. These and her wit and debating skill counterbalanced the hectoring of Knox, whose influence was, by the mid-1560s, less than what he had hoped for. Then, for reasons far more personal and passionate than anything which would have appealed to Elizabeth, she put all her advantages at risk. Mary was courted (at long range) by the kings of Sweden, Denmark, and France, as well as by the earl of Arran, but she chose to marry in July 1565 her cousin Henry Stewart, Lord Darnley, who was also James V's heir. Darnley was handsome and poetic; his court a great success. Mary deferred to him as 'King Henry' and was pregnant by October. He was also Catholic, overambitious, probably syphilitic, and generally unstable.

Mary's political skills dissolved as rapidly as her marriage. She openly opposed the reformers and hunted the pro-reform nobility out of the country. Darnley seems to have reacted by going pro-English. He involved himself in the murder of Mary's secretary, David Rizzio, regarded as a French agent, who was stabbed before her eyes at Holyrood on 9 March 1566. Mary then rejected her husband, even before her son James's birth in June. She moved diplomatically towards England, and physically into the bed of James Hepburn, earl of Bothwell. Clever, ruthless, and Protestant, Bothwell managed, with Mary's acquiescence, the murder of Darnley at Kirk

O' Field, Edinburgh, on 10 February 1567. Her counsellors regarded him as dispensable; the queen did not, and married him three months later. The nobility had had enough and on Carberry Hill, east of Edinburgh, they captured her on 15 June; confined in Loch Leven Castle, she was forced to abdicate on 24 July in favour of her infant son. Bothwell fled. A year later Mary escaped and attempted a last armed resistance, which ended with her defeat at Langside, near Glasgow, on 13 May 1568. She rode south to the protection of Elizabeth: the last and most dangerous of her mistakes. Bothwell, jailed in Denmark, died insane in 1578.

Mary Stewart was a drama that would run and run, like Ludwig II of Bavaria or the end of the Romanovs: aided by Schiller, Swinburne, Thomas Cook, and Hollywood. Passion, sex, intrigue, religion, violence, death, and Scottish scenery and weather in appropriate mood. All of this came very late. George Buchanan, once the queen's rhapsodist, provided the immediate, official version. Mary was a papist adulteress and murderess: end of story. The romantic version was a product of the later eighteenth century and after, which embroidered Mary's career—remarkable enough—with whatever appealing motifs from the Stewarts, or any other doomed dynasty, came to hand. In a land notoriously lacking in theatres, Mary would stay the course as Scotland's documentary competitor to Shakespeare.

At Stirling on 29 July 1567, yet another infant was crowned. But this time with a difference: the Scottish Reformation was confirmed. Knox wrote its (strictly contemporary) history as his memoirs—the first 'modern' revolutionary to do so?—and enjoyed the embraces of his new, 17-year-old wife before he died in 1572. Melville reformed and greatly expanded Glasgow and St Andrews Universities as Calvinist seminaries, and the burgesses of Edinburgh built in 1583 a 'Tounis College' of their own. In burghs throughout the country 'black Genevan ministers' and kirk sessions had it in for the ungodly and unchaste, and at one palace or another Buchanan beat learning into young King James.

'MOST HIGH AND MIGHTY PRINCE JAMES . . .'

Twenty years later, still under 40, James went south to claim his inheritance. He revelled in the cheering of the English along the way—'the appearance of Your Majesty, as of the *Sun* in his strength, instantly dispelled those supposed and surmised mists'—and in the evidence, parish by parish, as he got further south, that he was taking over a country, and a capital, of vast wealth and culture. For him, as a courtier remarked, every day would be Christmas. The Edinburgh Parliament and administration stayed, though the crowns were united and after 1608 the 'Union Jack'—St George's Cross imposed on the saltire—fluttered at the mastheads of Europe's most formidable fleet. A union of equals it was not.

Scotland wasn't by European standards backward. Its landscape of small towns, harbours, new stone-built warehouses and kirks—and hundreds of recent tower-houses for lairds who wanted comfort plus security—would compare decently, socially and intellectually, with much of that arc which ran from northern France to the Baltic. John Napier of Merchistoun, as creator of logarithms the founder of modern mathematics, was also an inventor of mining and military equipment, as was William Drummond of Hawthornden, who wrote elegant poetry in English; Sir Thomas Urquhart of Cromartie, translator of Rabelais, satirist, inventor of a universal language, and cavalier-patriot, was less classifiable. With the exhaustion through the Wars of Religion of France (1562–89) and through the Dutch revolt of Spain, things were moving in favour of Protestant states of similar size, such as Holland and above all Sweden; Scots would involve themselves in both.

But England, and particularly London, Europe's biggest city, was something new. It had managed to combine the traditional mercantile and craft prosperity of the Low Countries—now, through religious upheavals, breaking their connection with Italy and shifting their business across the Dover Straits—with a dynamic combination of plunderers, pirates, planters, and Protestant imperialists who looked westward. The English were looting the Spanish, enslaving the Africans, transforming the cash gained by selling off their medieval patrimony, and the coal hewn from their provinces, into a truly extraordinary epoch in human culture. The fat, opulent, experimental country mansions with their 'walls of glass' housed or patronized the polyphony of Byrd and Tallis, the miniatures of Hilliard, the masques of Inigo Jones. The urban comedies of Ben Jonson (of Scots descent) or the melodramas of Kyd, Marlowe, Beaumont and Fletcher coexisted with the private eroticism of John Donne or the piety of George Herbert, and the butterfly fashions of the court—tights, padded breeches, stomachers, hairdos, earrings (and wait till you saw the women!).

It might be ruled by a Scot, who—with his wife—proved shrewder and more enlightened as a patron than Gloriana. It was often managed by crafty Welsh squires—Cecils or Myddeltons who had followed the Tudors eastwards—but this was a civilization which was English in speech and writing: the scientific discourse of Francis Bacon, the topographical information of Richard Hakluyt or Celia Fiennes or Fynes Morison, above all the existential genius of Shakespeare, stitching chronicle and classic, masque and myth together in the wattle and plaster of his 'Wooden O' for his nobles and groundlings, and creating an indispensable, unavoidable text. Perhaps the finest passage of the translated Bible which James determined on at Burntisland in June 1601, from Paul's Epistle to the Corinthians, captured the king's attitude to his dominions: 'when that which is perfect is come, then that which is in part shall be done away.' This went far further than religion. The same melding of experience, power, and reason figures in Canon Donne making orgasm (however ironically) an imperial act: 'O my America, my new-found-land I My kingdom safliest when with one man man'd!' With Francis Bacon's image of instauration or enlightenment, the cusp of the Tudor-Jacobean age exemplified the sense of the undivided sensibility—a potent unity of commodities, precepts, ideas, and images— that the Victorians from Arnold to Marx, and later T. S. Eliot and the Modernists would try to recover. It would alter indelibly, though not suppress, the Scots intellect.

For the bright young prince growing up in Holyrood, Linlithgow, or Stirling, this paradise was imaginable, however dimly, south of the bald hills. As he matured the marvels of dynasticism got real enough to salivate over, despite the near-chaos of a long minority further agitated by religious revolution. The regency broke down into civil war, not as bloody as in

France (the Massacre of St Bartholomew hit the Huguenots in 1572) but as prolonged. In 1571 his mother's half-brother, Regent Moray, got shot at Linlithgow. He wasn't the one of

> Ye highlands and ye lowlands,
> O whaur hae ye been?
> They hae slain the Earl o' Moray,
> And laid him on the green.

(that was his son, killed in 1592) but the ballad captures the casual violence of the period. The earl of Lennox, James's grandfather, was stabbed in a brawl by Mary's partisans. The earl of Mar's effort was only an interregnum, but he died of it. Then James Douglas, earl of Morton, took Edinburgh Castle after a two-year siege, crushed Mary's last supporters with English 'help' as destructive as that of Hertford, and ruled ruthlessly until the young king—at 12—began his personal reign in 1578.

James was impressionable. Two years later Esmé Stewart, Sieur d'Aubigny, came from France, captivated him, and overthrew Morton, who was executed by a guillotine of his own invention 'The Maiden' in June 1581. By then Mary was intriguing from her English prison, and Aubigny, now duke of Lennox, became in Elizabeth's eyes a liability. The king paid for his enthusiasm when he was seized by extreme Protestant noblemen in 1582 in the 'Ruthven Raid' and held for a year. Lennox fled. The earl of Arran staged a Protestant but pro-monarchical counter-coup, annexed James, and ruled until he was expelled in 1585. A year later Elizabeth, who was facing invasion from Spain, came to an agreement with the young king, who accepted a subsidy and (somewhat mutinously) a London-determined foreign policy, and left her to settle accounts with his mother. Mary was beheaded at Fotheringhay on 8 February 1587. A year later, secure in the north, Gloriana's licensed pirates in their gun-crammed galleons, aided by a storm, saw off the Spanish Armada. Its ships were beached or wrecked along the northwest coast, with some interesting ethnic consequences. Her greatness lasted another decade and a half.

James's reign was one of Britain's longest: from 1567 to 1625. His ideal—quite different from any of his predecessors—was the crown of England, and his appetites shifted as his power of manoeuvre increased. Gawky, learned (right about tobacco, horribly wrong about witches), gannet-like as an eater, and maybe bisexual, he was a realist—sharp, unflattering portraits contrast with Van Dyck's idealization of his son. He extended his domestic power northwards, imposing his will on at least part of the Highlands, and in 1589 married Princess Anne of Denmark, whom he allowed to spend on art and fashion and to convert to Catholicism in 1600, perhaps to insinuate a middle way into his European diplomacy by conciliating the Catholic powers.

Confronted with depleted royal finances in Scotland, James deployed a board of low-born but able court administrators called the Octavians, and sold enough titles to near-double the Scots peerage from forty-nine to ninety-two. He ratcheted up taxation, bullied town councils, and made the Kirk's representatives in Parliament effectively a pliant hierarchy. He could use them to manage it via the Lords of the Articles, its agenda committee, or he could avoid approaching it by using the Privy Council and private financiers such as the Edinburgh goldsmith 'Jingling Geordie' Heriot, who made thousands out of bankrolling the queen.

In the longer term the Kirk spelt trouble. Lowland Scotland was evangelized from the burghs, but the Highlands were scarcely affected and the Kirk continued underfinanced. James had an initial advantage: in 1592 he played off the clergy against each other, building up the northern, conservative element in the Kirk's General Assembly. In 1596 he outmanoeuvred Melville, his formidable Calvinist opponent, and in 1611 would expel him. He constructed an alternative, derived from the political writings of Jean Bodin and Richard Hooker in the 1580s and 1590s: the Erastianism which saw the 'two kingdoms' of Church and State in partnership under his personal headship, as he wrote in his *Basilicon Doron* (1598). But he could not check popular, print-fed Calvinism. Despite one last conspiracy, James was ready for the summons from London when it galloped north, on 24 March 1603.

Emerging from his grimly contested kingdom to three times the income (admittedly from a fast-dwindling royal treasury) James luxuriated. Following the 'pacification' of the north he was moved to tell the English Parliament in 1607: 'This I must say for Scotland, here I sit and govern it with my pen. I write and it is done, and by a Clerk of the Council I govern

Scotland now, which others could not do by the sword.' Although his scheme for an incorporating union failed in the same year, James's consciousness and furtherance of the 'crown imperial' disadvantaged Scots culture. The translation of the Bible, finally authorized in 1604, was a triumph of the English tongue, and evicted the Scots language from a central religious-political position. The London theatre blossomed, Shakespeare in *Macbeth* stressing union, reform, dynasticism, and rationality against triadic, occultist, blood-feud. Thanes weren't what they used to be, in a world-view of politics and morality in which the Globe Theatre marginalized Celtic Scotland as firmly as it had the Wars of the Roses.

James enjoyed the fruits of Elizabeth's enterprise, but knew that his income was wasting away. He favoured empire, not least because 'plantation' in the Americas and Ulster helped pacify the troublesome Borderers. He was against adventures and sought European peace, though by one fateful act of 1613, marrying his daughter Elizabeth to the dim but determined Frederick of the Palatinate, he would trigger the horrors of the Thirty Years War (1618–48). Scotland he treated gingerly, from his private office, the Bedchamber, and through low-born Scots advisers and administrators. Ideas of socially engineering the Gaels out of existence were played about with, but not imposed on the Highlands; instead, the power of the clans on their borders, most notably the Campbells, was strengthened. Not much enthusiasm came the way of James's hybrid, Calvinist yet monarch-dominated Kirk, only a mass of 'nominal' adherents. At one level the balance of power between nobility and monarchy had changed to the latter's advantage, and the country's prosperity allowed the king's policy of devolution to work, but at another the removal of the court and the diplomats created a political vacuum into which there flowed the business and ambitions of the magnates and a highly political Kirk. All of this was observed by fighting men who were doing well out of continuous European conflicts.

CULROSS AND VEERE

When James visited the mines of Culross there was a sudden frightening episode when the royal party clambered up a shaft to find itself on a tiny islet in the Forth: this was Sir George Bruce's pièce-de-résistance: an offshore loading point. Culross was new technology, but it was also venerable. It was known in early Scotland as the birthplace of the legendary Kentigern or Mungo. The earl of Fife founded a Cistercian abbey here in 1217, but its property passed to the Colville family after the Reformation. The monks had mined coal and the town, made a burgh of barony in 1484, and a royal burgh in 1588 (giving it the right to international trade), rose to prominence as an exporter of hides, coarse woollens, salt, and in particular coal. It was the main port of the western Firth, as it was difficult to get to Stirling under sail, and like other Forth ports it bucked the falling trend of Scots urban prosperity. Sir George Bruce of Culross prospered on mines and salt-pans and between 1587 and 1611 built his 'place' or 'Palace' with its storerooms and painted ceilings as an outstanding example of the domestic architecture of the time; his family are buried under a sumptuous tomb in the abbey church. Other Culross buildings reflect the town's prosperity in the early seventeenth century, when up to 170 vessels could stand off its harbour waiting for cargoes. Culross Abbey House, the seat of Lord Bruce of Kinross, was built in 1608, and the Town House's architecture recalls the Dutch towns with which Culross traded, among which was Veere. But Culross was hit by the Union and the shift of trade to the west coast, and by 1881 had declined to a population of 370. A restoration project of the new National Trust for Scotland in the 1930s, it survives, frozen in time.

In 1540 the Scots shifted their European 'staple' from Bruges to the port of Veere in Zeeland, a low island formed by the Rhine delta. For over 250 years this was the centre of Scotland's trade with the Low Countries and the lands which were connected to them by the Rhine. Hereditary Curators of the Scots Privileges, meaning the right to use Scots law—Davidsons, Armstrongs, Buchans—established the export trade in fairly basic goods. A cistern was built in 1551 to wash Scots wool, near the great church, and from Scotland were dispatched 'all sorts of wool, wollen and linen yarn, all wollen and Linen Manufactures, Hides and Skins of all sorts, Playding, Kersies, Scots Cloath, Stockings, Salmond, Tar, All sorts of Barrel Flesh, Pork, Butter, Leather, Dressed and Undressed . . .'. Luxury goods were dispatched north in return, by the merchants of the 'Schotse Huizen', offices and warehouses, from which this list (of 1676) comes. These still stand on the quay, but other ports competed for Scots commerce in the eighteenth century, and French

6. *The Palace at Culross, Fife. Sir George Bruce's seat was the house of a boomtown trader showing off. This distinctive domestic architecture, sparing of glass and juggling the geometric shapes of its building in a almost abstract way, would be used three centuries later as the inspiration of the art of Charles Rennie Mackintosh.*

invasion in 1793 ended the wool trade. The population of Veere, reputedly 10,000 in its glory days, is now scarcely 440.

CHARLES AND THE COVENANT

James ruled as an absentee. After 1603 he visited Scotland only once, in 1617, but he conciliated the gentry and, through the 'Scottish Council', got his way in Parliament. He compelled the return of bishops in 1610, and got essentially Anglican practices through the General Assembly as the Articles of Perth between 1615 and 1618. Despite his divine right views, he was too canny to tackle English Puritans and Scottish Presbyterians simultaneously, but the latter would confront his small-bodied, small-minded son Charles.

7. *Charles Rennie Mackintosh's 'Hill House', Helensburgh, 1909.*

The Scots decision for Calvinism in 1560 had been narrow; it could have gone the other way. But the reforms of Melville established, in the towns, schools, and colleges, the Kirk's strict control of social order and sexual morality. By the 1620s this had, bishops or no, rooted itself as a 'national' attribute.

Charles I (1600–49), born in Dunfermline, became heir on his elder brother Henry's death in 1612 and succeeded James in 1625. He came north to be crowned with great ceremony eight years later (Edinburgh's new Parliament House was then opened: the council, tight-lipped, paid). He took his father's beliefs seriously, but his taciturnity implied not strength but inflexibility; he attempted to use his control of the Church and (after 1629) his suspension of the English Parliament, to impose 'autocracy, assimilation and Anglicanism'. There were two responses to this: English MPs like John Hampden and John Pym deployed the common law tradition against Charles and his lieutenants Thomas Wentworth, earl of Strafford, governor of Ireland, and William Laud, archbishop of Canterbury; the Scots, who had read Livy on Roman history as interpreted by Machiavelli, fused this gentry-republicanism with Calvinism in the writings of Buchanan, particularly *De Jure Regni apud Scotos* (1579) and his follower Samuel Rutherford's *Lex Rex* (1644). The Scots insistence on a Covenant between God and man—Calvinism combined with the bond of manrent tradition—had the political implication that the king was simply a party to a contract, not possessed of any individual sanctity.

The confrontation came to a head in Scotland after 1633, when Charles and his new archbishop set out to assimilate the Scots Kirk to the English episcopalian model, 'revoking' the secularization of Church lands since 1540 and applying the gains to Church reform. James had persuaded the Scots to tolerate episcopacy, however unwillingly; Charles's plan would also bleed the nobility. Laud's new Prayer Book fired riots in Edinburgh in 1637 and at the end of February 1638 the Scots magnates felt that they had to intervene before things got out of hand. The result was the signing of the National League and Covenant in the kirkyard of Greyfriars, a church built only in 1612 for the Presbyterian rite.

EDINBURGH

So dominant is the image of Edinburgh, its great castle riding above the roofs of the Old Town, the squares and quadrants of the New Town marching off to the north, that it comes as a shock to realize that it was only really recognized as the Scottish capital in the fifteenth century. David I chartered the town in 1124–7, but in his day Berwick was the largest burgh, and royalty shifted around a range of palaces and castles—Scone, Dunfermline, Linlithgow, Falkland. Edinburgh's growth, however, was rapid and ran against the prevailing depression in late-medieval Scots trade and urban life. Its share of Scots exports—through its harbour at Leith, 3½ kilometres to the north—increased to a 72 per cent dominance by the end of the sixteenth century, after the prestige of the city was reinforced by James IV's building of a Renaissance palace at Holyroodhouse. Edinburgh was a firmly Scots city, while Dublin was an English implant in Ireland. It thus became crucial for the success of the Scottish Reformation in the 1560s. Why was this? It was

The Arch-Prelate of St Andrewes in Scotland reading the new Service-booke in his pontificalibus assaulted by men & women, with Crickets ftooles Stickes and Stones.

8. *A well-organised and rather learned Edinburgh crowd riots against the use of the English Prayer Book in 1637. Its leader, Jenny Geddes, was not 'legendary' but recovered from documents years afterwards by Sir Walter Scott:*

As the reader of the prayers announced the collect for the day, an old woman named Jenny Geddes, who kept a green stall in the High Street, bawled out 'The deil collick in the wame of thee (stick in your throat) thou false thief! Dost thou say mass at my lug?' With that she flung at the Dean's head the stool on which she had been sitting and a wild tumult commenced. The women of lower condition (instigated it is said, by their superiors) flew at the Dean, tore the surplice from his shoulders, and drove him out of the church.

> Sir Walter Scott, citing the Edinburgh Town Archives, in *Tales of a Grandfather,* 1828, p. 446. He checked later papers, showing that when the service was returned to its Presbyterian form, Jenny was good as gold.

---

probably bound up with the vulnerability of small towns to raids by the English and the relative impregnability of the city, walled after 1513 and increasingly stone-built, and its sense of a 'burgh community'.

Seventeenth-century Edinburgh crammed into a space of about 900 by 450 metres a population of 30,000 in 1660 and perhaps double that in 1760, the date when it burst out of this medieval chrysalis to become the Athens of the North. This was the Edinburgh depicted by John Slezer (John the Silesian), the luckless commander of the Scots army's artillery (they never paid him, so he made his money by engraving Scots townscapes). Its density would be staggering in contemporary Calcutta: the city's narrow, continuously built-up 'wynds', awash with human and animal filth, stretched almost 60 metres from the spine of its single street, and their 'lands' rose up to thirteen storeys. How could such a society produce, as it did, Adam Smith, Adam Ferguson, and David Hume and the cool rationality of the 'Scottish Enlightenment'?

The burgh itself wasn't finite, and took only a few minutes' walk to quit. Canongate, to the east, expanded, and so did Leith; country houses rose on former religious land to the south. Yet a sense of community thrived in its taverns, bookshops, lecture rooms, and flats, more powerful than the various, deeply divided, loyalties of early modern London. Out of this grew the literati—the likes of Allan Ramsay the poet and his son the painter, Hugh Blair, Robert Fergusson, Henry Mackenzie, and Walter Scott—continually reinforced by advocates of gentry background fighting out the old blood-feuds through 'guid-gangin' pleas' in the courts, in an Old Town where distances were vertical as much as horizontal. Scott's Guy Mannering (1815) presents the place at its hugger-mugger zenith, in the 1750s, just after occupation by the Jacobites. This was when 'national disturbances', culminating in the Porteous Riots of 1736, were giving way to more class-driven upheaval—and the physical splitting of the city.

Lord Provost Drummond and James Craig planned the New Town in the 1750s, and after 1762 it developed to the north, in its broad, straight streets of silver-grey, incredibly hard Craigleith sandstone, interspersed with severe neo-classical buildings: the Royal Scottish Academy, the Royal High School, the chambers of 'Writers to the Signet' (senior solicitors) and the major Scottish banks: this was Dr Jekyll's city. The Old Town remained a cross-class community for a long time, though the 'burgh community' waned and was replaced by a lifestyle which reflected political control and elite affluence. Social policy shifted after about 1730, away from outdoor relief towards either institutions—the infirmary, the poorhouse—or expulsion to parishes of origin: anticipating the fusion of Calvinism with classical economics. The Old Town, ruinous and insanitary, remained 'Mr Hyde', until it was radically rebuilt in the middle years of the nineteenth century through the efforts of the City's pioneer Medical Officer, Prof Henry Littlejohn, and the

City Improvement Trust. It was not forgotten, particularly by its literary
custodian, Mr Hyde's creator, on his Samoa estate:

> *I saw rain falling, and the rainbow drawn*
> *On Lammermuir. Hearkening I heard again*
> *In my precipitous city beaten bells*
> *Winnow the keen sea wind. And here afar,*
> *Intent on my own race and place, I wrote.*

By Robert Louis Stevenson's time, Edinburgh's industries were not just those
of a national capital, with professional life bringing in printers and
publishers, furnishers, coachbuilders, and brewers. It had coal mines, one
of Scotland's first American firms, making rubber, foundries, electric
equipment, and engineering works, and in Leith shipyards and locomotive-
builders. It was, by European standards, an unusually multifaceted
industrial town, though overshadowed by the Clydeside giant to
the west.

The Scotland thus stirred up was a puzzling hybrid. Her power of
independent manoeuvre had gone with the French alliance, but her manpower and resources were attracted to places other than England. Would
the rise of Dutch trade, or the transformation of Gustavus Adolphus's
Sweden into a Baltic empire, have happened without a lot of Scots involvement, as fishermen, traders, pedlars, or mercenaries? Such diffused
activities—whose cash outcomes have never been calculated—may have
helped the Stewarts keep the place tranquil.

The country remained agricultural. Trade, manufacturing, and population had accelerated since 1550, keeping it ahead of inflation and making it
catch up on most smaller European countries, but it still lagged behind an
England which was powered by its contribution to the woollen industry
and a growing Atlantic trade. The mass of the sixty royal burghs were small,
under 3,000 population—although Edinburgh had 40,000 inhabitants in
1700 and was Britain's second city, London had a quarter of a million—but
in the absence of regular Parliaments they summoned their own
Convention with great regularity. The burghs, and not the empty palaces,

were where preachers were listened to, books were printed and sold, and politics happened.

Cultivation had only in a few places changed from the township and the run-rig system, and a phase of prosperity petered out in severe famines in the 1620s. Country farms, lacking much wood, remained primitive, and conditions were even worse among the third of the population who lived in the Gaelic-speaking Highlands. Glass- and iron-making had started, but only in the burghs was anything comparable to the European style of the Renaissance period to be found, evidence of the rise, despite the violence of the 1570s, of one dynamic group: lawyers. 'A tower-house, a midden, and a gude-gangin' plea': the last rapidly supplanted the blood-feud and the bond of manrent. The main pro-urban influences were French and Dutch, something that can still be seen in the small coastal towns of Fife (roofed with red pantiles brought in ballast from Holland) and their trading-vessels, on which it was easier to reach Rotterdam than London. The landward 'tower-houses' themselves, seats of the rising class of lairds or small gentry, were often L-shaped in plan. A circular stair-tower in the angle gave access to the upper storeys, while the ground floor was used for animals. This type was built until the latter part of the seventeenth century. Why? Because the prospect of clan feud or English invasion remained? Or because the laird was away marching through Brandenburg, and wanted to see his family secure, and his reputation martial? At Fyvie or Drumlanrig or Thirlestane, the tower-house went classical-fanciful but the defensive structure remained.

The other building to be found in every Scottish parish—and there were over 850 of these—was the kirk. The pre-Reformation parish churches, with their thatched roofs and unglazed windows, crumbled. The Reformation meant a revolution in church design—not just because of image-breaking but because activity was centred on the pulpit. A remarkable square church of 1592 at Burntisland, after a Dutch plan, was unique, but in the seventeenth century many T-shaped kirks rose in the villages, plain and functional but often well proportioned, a tradition that lasted to the 1800s, when Thomas Telford broadcast a standard design in the Highlands. To these were added 'lairds' lofts', where the 'folk above' could fortify themselves against hours of Calvinist eloquence with meat and drink, and other cottage-like buildings: a schoolhouse—to meet the education acts of 1596 and 1696—and a manse. Later, as enclosures took effect, there came stone-built farmhouses and 'steadings' or rows of cottages for former peasants turned 'hinds' or farm labourers.

'THE WARS OF THE THREE KINGDOMS'

Nine months after the signing of the Covenant, the first General Assembly of the Kirk for two decades met in November 1638 in the cathedral of Glasgow. It deposed the bishops, rejected Charles's Prayer Book and the Five Articles, and accepted the great west Highland magnate Archibald Campbell, eighth earl of Argyll, as leader. The king's response was furious. He wanted to launch a Hertford-style attack but discovered just how far his father had created his 'Great Britain' on the cheap. Lacking funds, Charles could only allow 'loyal' clans to skirmish north of Aberdeen in what called itself the first 'Bishops' War'. His army, poorly financed and equipped, got as far as Duns by 5 June, and sat there until a truce was patched up. On 20 August 1640 the Scots Parliament, already negotiating with Pym in London, sent a force south under Alexander Leslie, Viscount Leven, formerly a Swedish field marshal in the German wars. Professionally commanded and ideologically stiffened by Calvinist chaplains, it defeated another inadequate royal army and occupied Newcastle, source of London's coal, on the 30th. It had to be bought off, and Charles had to summon a London Parliament to do this. The Parliament was circumspect (though it got Strafford's head); the king grudging and untrustworthy. He was further pressured by the Scots when he came north in August 1641, and their Parliament emerged with autonomy. The Catholic Irish, observing royal weakness and fearing parliamentary repression, rose two months later against the 'planting' of colonists. The massacre of Protestants made Parliament in London demand an expeditionary force, but it had no trust in the king. Tensions steadily worsened and Charles turned on Westminster. Civil war in England broke out on 22 August 1642.

The Scots were at a military advantage; in 1641 they and English parliamentary commissioners negotiated a union which would preserve the separate Parliaments, and put the monarchy under restraint. In support of the invasion of Ireland by the English Parliament-sanctioned army, a Scots Covenanting force occupied Ulster, but rather reluctantly. So Pym, who (rightly) feared Royalist military resources, came via Argyll to an agreement with the Edinburgh Parliament, 'The Solemn League and Covenant' of August 1643. This promised aid to the English Parliament on the condition that Presbyterianism would be made the religion of the United Kingdom. Leslie led 20,000 men south to Marston Moor in Yorkshire in July 1644, where Charles's forces suffered a crushing defeat.

This was as good as it got. Within a month the Scots faced a new Royalist front. The marquess of Montrose, initially a Covenanter, leagued with the Irish to invade in the north-west and with Alasdair MacColla turned a feud between the Scots-Irish MacDonalds and Argyll's Campbells into a powerful threat. Harrying as far south as Kilsyth, he put Argyll to the worst of several defeats, on 15 August 1645. On 14 June, however, Oliver Cromwell, Parliament's coming man, had won at Naseby, deploying the discipline and skill of General Fairfax's New Model Army, and a month later Montrose ran into a returning Covenanting force under General David Leslie, Leven's nephew, at Philiphaugh, near Selkirk, and was shatteringly defeated. The subsequent slaughter of his Irish troops and their womenfolk echoes the bigotry and racism which disfigured the Covenanting spirit: the brutality of the Thirty Years War had left its mark.

In May 1646 the Scots received the surrender of the king at Newcastle. The programme of the Solemn League was achieved—on paper. But the experience left the Scots exhausted, just as the English army was dividing into Parliamentarians and visionaries.

Negotiations with the Presbyterian majority in the English Parliament withered into confusion and division, while at Putney and elsewhere a new *English* age seemed to dawn. Milton's 'Liberty, which is the nurse of all great wits ... which hath enfranchised, enlarged and lifted up our apprehensions' created a new debate and a new vocabulary, from Lilburne to Hobbes. Aggrieved at this, and at the threat of army centralism, the Scots reversed into a clumsy alliance with the king in December 1647. Next year their army marched south into defeat at the hands of Cromwell at Preston on 17 August. Covenanting radicals from the south-west—shouting 'Whiggam! whiggam!' as they marched, a name that would last over two centuries—took over in Edinburgh. There were some attempts at social change, abolishing patronage in the Kirk and extending education and the Poor Law, but more at repression, notably of witches.

Charles was now formally in the hands of the Presbyterian Parliament in London, with a better-than-even chance of recouping his position. But the army and the English Independent radicals under Cromwell had had enough. They purged Parliament in December, tried him, and had him executed in January 1649. England became a republic, but the Scots Parliament accepted Charles II, who landed at the mouth of the Spey and was crowned by Argyll. Cromwell thereupon invaded. His forces were stalked by David Leslie and he was about to evacuate, humiliatingly, when Leslie's religious commissars forced him to fight in the wrong place, on 3 September 1650, at Dunbar. 'The Lord hath delivered them into mine hands,' Cromwell noted, incredulously. A huge Scots army was decimated, thousands killed, enslaved, or exiled. It remained in being, only—and finally—to go down in blood at Worcester exactly a year later.

Cromwell lost patience, both with Parliament and the Scots. Scotland would be united with the rest of Britain, to form the Commonwealth of Great Britain and Ireland, ruled directly from London. His eye was on destroying the power of the nobility and promoting the interests of 'the meaner sort'—as well as, inevitably, trying to stop Charles II invading, and if he did (as in 1653–4) pinning him down in the Highlands. To this end 10,000 troops were quartered on the land, in great citadels at Leith, Ayr, and Perth, and a score of smaller forts. Cromwell's 'total union' functioned. Even a hostile Inverness minister wrote well of the occupiers: 'Never people left a place with such reluctancy. It was even sad to see and heare sighes and teares, pale faces and embraces, at their parting farewell from that town. And no wonder. They had peace and plenty for ten yeares in it. They made that place happy, and it made them so.' In fact, the whole episode cast long and ambiguous shadows. The wars exposed the 'federal Calvinist' tradition as long winded, incompetent, occasionally vicious; the brave and eloquent Montrose, who *did* believe in the division of powers, was gibbeted in 1650 for a course which the sanctified imitated, clumsily. By contrast Cromwell exemplified buff-coated good sense, tolerance, and force. He forwarded 'England's treasure by foreign trade' by successful wars against the Dutch and Spanish, and by passing the navigation acts; the Scots took notice of this, and wanted in on it. 'God's Englishman' was celebrated by such post-Calvinists as Carlyle and later on John Buchan. Hence that long Scots tolerance of federal Calvinism's ideological opposite, Thomas Hobbes's doctrine of unqualified sovereignty: 'By Arts is formed that great Mechanical Man called a State, foremost of the Beasts of the Earth for Pride.' Mechanical Man *got things done.*

In fact, Cromwellian Scotland was as expensive to run as Jacobean 'Great Britain', one of the central circumstances which, after Oliver's death, and his son Richard's inadequacies, brought about its fall in 1660, when General Monck marched his Guards south from Coldstream. On hearing in his exile of Charles's return to London, Urquhart of Cromartie burst out laughing, couldn't stop, and died.

KILLING TIME

Westminster, not Edinburgh, voted the restoration of Charles II. It also inaugurated a phase in which a strange, archaic radicalism was born, and Scotland drifted alarmingly far from England. Two and a half centuries later the word 'Covenanter' would still denote opposition to London *diktat*, in Ulster 1912–14 and in Scotland in 1948–51. The conflict between 'Planters' and 'Papists' in Ireland has never died out of a particular Protestant consciousness, yet when the 'Red Clydesider' MPs went south in 1922, they were seen off by the singing of Psalm 124:

> Then Israel may say
> And that truly
> If that the Lord
> Had not our cause maintained,
> When cruel men
> Against us furiously,
> Rose up in wrath
> To make of us their prey . . .

which their ancestors had sung at moorland conventicles. Union in 1707 would end one political crisis, but it would leave a lasting religious residue.

Charles II was greeted with enthusiasm for restoring the Parliament, which first met in January 1661, but he ruled from London, through a Scottish Council of his own nominees, and trusties who were sent north as Commissioners, appointed by his confidant James Maitland, earl and later duke of Lauderdale. Serial adulterer, intellectual, wit, Charles was quite different from his honourable bonehead of a father, which made him dangerous: the example of Louis XIV (who reigned from 1643 to 1715) beckoned. In France the conservative opposition of the regional *parlements* had been crushed, the nobility neutralized. Something of the kind was tried, less systematically, in Scotland. Colbert's new roads helped the French absolutists: Lyons was only five days by coach from Paris, Edinburgh a fortnight from London. Arguably, Scotland was now more distant from metropolitan politics than it had been in 1603.

In July 1661 leading anti-Royalists—Argyll, Guthrie, Govan, and Warriston—were hanged, Charles's earlier compromises with the Presbyterians repealed. Episcopacy wasn't only seen in religious terms: it was a way of imposing a type of bureaucratic royal authority, which could take on the regional nobility and their 'heritable jurisdictions', as well as the Presbyterians. Various of the latter, including James Sharp, were more or less bribed into line—the minister of Crail became archbishop of St Andrews in 1661— and up to 270 of the clergy left. Having done its work, Parliament wasn't summoned for another seven years. In the interval a revolt of south-western Calvinists broke out, to be put down at Rullion Green in the Pentlands in late 1666. This episode—both through the hopelessness of the insurrectionists and in the hangings and deportations which followed their defeat—created a long-enduring folk myth. In comparison with the butchery of the Thirty Years War and Ireland (and the mayhem wreaked in both by Scots soldiers) casualties were trivial. But the hangings and shootings were meticulously recorded, preserved in the glens of the south-west on the lonely memorials which Walter Scott's 'Old Mortality' chiselled.

His servants Earl Middleton and the duke of Rothes having failed him, Lauderdale took direct control. Operating from his grand new house at Thirlestane, he could count on the tacit support of two-thirds of the clergy, ever in search of a quiet life, but when Archbishop Leighton of Glasgow attempted reconciliation, he failed and retired in 1675. Lauderdale proscribed all forms of dissent and severely fined offenders, not least because Charles needed the money for his wars against Holland; later in 1678 he battened the 'Highland Host'—6,000 Catholic Gaels from the Isles—on the lands of Ayrshire and Galloway. But within a year the renegade Archbishop Sharp was dragged out of his coach and murdered on Magus Muir, near St Andrews and another revolt broke out in the south-west. After a victory at Drumclog, on 1 June 1679, a Covenanting army marched on Glasgow. It was met at Bothwell Bridge and cut down by the duke of Monmouth, Charles's bastard son. The usual vengeance was exacted, but Lauderdale, who had made a killing in every sense of the word, was finished.

In 1679 James, Catholic duke of York, came to Holyrood, which his brother the king had grandiosely extended and 'classicized'. A Dutch artist called de Witt churned out portraits of all the kings back to Fergus mac Erc, to fill the state apartments. In 1681 York came north again as Royal Commissioner, just as resistance swelled, this time headed by the near-republican Cameronians. York tried a dual strategy: to encourage local industries with various privileges—some succeeded, notably sugar and paper—but otherwise to enforce his will in Parliament and in the south-west: a policy enforced by James Graham of Claverhouse, Viscount Dundee, and the Lord Advocate, Sir George MacKenzie of Rosehaugh.

Charles II died in February 1685, and his brother—very much a reversal to his father's type, succeeded as James VII and II. He tried to reconcile dissent *and* create a Catholic community, but 1685 was the year of Louis XIV's Revocation of the Edict of Nantes, outlawing the Huguenots, and trust in royal tolerance was limited. Interference with the Court of Session even brought the advocates out on strike. Yet in 1688 the Scots hesitated before attaching themselves to the English appeal to his Protestant daughter Mary and her husband William of Orange. On 23 December, when James fled from London, his cause in Scotland, with its highland supporters, might have been rescued, but he killed it off when he failed to conciliate the Scots Estates (effectively an unofficial meeting of Parliament) on 11 April 1689. Instead, they issued a radical Claim of Right: an explicitly republican document, which implied, by abolishing the Lords of the

Articles, an unmuzzled Parliament. A deputation went south to treat on it and, grudgingly, William assented.

The Covenanters retained a place in Scottish radical iconography, although comparatively few were actually martyred, and they, too, treated opponents with great brutality. Accounts of Prophet Peden and the *Fourfold State* of the Calvinist theologian Thomas Boston became fixtures in the small libraries of local sects, and works such as Robert Wodrow's *History of the Sufferings of the Church of Scotland, 1660–1688* (1721–2) ministered to a steady 'secessionist' opposition to the Kirk in the eighteenth century, as well as to the radical and democratic ideas the Scots carried into the New World (Woodrow Wilson was of Galloway stock: his League of Nations project was grounded in a Covenant, making Woodrow/Woody an unavoidable name in the USA). The Glorious Revolution divided Scotland as much as Ireland. After James's overthrow the north rose for him, led by the 'malignant' Dundee. His army struck south and routed a Williamite force at Killicrankie in Perthshire, but Dundee was slain and his cause lost. In 1689 the Presbyterian Kirk and its federal government triumphed.

Unionist historians from Bishop Burnet's *History of His Own Time* (1723) onwards regarded the seventeenth century as a grim lapse from the cultivation of Renaissance and Reformation Scotland, a line unconsciously seconded by partisan Calvinist history. This view must be revised. Certainly, at the mid-century, the general European crisis exerted its influence, and sucked the Scots into its turbulences: hence the mercenaries and pedlars, displaced and perhaps dangerous people in a divided continent. Yet continental wanderings could be put to good use. Scots commercial skills may have been developed here; medical and legal skills certainly were, notably at the Dutch universities. In John Buchan's first novel *John Burnet of Barns* (1895) he takes his hero, a fictional kinsman of the bishop, out of Covenanting Peeblesshire to Leiden and the entourage of Leibnitz, and similar trajectories were described by Jacobites chased out by the Williamites. In many respects, in fact, the Enlightenment starts here: with the first members of the cousinhood of architects, scientists, and lawyers, and the principles which underlay their work. Scottish architecture had been a hybrid of defensiveness and display. With the end of hostilities, display won out. The classicism which Sir William Bruce (d. 1710) adopted for extending Holyrood

(1671–80) and for Kinross House (1681) was used by him to begin a small Scottish Versailles at Hopetoun, west of Edinburgh, in 1696. In 1681 Viscount Stair edited his *Institutes of the Law of Scotland*, covering civil law; 'Bluidy Mackenzie' of Rosehaugh did the same thing for criminal law in 1684.

The Covenanters emphasized the way in which modernity and conservatism in seventeenth-century Scotland clashed violently, yet were also awkwardly linked to one another. They could be described as advanced republicans, yet also as credulous and authoritarian primitives, whose redistributive politics were caught up in and perverted by religious mania. They were not alone in their fanaticism. Also to Scotland's discredit was the witch-hunting which probably claimed 3,000 lives. Sweeping across the country in waves, in the 1590s, around 1649, again in 1661–2, and finally in the 1690s, it was directed by the local elites, by ministers and lairds. Its victims were nine-tenths of them women, old, isolated, and poor. It was an extreme form of Calvinism's anti-feminism, but it was also a reaction of a semi-modern people trapped between the rationalism of Newtonian science or the commerce exemplified by the pamphleteer and financier William Paterson, who founded the Bank of England in 1694, and the old horrors of war, plague, and famine.

DARIEN, FAMINE, AND CRISIS

> What force or guile could not subdue
> Through many warlike ages,
> Is wrought now by a coward few
> For hireling traitor's wages.
> The English steel we could disdain,
> Secure in valour's station
> But English gold has been our bane;
> Such a parcel of rogues in a nation.

Not content with founding the Bank of England in 1694, Paterson went on to found the Bank of Scotland a year later and also 'The Company of Scotland, Trading to Africa and the Indies'. This was in part an attempt to reverse what the Scots saw (with reason) as their creeping exclusion from traditional North Sea and Baltic trades, and instead to compete with the monopolistic Chartered Companies of London, but its geographical focus was peculiarly ambitious: the isthmus of Darien, between the Caribbean and Pacific, through which the Scots believed they could establish an alternative route to the Far East. Paterson appealed for funds in England, in Bremen and Hamburg. But he ran into the opposition of the English government and its commercial allies. Eventually, in a spirit of patriotic fervour, the Scots, their new free Parliament in the van, decided to go it alone and subscribed £300,000, about a quarter of the cash in the kingdom. In 1698 2,000 settlers, Paterson among them, landed at Darien and founded New Edinburgh. But the Spanish were hostile; no help was forthcoming from Amsterdam or London. Ill-selected trading goods, endemic fever, and dogmatic Calvinist preachers swelled the disaster. A Spanish attack was beaten off but the colony was unsustainable. Only 300—including Paterson—came back.

The Darien failure, coming on top of three catastrophic harvests, and the squeezing of Scots merchants out of many of their accustomed trades because of the ten-year conflict between William and France, sealed the fate of the Scottish Parliament, though never were its 315 members to be so preoccupied by it as in the last decade of its existence. Darien wrote *finis* to an experimental period, but more than anything else, it showed the impossibility of an independent Scotland making its way in a Europe of mercantilist carnivores. By 1704 half of its sadly diminished trade was with England. Paterson himself started pamphleteering in favour of a Union while an already rather notorious young rake and speculator, John Law of Lauriston, proposed in 1705 to save the country through the use of paper money and a commitment to economic growth. Law would go on to become the finance minister and—for a few dizzy months in 1718—the most powerful man in Louis XV's France. His ideas, deemed outrageous at the time, would underwrite much of modern public finance.

But English affairs of state were dominant. In 1700 there died the 11-year-old duke of Gloucester, the last surviving child of William's heir, his sister-in-law Anne. A settled Protestant succession became imperative. France was hostile, and a mutinous Scotland couldn't be left on England's northern flank. In Edinburgh, resentment of England and a desire to survive economically were there in equal measure. So the years 1701–7 were fraught with the politics of declaration and intrigue. In 1701 Westminster was anticipating a further war, because of a crisis over succession to the Spanish throne and by the Act of Settlement; it determined that the British throne should go to the royal family of Hanover, descendants of the luckless Frederick and the Winter Queen. The Scots Parliament was not consulted, and even its High Commissioner, the duke of Queensberry, was apprehensive. When William died in an accident the following year, only the new Queen Anne favoured an incorporating Union.

The old instrument of management, the Lords of the Articles, was dead. Perhaps it could have kept a pseudo-Parliament in being. In the real one Queensberry's Court Party faced the duke of Hamilton, leading a 'Country Party', the earl of Roxburghe leading the Whiggish *Squadrone Volante* (which might go either way), and the Jacobites. The last two were successful in the election of 1703, and the new Parliament passed acts defending Presbyterianism, Scotland's autonomy in foreign affairs, the wine trade with France, and the right of the Parliament to choose a monarch on its own. A moving force here had been the MP for East Lothian, Andrew Fletcher of Saltoun, an eloquent, choleric philosopher whose own vote would have gone for a federal Britain under the Hanoverians. But the clause appended silently but implicitly to all these declarations, by an increasingly insistent Whitehall, was that the pockets of Scots interest groups would have to be filled: in terms of continuing institutional rights, trade concessions, or outright bribery.

This was the crucial issue, and one which didn't promise much in the way of principle. The mass of the people—the mobs who rioted frequently in the Edinburgh streets—were hostile to Union, but the Scots ruling classes were there to be bought, disquieted only by being in such a poor bargaining position. In 1705 Westminster carried an Alien Act, by which Scots should lose all privileges in the south and abroad, a measure that has to be seen against the 'Worcester' incident, in which an English shipmaster, Captain Green and his crew were shanghaied in the Forth in August 1704, accused of piracy against the Company of Scotland on flimsy grounds, and condemned to death. Three were hanged in April 1705, in a crescendo of wounded national pride that ebbed as fast as it had swollen.

On 1 September Hamilton sold out, committing the Scots Parliament to accept royally nominated (and hence pliable) Commissioners to draft a Treaty of Union. Thirty-one were appointed from each country, and met in Whitehall from 16 April to 16 July. The Treaty had twenty-five Articles, fifteen of which were economic, and was debated in Edinburgh between October 1706 and January 1707, under the watchful eyes of the duke of Argyll and the earl of Mar. The issues, hard fought, were transmitted south by Defoe: the nobility, roughly half the Parliament, were bought by £20,000 in bribes. But, partly because of external agitation, the Treaty was made to guarantee the powers of the Scottish 'estates' of law, Church, local government, and universities, providing an 'equivalent' to foot Scotland's share of the British national debt. It underwrote the Darien losses, opened English trade to the Scots (something carried with a much bigger majority than the final vote of 110 to 69 on 16 January 1707), and promised help with the development of Scottish industry.

The Parliament was dissolved on 28 April. Scotland would send forty-five MPs (thirty from the counties, fourteen from the sixty-five royal burghs, voting in groups, and one for Edinburgh) and sixteen peers (elected by the Scots nobility, who numbered 154) to Westminster. Unionists would praise the prescience of the men of 1707, Jacobites and nationalists would execrate them, but in itself such a union was probably no more momentous than its architects were moral. Within a decade Hamilton would anyway be dead, shot in a duel, and Mar a Jacobite exile. The Union might have gone the way of other such compacts elsewhere in Europe and been, for one reason or another, dissolved. That this didn't happen was because Parliament was only one of several representative bodies—the General Assembly, the Faculty of Advocates, the Convention of Royal Burghs—which could move into the vacuum it left. As Burns's fervent poem indicates, resentment of the Union continued to fester in the north—as did advocacy of it. Not so in London: the English forgot about it—and the start of the 'British' experiment—almost completely.

4 | UNION AND ENLIGHTENMENT, 1707–1815

There is no European nation which, within the course of half a century or little more, has undergone so complete a change as this kingdom of Scotland . . . But the change, though steadily and rapidly progressive, has nevertheless been gradual; and like those who drift down the stream of a deep and smooth river, we are not aware of the progress we have made until we fix our eye on the now-distant point from which we have been drifted.

(Sir Walter Scott, *Waverley*, 1814)

But, Mousie, thou art no thy lane,
In proving foresight may be vain:
The best laid schemes o' Mice an' Men
    Gang aft agley,
An' lea'e us nought but grief an' pain
    For promis'd joy.

Still thou art blessed, compar'd wi' me!
The present only toucheth thee:
But Och! I backward cast my e'e
    On prospects drear!
An' forward, tho' I canna see,
    I guess an' fear!

(Robert Burns, 'To a Mouse', 1785)

A CAUSE LOST FOREVER

'The motives will be, trade with most, Hanover with some, ease and security with others,' wrote Roxburghe (now a duke), whose *Squadrone Volante* had done much to bring the Union about. Initially, its 'boasted advantages' were in short supply, and might have evaporated altogether in 1708 when the French King and the Pretender launched an invasion attempt. Visible from Edinburgh Castle, their fleet failed to make a landing. Native opinion was divided, between Jacobites and Calvinists, highland and lowland, as the new arrangements took effect. The Scots ought to have condemned the abolition of their own Privy Council in 1708, but didn't, regarding it as a centre of Jacobite intrigue, yet many Union supporters were scandalized when Westminster reintroduced patronage in the Church in 1712, as a result of Tory-Jacobite pressure. The right of landowners to appoint ministers caused steadily mounting conflict, and finally exploded in 1832–43. Yet it was not the immediate problem which confronted Whitehall, and would make Scotland more dangerous than Ireland for forty years.

'We could aye peeble them wi' stanes when they werena' gude bairns,' complained the Edinburgh folk when the Parliament men departed. Discontent over remote, manipulative government throbbed away—the Union only just survived a repeal motion at Westminster in 1713—and expressed itself in the Levellers' rising against enclosures in Galloway in 1724 and the bloody riots against the Malt Tax in the following year. London discovered how expensive Union was proving, but trying to recover costs with new taxes was risky. A rather circumspect Edinburgh mob hanged the captain of the town guard, 'Black Jock' Porteous, in 1736 (they bought the rope and got a receipt). He had shot demonstrators protesting against the execution of a popular smuggler at a time when smuggling may have made up a third of the country's trade. But there were few reasons for Jacobite and Presbyterian to coalesce. The latter's furious reaction to Kirk patronage meant that by 1820 a third had joined 'seceding' bodies, whose doctrines were hair-splittingly complex. 'Controversial divinity' in Scotland meant arguments about Church government, not theology, and involved by the end of the century a bewildering variety of sects—Auld Lichts and New Lichts, Burghers and Anti-Burgers, Lifters and Non-Lifters. A common quality was the conviction of even the tiniest group that its conventicle represented the True Kirk, from which 'the others' were backsliders: an ideological thrawnness (stubbornness) passed on almost *in toto* to the Scottish socialist movement. The towns were penalized by the abolition of protection on Scottish manufactures. Though grain and cattle exports—the latter driven on the hoof via the markets of Crieff and Falkirk—increased, Yorkshire and Cotswold competition shrank a woollen industry which had long and ineffectually tried to improve its quality, and linen stagnated.

In 1715 regal union with Hanover began, and lasted until 1837. George I was crowned, and the Jacobites rose under the Earl of Mar, under Queen Anne a maker of the Union. In the Highlands, he marshalled a force of 12,000, winning over government commanders, but at Sherrifmuir just north of Stirling on 13 November he was checked by a much smaller army under the duke of Argyll. His English allies surrendered at Preston, and by 22 December, when 'James VIII' landed at Peterhead, his forces had melted away. After a small, half-hearted attempt in 1719 in the west Highlands, the land went quiet for a quarter-century. Peace of a sort with France lasted until 1740. In England the South Sea Bubble of 1720 gave London a taste of Darien, disease and gin-drinking ravaged the English population (which remained pretty static until 1750), and Sir Robert Walpole stitched up the political system. In Scotland, after 1724, while Rob Roy MacGregor was doing his stuff as 'gentleman-drover', the government laced the Highlands with military roads, laid out by the Irish General George Wade, and tactfully demilitarized such clans as it could, while promoting the interests of one: the Campbells.

GLENCOE AND INVERARAY

The steep-sided, dark crevasse of Glencoe, with buttresses of peaks—Buchaille Etive Mor, Meall Derg—rising to over 1,000 metres from sea level, has spelt highland tragedy and grandeur to many generations of visitors and film makers, the more so as it is inextricably linked with the 'slaughter under trust' of 1692. That February a detachment of soldiers under the command of Captain Campbell of Glenlyon was sent on a punitive expedition against the

MacDonalds of Glencoe. After Bonnie Dundee's abortive attack, all northern clans had to attest to a bond of fealty to William III but that of MacIan of Glencoe had failed to do so on time. Lord Advocate Stair, kinsman of the great lawyer, determined on a punishment, instructing Glenlyon to kill every man in the glen under 70. After enjoying the clan's hospitality, the soldiers struck on the morning of 13 February, and put MacIan and his family, and upwards of thirty clanspeople, to the sword.

The massacre has been linked to clan wars, but these were fast dying out. The culprits were investigated—in a remarkably judicious way—by the Scottish Parliament in 1695, and Stair was censured. The background was a confusion between approaches of coercion and subtler 'divide and rule', which could lead to scores being settled with official sanction. Glencoe poisoned relations with the highland clans for two generations: in 'making an example' of the MacDonalds, it has the jarringly modern tone of ends justifying means, the tidying-up of what Marx and Engels called 'national refuse'. Their contemporary T. B. Macaulay, the grand Whig-imperial historian, devoted a surprising length of his History of England (1848) to this horror, slightly baffling until one realizes that he was 'national refuse': a Lewisman by descent, and only a third-generation English-speaker.

Mrs Marx, Jenny von Westphalen, was kin to the Campbells, and 80 kilometres south of Glencoe, on the shores of Loch Awe, the clan's new Inveraray Castle was rising as Jacobitism came to its bloody end on Culloden Moor. Built by Archibald, third duke of Argyll, between 1744 and 1761 at a cost put at £300,000, standing in a huge planted park and ringed by the spectacular mountains of Argyll, it was a fortress in name only and reflected the change from 'militant' to 'civil' society. The original town, a burgh of barony in 1472 and a royal burgh in 1648, had clustered round the old castle, which was burned in the Civil War in 1644; its master the earl of Argyll had crowned Charles II in 1651 and then deserted him; the restored monarch executed him in 1661. His son died in 1685 for his part in Monmouth's rebellion against James VII and II. But the first duke got his title by backing the Revolution in 1688, and the second duke, the effective ruler of Scotland, demolished ruin and town in 1742, and resettled the folk on the promontory. With only one unhappy gap in 1736–45 when he lost control because of the Porteous Riots, Argyll won Scotland for the Union, rooting it in shrewd *patronage and economic improvement, and pioneering the replacement of military tenures by commercial rents. Inveraray could almost be a miniature of this, with its terrace of classical houses fronting the bay and its main street running at right angles to kirk and courthouse. Robert Morris's four-square castle, built almost like a child's toy, was a first fruit of the Gothic revival; south of the town, at Furnace, was from 1775 to 1813 one of Scotland's first ironworks, using charcoal taken from the local forests. Inveraray's prosperity was based on fisheries—its seal showed herring streaming into a net—but started to recede as the herring shoals left Loch Fyne in the later nineteenth century. By 1891 its population, 1,233 in 1841, had fallen to 816.*

After the violent quasi-religious conflicts that had convulsed the European powers in the seventeenth century, the configuration of the pre-Reformation period had been resumed, though the now United Kingdom was still faced with France, which had twice the population, was technologically advanced, and efficiently and autocratically run. Anglo-French conflict would be imperial—in India and North America—and the Scots would contribute mightily to it. But the 'Auld Alliance' role of diverting English forces was about to kick in, for the last time. In 1745, five years into the War of the Austrian Succession, a determined Franco-Jacobite assault on Scotland was planned as a diversionary measure. But it was the personal initiative of the Pretender's son, Prince Charles Edward, that raised the discontented highland clans in the summer of 1745. Travelling swiftly along Wade's roads with Lord George Murray, a gifted commander, he left Glenfinnan on 19 August and reached Holyrood on 17 September. On the 21st his troops routed Sir John Cope, the government commander, at Prestonpans, 9 kilometres east of the city. The court was briefly re-established, but shunned by Edinburgh's Hanoverian majority. George II's garrison still held out in the castle.

Charles moved south to take Carlisle in November. But the English Jacobites did not rise—did not perhaps (beyond a few recalcitrant families) even exist. The 6,000 highlanders got as far as Derby by early December, shadowed by Wade's forces moving down the east coast. Helped by French invasion preparations at Dunkirk, they caused panic in the capital but, gaining no English support, started to melt away. Charles retreated, losing more troops en route. A victory at Falkirk postponed the reckoning, but on 16 April 1746 at Culloden, east of Inverness, his dwindling army was over-hauled by a Hanoverian force—in fact mostly Scottish—under the 24-year-old duke of Cumberland, son of George II. The prince proved incompetent, making his clansmen—whose wild charges had earlier been terrifying—keep in line while being riddled by grapeshot from Cumberland's cannon. The result was about 1,000 dead, followed by a mopping-up operation which, certainly ruthless, checked the real possibility of further outbreaks. About 8,000 died in the rising (1798, in Ireland, would claim 30,000) but after a spectacular chase through the Hebrides, Charles escaped to France. Perhaps unfortunately: martyrdom might have given his cause a dangerous edge. When in Voltaire's *Candide* (1759) he surfaces in Venice, it's as a pitiable shade.

In *Redgauntlet* (1824) Scott has the Chevalier come back in the 1760s, to an improving land forgetful of Jacobitism. A government general rounds the prince and the would-be rebels up and tells them that if they disperse, he'll forget the whole thing. Disperse they do. '"Then, gentlemen," said Redgauntlet, clasping his hands together as the words burst from him, "the cause is lost forever!"' But it left traces, and rather paradoxical ones. Senti-mental ballads, by Burns among others, celebrated Charles—once he was safely out of the way. The prince regent himself quietly pensioned Charles's brother Cardinal Henry Stewart, and had Canova build the Stewarts their tomb in St Peter's, Rome; his 1822 visit to Edinburgh—'a gathering of the Gael'—was an attempt to annex their glamour. Villagers continued for over a century to enact Allan Ramsay Senior's musical pastoral *The Gentle Shep-herd* (1725), in which an exiled Jacobite laird returns to right his former tenants' mistreatment. Yet it was in 1720 that a Jacobite Catholic scholar, Father Thomas Innes, exploded the 'ancient constitution' of the Pictish king-lists on which Scottish nationalist history had depended, clearing the way for the Whigs and their ahistorical 'civic virtue'.

The Secretaryship for Scotland was abolished even before Culloden. The 'territorial jurisdictions' of the great highland magnates followed. The third duke of Argyll was back as manager, with the confidence of the Presbyterians and burghers of the Lowlands. He was ably assisted by a

9. *The battle of Culloden, 1746. The last battle to be fought on British soil was a brutal affair, but a battle between Scots rather than a repetition of Flodden or Dunbar. The classical Culloden House of Lord President Duncan Forbes, Whig and ally of the Argylls, spectates on the end of the old Scotland.*

new sort of politician: Andrew Fletcher's nephew, Lord Milton, agricultural and industrial improver (his mother had sailed to Holland and stolen the secret of high-quality linen-making, and established it on the family estate at Saltoun). As Lord Justice Clerk, Milton knew the electoral geography of every Scottish seat—and probably the electors, there were hardly 4,000 of them. This facility had its pay-off in the speed with which, a decade after Culloden, a menace was turned into a weapon. The War of the Austrian Succession had been merely a qualifier—showing the main stadia of Franco-British conflicts. The Seven Years War (1756–63) was the decider, and the premier, William Pitt the Elder, simultaneously solved the strategic problem *and* the highland threat by embodying the clansmen in his army— 'hardy, intrepid, accustomed to a rough country, and no great mischief if they fall'. The author of that was James Wolfe, who took Quebec in 1759, largely thanks to them. Not only were the French evicted from Canada and India, and the 'first' British Empire secured, but their commerce fell by nearly half, a vacuum into which rapidly developing British trade and industry flowed.

As Carlyle was wont to say, one silk-stockinged group trotted to power over the bodies of their poor brothers, dead in the trenches. In 1761 Argyll died, and authority over the whole of Britain passed to another Scot, and a kinsman, John Stuart, third earl of Bute (1713–92). Like the Argylls, Bute, at his Scottish estate, Mountstuart, was occupied with farming, botanizing, and building. He succeeded at court, and became tutor to the grandson and heir of George II. As George III's first premier, he was faced with bitter party conflict. Bute was inept rather than, as his opponents alleged, authoritarian, though lured to the regal Jacobitism of Henry St John, Viscount Bolingbroke. With the support of the king he made peace with France in 1763, but for this was venomously assaulted by the London radical John Wilkes (1727–97) in his weekly The *North Briton*, establishing a strong line in anti-Scottish vituperation. John Bull (then rather a slight, put-upon cartoon figure) did not much like a 'British Empire' which rolled out jobs for sharp-eyed Caledonians, even if two of them, James Thomson and Thomas Campbell, wrote 'Rule Britannia' and 'Ye Mariners of England'!

IMPROVEMENT

'There's ane end of ane auld sang,' commented the earl of Seafield, Lord Chancellor of Scotland when his colleagues voted their Parliament out of existence in 1707. In a way he was indicating that what should begin was another song, an epic rather than a straightforward political process. Indeed, what happened involved an intertwining of ideas and programmes, social and technical change, and efficient if unelevated political dealing which, under the overall rubric of 'improvement', proved remarkably dynamic—so much so that the literati began to mutter, not always reassuringly, about 'unintended consequences'. Scottish innovation was intensely literary, self-conscious, commercial, and well organized: the publishing and print-making activities of the Foulis Brothers at their 'academy' in Glasgow, 1752–75, were integrated with the rise of the university, the study of the classics, and painting. Colin Campbell's *Vitruvius Britannicus* (1717–25) acted as a pattern-book for countless lairds and master masons, the Edinburgh bookseller William Creech published Burns and Henry Mackenzie, and in 1769 the *Encyclopaedia Britannica* emulated Diderot's *Encyclopédie* of 1751–65. The clubs and discussion groups which abounded have been compared by Nicholas Phillipson to the vanished Parliament: this lodgement in 'print capitalism' meant that they were much more effective.

Reflecting the 'Moderate'—liberal and constructive—politics of the Kirk and its 'parliament', the General Assembly, it was a minister, the Revd John Webster, who pioneered a census in 1755: he found a population of about 1,265,000. By the time of the first official census, in 1801, this had risen to 1,608,000. By then the project of Sir John Sinclair of Ulbster to form a parish-by-parish *Statistical Account* of the country had been realized, between 1791 and 1799. Nothing similar existed south of the Border.

Trade, indeed, took some time to recover from the shocks of 1688–1720. Observers wrote of declining east-coast seaports, but the Scots, unlike the Irish, had kept control of their merchant fleet, and they now possessed a banking system which was more helpful in developing business than London's (the South Sea Bubble made the government ban joint-stock banks in England). By the 1730s trade in the west was sufficiently energized for some, like Scott's archetypal Glaswegian Bailie Nicol Jarvie in *Rob Roy* (1816), to feel annoyed at those who would 'grumble at the treaty that opened us a road west-awa' yonder'. Jarvie was one of about 10,000 speculator-migrants—among a much larger total—who crossed the Atlantic in the eighteenth-century. About a third returned, not always welcome, but often rich.

Early eighteenth-century Scotland was overwhelmingly rural, and the process of modernizing agriculture, anticipated by some acts of the pre-Union Parliament, had a long way to go. Much of the country was still held in multiple tenures—infield and outfield, with the remainder still held as 'commonties' by the local community. Subsistence agriculture functioned fairly effectively, with the exception of the 1690s, though large numbers of Scots cleared off to Europe, Ulster, and England. But from the 1720s on, and relentlessly after the 1760s, energetic attempts were made to boost production of cash crops by enclosing the former great fields with hedges, fences, and dykes. This enabled cattle and sheep to crop on sown grass and turnips—with the land limed and manured as part of a rotation. Small tenants and cottars had been over 50 per cent of the rural population in the 1720s, organizing cultivation collectively. 'Regulation and cooperation', Tom Devine writes, 'had to be at the heart of the old system.' Profit and expert management—coupled ironically with the pride of the workforce (the ploughman with his iron plough and glossy Clydesdales, the herdsman who was 'fair daft aboot sheep')—dominated the new, directed from the classical mansion and the smaller but similar houses of the 'muckle fermer' and the factor.

The 'notion'—mark that word!—was that cottar and 'kindly tenant' could be 'proto-industrialized'. In the time when the ex-cottar wasn't working as a labourer to produce cash crops (some three times as efficiently as under the old system) he would be powering some local industry—weaving, tanning, quarrying, or fishing. Through this transition he would, supposedly, retain his pride. Burns's fulsome 'The Cotter's Saturday Night' dates from 1786:

> From scenes like these, old Scotia's grandeur springs,
> That makes her lov'd at home, rever'd abroad:
> Princes and lords are but the breath of kings,
> 'An honest man's the noblest work of God.'

Radicalism and patriotism consoled. The cottar would never see the dawn.

Transport was supposed to knit such communities together. It started, however, primitive. Even the run-down Roman roads which served England after a fashion petered out in Scotland. Roads of a sort, fitfully maintained by statute-labour, existed in an arc from the Moray Firth to the central belt, but were often so primitive, rutted, or miry that they got worse as traffic increased. It was easier to use them as a guide and ride or walk alongside them, or even follow beaches or stream-beds. It could take a fortnight to get by coach from London to Edinburgh, though this would change as £2–3 million surged into roads which linked farms to the growing towns. Many opted to sail; this could be faster, but also subject to long delays from bad weather conditions and the threat of being wrecked on coasts still unmarked by buoys and lighthouses. But the 'inland sea' between Fishguard and Portpatrick was both easy of access and dynamic in a mysterious way.

Here was the secret of the 'creative chaos' of capitalism: an area bounded by rich mineral deposits, growing ports like Dublin, Belfast, and Whitehaven, dominated by the huge slave and cotton centre of Liverpool, and quiet creeks where smuggling was rife, migration a matter of course, and state authority limited.

> The big ship was leaving Bombay,
> One day,
> To sail to the Isle of Man,
> So they say . . .

is a song still sung by Scots children. Where it went after the Isle of Man was another matter, but the result was an energetic and resourceful business class, from the pedlars of east Europe (where *Schotte* meant dealer and still means hard bargainer) to the Nabob: unconfined to Scots ports, habitually speculative, and unfastidious about where its profit was coming from.

One group which, early on, took advantage of the Union's protection of their trade—and their distance from government—was the merchants of Glasgow. Many had been peddling (with a bit of fighting thrown in) in east Europe. After the 1720s they looked west and moved in on the tobacco trade. In and out of their harbour at Port Glasgow, between 1741 and 1752, their import–export business rose from 7 to 21 million pounds, making Glasgow *the* European entrepôt. In 1775 they reached nearly 46 million, imports being largely sent on to Holland and France. English pirates were no longer a worry, and French raiders were much less troublesome than they would be to London merchants. Cash from tobacco would find its way into the sugar, linen, and cotton trades, and indeed into manufacturing in general, to furnish outward cargoes to the plantations. The swaggering, red-cloaked Tobacco Lords in their 'beautifullest little city' embodied 'polite-ness' and its consumer goods possibilities just like the *bon ton* of Bath. They came to grief through the American revolt of 1776. But by then a new driving force had developed: textiles.

Scotland's major textile product in the early eighteenth century was linen. Flax was grown in the country districts, 'retted' and 'heckled' in small ponds and mills, spun and woven in the single-storey 'improved' cottages of the villages. Over the century 120 of these were actually built as 'new' settlements, affecting about a sixth of Scotland's 836 parishes. These were often laid out by landowners and bore the names of them and their families—Gavinton, Fochabers, Grantown, Pulteneytown, Helensburgh. In accordance with a clause of the Union, funds were made available, after 1728, by the 'Trustees for Improving Fisherys and Manufactures', which were ploughed into scientific projects, notably new ways of bleaching linen. Between 1728 and 1750 production of linen cloth increased from 1.8 to 6.9 million metres. Most of it was exported to the Caribbean and the Americas, where it would clothe slaves in the tobacco, sugar, and cotton plantations.

Cotton gave nearly the quality of linen but, when production was mechanized, cost far less. The entrepreneur who used new techniques to manufacture cheap but sell as close as he could to the linen price was onto a winner, until competitors caught up. Such huge profits were the dynamo of early industrialization, kept going by slaves in the continuously expanding plantations. Here, Scotland moved directly in step with the south. In 1771 Richard Arkwright's water-powered spinning frames started working in factories in Derbyshire, but they were soon installed in Scotland in Catrine in Ayrshire, Deanston in Perthshire, and Spinningdale in Sutherland. However, within a few years the real expansion was concentrated in Glasgow and Renfrewshire around Paisley, which had good communications and water supply and lots of rain, just like Lancashire. Soon, specializations developed. Paisley became the centre of the thread industry and its Indian-style shawls were treasured. But one works in particular projected itself worldwide.

NEW LANARK

In 1784 the Glasgow yarn importer David Dale took 'the pot-bellied, bag-cheeked barber' Richard Arkwright to view the Falls of Clyde, 32 kilometres south-east of Glasgow. Within two years he had built four cotton mills in the gulch formed by the river, using Arkwright's patent water-frame, and within ten he was employing nearly 1,500 workers, many of them highlanders, accommodated in a dozen tenement blocks. He sold the works in 1799 to a Manchester company who appointed as manager the 28-year-old Welshman Robert Owen, who also married Dale's daughter and had already made

£40,000 *in cotton. Under Owen the mills became the most famous factory in the world until Henry Ford built his Dearborn automobile assembly-line a century later. Owen was both a clever manager and a bold utopian. He believed that workers would produce more if treated well, yet he was also eager to remodel society. New Lanark, whose site he actually rented from the monstrous reactionary Lord Braxfield, provided advanced education and communal cooking and entertainment for its employees. The crowned heads and clerics of Europe came—among an annual 2,000 visitors—to investigate, hoping that they would find some paternalist way of guiding the energies of the new urban industrial masses. They were fascinated and almost frightened by the energy—coupled with the wealth—of their host.*

Owen kept his connection with New Lanark for thirty years. Worker behaviour was marked by a 'silent monitor' (a multicoloured block on each machine, showing how well the operative was performing), children were instructed, without physical punishment, in singing, dancing, and drill: the beginnings of the 'child-centred' teaching that such as A. S. Neill would later develop. 'The Character of Man is Formed for and not by Him' was painted above the classrooms: not exactly the message of the Enlightenment, but Owen drew on its connections. He travelled widely in Europe and later in the Americas to advertise New Lanark, yet he was not satisfied with the factory system, believing instead in intensive cultivation—spade-culture—by self-governing communes. One socialist community was set up in 1831 at Orbiston, near Motherwell, with the radical laird of Dalzell, but soon broke up: 'Babylon' the locals called it. Owen went in 1834 into a near-revolutionary phase, advocating a 'general' trade union which would, by provoking a 'grand national holiday' bring the capitalist system to an end, and usher in a co-operative commonwealth. Latterly, and by now mainly settled at New Harmony in the USA, he adopted spiritualism and in seances contacted Milton and Shakespeare, who responded with helpful messages along the lines of 'Carry on Owen, you're doing a great job'.

Owenite ideas, preached by enthusiasts like G. J. Holyoake and Sandy Campbell, diffused themselves over the political left, particularly affecting consumer co-operatives, education, and ideas of workers' control. While these revived in the 1960s, New Lanark's mills were on the point of closure,

10. *New Lanark mills and village in 1818 by John Winning. David Dale and Robert Owen's mill village has changed little externally since it was built in the 1780s. Hotel staff have replaced the cotton-spinners, and 200,000 tourists the crowned heads and theorists who once viewed the social laboratory.*

and were then threatened with destruction. They were rescued in 1971 and have now become a tourist centre, museum, and luxury hotel, with 200,000 visitors annually. What Owen would have made of that, we will have to enquire of him on 'the other side'.

The textile boom, along with the growth of the sugar and salt industries, swelled the demand for iron. In 1759 two English entrepreneurs Samuel Garbett and Dr John Roebuck and a Scots timber merchant William Cadell set up the Carron Ironworks, using coke for smelting (earlier furnaces had used charcoal and been sited in the forested Highlands) and drawing on the big central Scottish coalfield. It gained a reputation by casting cooking-pots and the 'Carronade', a light cannon for ships. Not long afterwards, trying to imitate the success of the duke of Bridgwater in

Manchester, speculators put money into a small ship canal which would connect it and the Forth at Grangemouth with Glasgow and with the Clyde at Bowling.

How Scottish was all this? Or was it in fact more of a collective effort of the western littoral settlements, from Cornwall to the Clyde? Not only in Scotland was the shift in trade from the North Sea to the Atlantic; her towns were part of a trading partnership that found Scots (mainly in partnership concerns) involved in Cornish copper and tin mines, Welsh ironworks and lead and slate mines, the docks of Liverpool, the cotton mills of Manchester, the linen works of Belfast—and the plantations of Jamaica, the shipyards of New Brunswick, the cotton warehouses of Charleston. All sorts and conditions of men from such places turned up in what the satirist and social commentator John Galt (1779–1839) termed 'the West': that necklace of towns stretching from Dumbarton via Glasgow to Paisley, Greenock, Irvine, and Ayr. Along this coast, the Irish one, which, only 23 kilometres away, confronted Portpatrick in Galloway, and the American one, which, nearly 5,000 kilometres distant, confronted both, a complex series of changes were going on.

They are the more complex because, even after the Union of 1801, Irish statistics were not combined with those of Britain. A unique European experience of famine, deindustrialization, population boom-and-bust doesn't register within the Blue Books which economists celebrated and Karl Marx quarried. Ireland supplied Britain with food and with strong, docile, cheap labour—Adam Smith wrote ingenuously about the potato having furnished London with its strongest porters and most handsome prostitutes—and this applied to Scotland in particular. Unskilled workers both liberated the skilled to be trained in the new technologies which were required, and reduced the wages of skilled men, to allow for capital investment: as with Germany in the 1960s, the *gastarbeiter* was essential. As for the 'men above', few thought of themselves *initially* as 'Scots' players—to Thomas Reid, the 'common sense' philosopher and improver, Buchan and Britain mattered more—but this strong sense of regional and urban identity reinforced industrial development. 'Scotia—my dear, my native soil!' was a concept as much as an emotion, contributed by the poets.

THE SCOTTISH ENLIGHTENMENT

The term 'enlightenment in Scotland' was coined by an Irishman, Professor W. R. Scott, towards the end of the nineteenth century. It was conjured up almost as a counterweight to the religiosity of Victorian Scots—here was a country which had produced the sceptic David Hume and the greed-driven 'progress' of *The Wealth of Nations* (1776). It took much longer for its elaborate ramifications to be identified, but by the end of the twentieth century analyses of the Scots experience had, if anything pulled ahead of study of the other enlightenments. After all, it didn't end in revolution and terror as in France, or in recrudescent militarism, as in Germany, but provided the orthodoxies of Western technological and social development: market economics, sociology, systematized and programmed knowledge. It had practical and democratic dimensions otherwise absent in Europe, a solidity absent in England. Yet the more its thinkers and actors were examined, the more complex their attitudes were.

Where did it come from? The historian H. T. Buckle in 1861, and Hugh Trevor-Roper, Lord Dacre in 1964, reluctant to give Calvinism any credit, put it down to a 'forced growth' or to Jacobite exiles. More subtly, Nicholas Phillipson claimed that it annexed the discourse of English *politesse* from Addison and the *Spectator*. But the picture is far more one of continuity from Scotland's acceptance of Renaissance learning, evident in the influence of the civic Machiavelli on George Buchanan, the development of mathematical logic by Napier of Merchiston, or the Euro-eccentric polymathy of Sir Thomas Urquhart, and the dialogue of this with the powerful Anglophone influences of Milton, Bunyan, Locke, and Defoe. Throughout the seventeenth century the Scots had visited the Low Countries, France, and Italy as traders, soldiers, or political exiles, Whig or Jacobite. They had explored cultural difference on the nearly 'internal' frontiers with the Highlands and Ireland, and converted the blood-feuds of clans and bonds of manrent into the unending litigation of Parliament House, in which the learned gentleman-advocate took over from the man-at-arms.

It seems that the political and social prostration of the turn of the seventeenth and eighteenth centuries—the lean years of the 1690s, the

Darien disaster, the Union—worked on Scotland like a catalyst. Ideas of local improvement and civic patriotism *divorced* from armed glory or 'the community of the realm' focused on intensely practical goals and on the 'scientific' examination of reforming schemes in practice. The Calvinist contribution was as various as that of other religions: ranging from the bigots who hanged the heretic Thomas Aitkenhead in the 1690s to the successors of Buchanan like Andrew Fletcher, whose lively continental connections linked Scotland with the new learning in law and medicine, of the Low Countries in particular. But there was also a strong 'push' factor, in the need of the Scots economy for accurate technical, economic, and social information, and the desire to establish Edinburgh as a capital prestigious enough to keep the Scottish gentry north of the border, instead of, like their Irish counterparts, flocking to London. So Edinburgh accumulated, in what Christopher Smout called 'a dizzy sense of opportunity', not just courts, infirmary, and University, but publishers, painters and sculptors, and even (in Calvinist Scotland!) actors and musicians.

The reputation of David Hume has tended to crowd out all of his contemporaries, save Adam Smith. Hume was a radical sceptic, and this, and his nomination of the emotions as the propellant of human behaviour, would lay the foundations of hedonistic individualism, utilitarianism, and perhaps later on Freudianism. His fretting about his Scotticisms made the Enlightenment an alien presence to robust patriots. Yet he made his considerable fortune not as a philosopher but with his *History of England* (1754–62). In the 1760s he gave up—'too lazy, too fat, too old and too rich'. That other pregnant refinement of hedonism, 'the greatest good of the greatest number' was coined early, by the Ulsterman Francis Hutcheson, while the word 'utilitarianism' itself stemmed from a novel of John Galt. This gives an idea of the variety of methods of broadcasting their ideas that the Scottish literati used, from the pamphlet to the *Encyclopaedia Britannica*. Yet the *Scottish* nature of the 'Enlightenment' was even more pronounced, if less optimistic.

The concerns of the literati were practical was well as theoretical. Reid, the philosopher of 'common sense' (technically, the assumption that a God-given faculty of 'conscience' mediated between the individual senses) worked for agricultural improvement in Buchan before his translation in 1764 to Glasgow. Smith, Ferguson, Hume, and others were in 1761 energetic supporters, in the Poker Club, of a militia for Scotland, when this was turned down by a Westminster Parliament fearful of Jacobite influence on any such Scottish body. The literati were thus not abstract *philosophes* in the French sense. Rather than relying on reason, they were continually concerned about the impact of economic success on the relations of civil society: its tendency to promote the twin pests of 'luxury and corruption'. In this sense they had a continual concern with the primitive and familial, as well as the sophisticated and progressive. How did societies hold themselves together? By the 'learned drive' of sympathy, answered Adam Smith. By fear of and conflict with 'the other', answered Adam Ferguson, whose view of man's capabilities was not so elevated.

The Enlightenment was a contradictory mixture of progress and conservatism, whose unity was both more poetic and more practical than ideological. It throve, economically, on the exploitation of Scots resources *and* the Scots drive *away* from historic Scotland and into Europe. There is truth in the allegations of its anti-national quality. Yet there was also its apparently paradoxical interest in the antique, typified by the furore over James Macpherson's *Ossian* in the 1760s. Macpherson claimed to have reconstructed a Celtic epic, comparable to the *Odyssey*, from oral tradition and old manuscripts. The latter never turned up, making *Ossian* look a total fake, yet enough was authentic to suggest to recent critics that it was meant to draw a curtain across the past. 'I look back, but all I see are the graves of my friends' implied that, henceforth, all would look to the future. The result, however, was a process of emulation throughout Europe. Goethe's doomed Werther clutched his copy, it inspired Herder's equation of language and nationality: no self-respecting national movement would be without its epic—*Nibelungenlied, Kalevala, Táin, Ossian* stimulated much genuine enquiry and folklore collection, by among others Burns, Hogg, and Scott, and these in turn served further to advance national distinctiveness. Generating a popular culture also emphasized elements, however sentimental, which pulled society together in the way advocated by Adam Smith in his other great text published in 1759, *The Theory of Moral Sentiments*. Henry Mackenzie's novel *The Man of Feeling* (1771) seems slight and slushy,

11. *Portrait of Adam Ferguson by Sir Henry Raeburn (1756–1823). To walk past the swooning saints of continental baroque, and then be confronted with the cool rationality and painterly flair of Raeburn's portraits of the Edinburgh literati is to realize how drastically Scotland—in this case exemplified by the sociologist Adam Ferguson—had overtaken Europe.*

but here was Smith's 'sympathy' in spades. It was wildly popular, Robert Burns's 'bosom favourite', though in 'To a Louse' he put over the Smithian message more pithily:

> O wad some Pow'r the giftie gie us
> To see oursels as others see us!
> It wad frae monie a blunder free us
>   An' foolish notion:
> What airs in dress an' gait wad lea'e us,
>   An' ev'n Devotion!

is almost word for word out of *The Theory of Moral Sentiments*. It lives because of its Scotticisms. Hume would have appreciated that.

With the other major area of the Enlightenment, its linkage with new technology, we come full circle. Joseph Black, professor of physics at Glasgow, assisted the university's instrument maker James Watt with the theory of heat. The search for new and cheaper methods of bleaching linen led to links with the Board of Trustees and the well-developed chemical works of France and the Netherlands. The mathematical skills of Napier and his successors influenced, besides Watt, the 'great civilians': Smeaton, Rennie, Telford, Macadam, the Stevensons. The systematic surveying of the country followed the 'Forty-Five, and the geology of Hutton followed *that*. In the mid-century technology moved from the medieval to the classical, partly through the application of English and European techniques, partly through the rapid accumulation of craftsmen—in clocks, locks, pistols, furniture—who could also serve manufacturing industry. The orthodox bridges of General Wade's roads gave way to the virtuosity of Telford's Dean Viaduct or iron Craigellachie Bridge. The early wooden tramroads of the Forth estuary—like the Tranent and Cockenzie, which had the battle of Prestonpans fought over it in 1745—led to iron-railed tramways but, more importantly, to the broadcasting by Robert Stevenson (lighthouse wizard and grandfather of Robert Louis) of the concept of the railway in the *Encyclopaedia Britannica* in 1823.

After the mid-century the interweaving of manufacture and infrastructure dramatically increased. Canal prospects were limited but strategic. The Forth and Clyde reached Glasgow and stuck there, because the outbreak in 1776 of the American War of Independence felled the Tobacco Lords—though it eventually broke through to Grangemouth in 1793. Rennie built the Crinan in 1793–1801, from Loch Fyne to the Atlantic. Telford engineered the Caledonian in 1802–22 through the Great Glen; it was a financial flop, but—to that generous and poetic soul—'a great working academy'. Turnpikes, often spectacularly engineered, ramified, providing easy and economical transport for the new spinning-mills, and reducing the time taken to reach London from two weeks in 1750 to two days by 1820. Graving docks for ship repairs—the first was at Port Glasgow in 1762—and 'wet docks', accessed by locks, followed: Greenock in 1805, Leith in 1800, and Dundee in 1815. Glasgow would only come late, in 1867, when the Clyde had been dredged, and transformed into a coal-black artery.

Steam power was to be Scotland's most famous contribution, though its dominance as an industrial prime mover came only in the 1820s. It had its roots in the expansion of the coal industry, in particular the driving of mines under the Forth which required constant pumping. This caused the installation of massive Newcomen atmospheric engines, and it was on one of these (whose cylinder, big enough to take a car, can be seen at Kinneil, near Falkirk) that James Watt experimented to see whether its efficiency could be increased by the use of a second cylinder in which to condense the steam. Although he broke through to success through his Birmingham partnership with Matthew Boulton, and the most demanding tasks for the new engines were in the very deep shafts of Cornish copper and tin mines, Scotland again assumed the lead in the technology, with the application of steam to water transport in 1803. The inventor was William Symington, born in the remote but very literate lead-mining village of Wanlockhead (its library, one of many, still exists); the name of his paddle-tug, the first technically successful steamboat, was the *Charlotte Dundas*. Almost a century later Professor Patrick Geddes would see these changes ushering in the 'paleotechnic age'—when man could liberate the stored power of carbon, without being able to control it.

THE WORLD OF HENRY DUNDAS

Everyone would know who Charlotte Dundas was. The year 1766 saw another 'Scotch manager' clamber up the rungs of power. Henry Dundas of Arniston, the son of a Midlothian laird, became Solicitor-General. More flexible than the great magnates like the Argylls, members of the Faculty of Advocates, largely drawn from the landowning classes, were penetrating and professionalizing government and administration. Dundas was representative of them, but he also had his eye on Whitehall, and proved a fixer of genius. Within nine years he was Lord Advocate, and by 1784 a member of the Board of Control of the East India Company. The period when Scotland's destiny and that of the Dundas family were intertwined would last for nearly sixty years. It combined unashamed venality with enlightenment and shrewd exploitation, generally on their countrymen's behalf, of the benefits of empire. Henry Dundas's likeness stands on a tall column on Edinburgh's St Andrews Square. For every hundred who recognize George Meikle Kemp's nightmarish Scott monument, about a hundred yards away on Princes Street, scarcely one will identify 'King Harry the Ninth', who bankrolled Scott, and Admirals Nelson and Rodney besides.

Dundas's opportunity came through the imperial success of the Seven Years War and mounting pressures on the Westminster government in the 1760s and 1770s: the coalitions formed by Lord North and Lord Rockingham were always under assault, notably through the French wars and the crises with the American colonies. They were only too glad of solid support from the forty-five Scottish MPs, which Dundas delivered with ever-greater efficiency. By 1791 he could engineer a pro-government member in thirty-four out of the forty-one contested constituencies. The pay-off for this was the patronage he distributed: a quarter of government pensions, a third of government sinecures. And, much more important, ready access to jobs in India after 1793 and in the navy after 1801. He was the buttress on which William Pitt the younger's rule depended.

Despite the involvement in it of many emigrant Scots-Irish—a tough-minded lot—the outbreak of rebellion in the American colonies in 1776 was unwelcome to the Scots in Scotland. So important were their links to government, and their interests in tobacco, that they were badly hit by the economic disruption and largely took a 'loyalist' position. Many Scots settlers were driven north, to settle in 'Upper Canada' (Ontario) and New Brunswick, among them Flora MacDonald, the rescuer of Charles Edward. The consequences of the rebellion stimulated pressure for constitutional reform on both sides of the Atlantic. In the liberated colonies Alexander Hamilton, son of a Scots West India proprietor, drafted the *Federalist Papers*, 1787–8, and then helped force through the United States Constitution, a conservative Covenant that Montrose could have commended. But the Scots version of the Association Movement campaigned for the introduction of constituencies broadly similar to those of England, and there was no assertion of independent political nationhood, as happened among the MPs of the Irish Parliament, which used Westminster's difficulty to increase its power.

The reform associations were only just getting into their stride when from France came the news of the 1789 Revolution. This was welcomed almost universally, from the aristocratic Whigs who formed the 'Friends of the People' and were close to the literati of the Enlightenment, to the workmen and weavers of the central belt who formed their radical clubs and sang the 'Marseillaise'. 'United Scotsmen' met their radical Presbyterian brethren 'United Irishmen'.

ALLOWAY, AYRSHIRE

> *She prophesied that, late or soon,*
> *Thou wad be found deep-drown'd in Doon,*
> *Or catch'd wi' warlocks in the mirk,*
> *By Alloway's auld haunted kirk*

The village, 4 kilometres south of the town of Ayr, has a ruined church, hump-backed bridge, and nearby a low white cottage in which in 1759 Robert Burns was born. Alloway figures in his most popular poem, ceremonially recited every 25 January on his birthday, 'Tam O'Shanter', a blackly comic, rollicking tale of liquor, superstition, and near-disastrous lust. While generations of Scots have celebrated their national poet as 'the heaven-taught ploughman', this son of a small Ayrshire farmer reflected far more vividly the decline of his own class, under the challenge of enclosure and landlord dominance, and the pervasiveness of the values of the Enlightenment. Burns's father had him schooled, with other local farmers' sons—including the founder of the St Rollox chemical works—by a university graduate, and he was well aware of the arguments of Hume, Adam Smith, and Adam Ferguson.

Burns's life was a succession of hopeless attempts to make himself a farmer, a task for which he fundamentally lacked the cash and credit, while his loving eye for the women frequently brought him to the notice of the Kirk and the 'stool of repentance'. On the verge of emigration, he published in Kilmarnock in 1786 his Poems chiefly in the Scottish Dialect. *This created a furore and got him acceptance in Edinburgh, though not enough to pay the rent. 'To a Mouse' verges on bathos, but is tragically honest about the solitary ploughman—a century earlier he would have been part of an eight-ox team—as naked to the new economic world as his 'fellow-mortal' the fieldmouse. He ended as an exciseman in Dumfries: 'Burns, Robert, the poet: does pretty well' reads his entry in the Customs Headquarters at Greenock. Burns's politics were radical, though a mixture of two, incompatible components—Jacobitism and Jacobinism. In 1789 he sympathized warmly with the French Revolution and in 1793, after the execution of the French king, wrote 'Bruce to his troops on the Eve of Bannockburn':*

> Lay the proud usurpers low!
> Tyrants fall in every foe!
> Liberty's in every blow,
> Let us do or die!

This goriness was qualified by the 'enlightened' ideas of 'For a' that', Germanized in 1848 by Ferdinand Freiligrath for the Berlin revolutionaries as 'Trotz Alledem'. It was sung out by the Members of the new Scottish Parliament two centuries later, as enthusiastic as the young American who devoured Burns in the 1920s and who bore the good south-western name of Woodrow Wilson Guthrie:

> Then let us pray that come it may,
> As come it will for a' that,
> That sense and worth, o'er a' the earth,

> May bear the gree, an a' that.
> For a' that, and a' that,
> It's comin' yet for a' that,
> That man to man, the warld o'er,
> Shall brothers be for a' that.

Burns was aware that he wrote in a tradition, though not wholly a Scots one. In the early eighteenth century James Thomson, born near Kelso, gained a huge reputation through his long formal poem The Seasons *(rarely heard today, though Vivaldi's famous suite was based on it), and Scots played a role in creating the idea of an English literature, something rather unwelcome to England, which had an elite whose education was narrowly classical. In 1724–7 the elder Allan Ramsay had collected old Scots verse, notably the ballads, in* The Evergreen *and later Robert Fergusson wrote— like Dunbar—of low life in Edinburgh, and Burns considered him his master. Nor was Burns alone in this Scots-English quandary. Thomas Campbell gained fame as a patriotic poet in the Napoleonic Wars: his most famous work was 'Ye Mariners of England'. And by 1810 Burns would be almost outdone—and totemized—by another amorous radical, George Gordon, Lord Byron:*

> *I am half a Scot by birth, and bred*
> *A whole one, and my heart flies to my head, –*
> *As 'Auld Lang Syne' brings Scotland, one and all . . .*

Most of the literati supported the aims, at least, of the Revolution. Sir James Mackintosh's *Vindiciae Gallica* (1791) was the intellectual's riposte to Burke, though the masses, in Scotland as in Ireland, read Paine's *Rights of Man* (1791). Some, like Adam Ferguson and Thomas Reid, even persisted when it was unpopular to do so, though the ailing Exciseman Burns was forced to toe the government line. The establishment hit back. After war had been declared with revolutionary France, 'Pitt's Reign of Terror' in 1794 saw radicals and liberals arrested, tried, imprisoned, and transported. Scots law and Scots judges like Robert MacQueen Lord Braxfield—the original of Robert Louis Stevenson's *Weir of Hermiston* (1896)—proved particularly effective at repression, condemning and jailing in the broadest of Doric. To a prisoner who claimed Jesus Christ had been a reformer came the answer 'Muckle he made o' that—he waur hangit tae!' 'God help the people who have such judges', was the verdict of Charles James Fox, the Whig leader. But the sufferings of the Scots (commemorated by a great obelisk in Edinburgh's Calton Cemetery) were few compared to the slaughter in Ireland in 1798, which led to the completion of the Union two years later.

IN THE SHADOW OF THE CORSICAN

Where Napoleon campaigned, from Italy to the Steppes, *Ossian* accompanied him in his command-carriage. The long war itself had other paradoxical facets. Relatively few British troops were involved in Europe until the 1812 Peninsular campaigns. But industry was boosted by the demand for ships, weapons, uniforms, and food. To the one great iron foundry at Carron were added others in Ayrshire, Lanarkshire, and Glasgow, turning out cannon and ammunition. Capacity rose eightfold, from 4,000 to 32,000 tons. Pressure for additional production—this time of coal—as well as moral pressure, brought about the liberation of the last collier-serfs in 1799, and the linen trade was boosted by the demand for sail canvas. Dundas, created Viscount Melville in 1802, put severe pressure on liberals while conceding some radical demands. Ending collier serfdom was linked to ending the slave trade in 1807 and Scots merchants did well out of the abolition of the East India Company's monopoly of Far Eastern trade in 1813.

Henry (later Lord) Cockburn, the Edinburgh Whig lawyer whose *Memorials* (1856) are the political history of the period, noted how many of his academic and legal colleagues opted for silence. Yet Dundas, with wartime opportunities for patronage gratifyingly increased, was prepared to compromise, notably with the Kirk's Evangelicals, whom he appointed to many government livings. He had to foster agriculture and to be generous to the labour force, in order to safeguard munitions production, so it was also a period of cultivation extension (the furrows of long-lost ploughlands can still be seen on the southern moors) and of experiments in economic organization, with notice taken of the ideas of such as Robert Owen. For the workers, living standards had probably increased overall by about a third since the 1760s, although they would face a choppy future once the wars ended.

War accelerated social change; demand for grain encouraged substitutes, notably potatoes, and the need for home-grown wool would have its effect on the fast-changing economy of the Highlands. At the same time Britain's foreign success—the capture or acquisition of the Cape of Good Hope, Singapore, Ceylon, and the strengthening of other imperial links and commercial opportunities—opened new fields to Scots administrators and entrepreneurs. Not least gardeners, as Scott would shrewdly note by creating Douce Davie Deans in *The Heart of Midlothian* (1818). Profiting from the importation of Dutch learning by Sir Robert Sibbald and the study of Linnaeus's works, they took the lead in trying to homogenize new cash crops: botanic gardens could matter more than battles. New and more efficient sailing ships enabled traders to break up the old imperial monopolies. With the end of the slave trade, Liverpool—a town with many Scottish merchants, Gladstones, Ewarts, Corries, and Parkers—moved further into cotton and grain. But most dynamic—and morally questionable—of all was the expansion into Far East trade of such Scottish firms as Finlay and Company, merchants in Calcutta, who assaulted the Indian cotton industry with machine-made fabric, and Jardine, Matheson and Company, who opened up China to Western trade, and in particular the import of opium from India.

More heroically, Admiral Cochrane, radical, speculator, and sailor of fortune, fought alongside Bolivar and O'Higgins in 1817–25 to gain the people of South America their freedom. This came at the end of a century in which Scotus Viator's repertoire had mightily increased. Boosted by patronage, linguistic interests, and sheer curiosity, James Bruce, Mungo Park, and Charles Clapperton explored the rivers of northern Africa. After recording their exploits in 1799, the polymath John Leyden—clergyman, folklorist, surgeon, linguist, and judge—burned himself out understanding and classifying the tongues of India and Indonesia. (He was the tiny village of Denholm's first philological genius: James Murray, who compiled the *Oxford English Dictionary* would be the other.) Not only had Frederick the Great's commanders been the former Jacobite brothers the Marshals Keith, but John Paul Jones founded the American, and Samuel Greig the Russian navy. Colen Campbell and Alexander Cameron built Adam-style palaces in St Petersburg. Alexander Hamilton crafted the American constitution, Robert Fulton armed America against Britain. Of Scots-Irish parents from Kilkenny, he had lodged with Robert Owen in Manchester, and seen the *Charlotte Dundas* under steam at Grangemouth. In 1808 he put his *Clermont*—the world's first commercial steamer—into service on the Hudson and in 1815 he built the armed catamaran *Demologos*: the world's first steam warship, the USA's first ultimate deterrent.

DUNROBIN AND STRATHNAVER: THE HIGHLANDS AFTER CULLODEN

The castle of Dunrobin, seat of the dukes of Sutherland on the shore of the Moray Firth 64 kilometres directly north of Inverness (and near 160 by road), might be on the Loire. From a rather grim Scots tower it was elaborated into a chateau in 1845–51 by Sir Charles Barry, architect of the Palace of Westminster. The locals had and have mixed feelings. Periodic resolutions are made to blow up the statue of the first duke on the top of nearby Ben Bhraggie. Why the 'gloomy memories'? We have to go back to Culloden, when the 'militant' society of the Highlands was dismantled. About a third of the land of the Jacobite clans was confiscated and managed by the crown. The kilt-plaid was forbidden—not irrationally, as it had always been the all-purpose garment of mobile fighting men, serving both as clothing and blanket—the clans were disarmed as the 'heritable jurisdictions' of the landowners were dissolved.

Around 1740 the first potatoes were planted in Scotland. They had three times the nutritive value that wheat or oats could give, and as in Ireland the population swelled, rising in the Highlands by about 30 per cent despite outward migration and recruitment into the British army. But since the old military basis of highland society was at an end, lairds treated their people as a resource. First they abandoned multiple tenancies and partitioned their land between tenants, the future crofters, a status which could at best be only part-time. With the additional labour power, they exploited the wartime boom, chiefly by grazing on it the 'all-weather' Cheviot or Blackface sheep.

But the boom years were coming to an abrupt end just when, between 1811 and 1820, the greatest of the clearances was that carried through by Elizabeth, countess of Sutherland and her husband George Granville Leveson-Gower, marquess of Stafford (and later duke of Sutherland) and their managers James Loch and Patrick Sellar.

The Sutherlands, though dripping with wealth from their Staffordshire coal mines, considered themselves progressive. They were fiercely against slavery and European reactionaries: their son would entertain Harriet Beecher Stowe (author of Uncle Tom's Cabin, *1852) and Garibaldi. They saw their role as social engineers, shifting the highlanders from subsistence agriculture to productive fisheries on the sea coast, or with subsidies to Canada. The locals had different views. They regarded the land as their right though they had no written title to it. Often, they had served in the army, and returned from Vittoria or Waterloo to deserted glens like Strathnaver, cleared by Sellar in 1812–14. Even Walter Scott, confirmed Tory, thought this was too much. He had one of his characters, a former sergeant, say: 'I cannot curse him, I will not curse him; he is the representative and descendant of my fathers. But never shall mortal man hear me name his name again.'*

Compared with the Irish Famine or the fate of the kulaks, the Sutherland evictions were minor stuff. The duke estimated that his philanthropy had set him back £60,000; he and his successors built roads and harbours, even their own railway, without altering the popular verdict. There was in fact little that any landlord, however benign, could do against developments which first commercialized the highland economy, and then abandoned it. But the 'Clearances' were, at the very least, assaults on a living culture by exploiters and would-be reformers who, lacking the language, had no real idea how it functioned, and no way of calculating outcomes other than profit and loss.

In 1828 Alexander Ranaldson MacDonell of Glengarry, who despite all the tartan in Raeburn's famous portrait, was a fierce evicter, tried to jump from the Caledonian Canal steamer *Stirling Castle* as it hit a reef at Corran, near Fort William, en route to Glasgow. He hit his head on a rock and drowned. Welcome to paleotechnic Scotland.

5 | THE WORLD'S WORKSHOP, 1815–1906

*Our old modes of exertion are all discredited and thrown aside.
On every hand, the living artisan is driven from his workshop, to
make room for a speedier, inanimate one. The shuttle drops from
the fingers of the weaver, and falls into iron fingers that ply it
faster. The sailor furls his sail, and lays down his oar; and bids a
strong unwearied servant, on vaporous wings, bear him through
the waters . . . We remove mountains, and make seas our smooth
highway; nothing can resist us. We war with rude Nature; and, by
our resistless engines, come off always victorious, and loaded with
spoils.*

(THOMAS CARLYLE, 'Signs of the Times', 1829)

It's a naked child against a hungry wolf;
It's playing bowls upon a splitting wreck;
It's walking on a string across a gulf;
With millstones fore-and-aft about your neck;
But the thing is daily done by many and many a one;
And we fall, face forward, fighting, on the deck.

(JOHN DAVIDSON, 'Thirty bob a week', 1894)

THE ROAD TO REFORM

In 1806 Napoleon ended a once-mighty polity when he named John Law of Lauriston, great-nephew of the wondrous financier, as French Governor of Venice. The last of the Doges had died in 1802. In 1815 a young Edinburgh cavalryman, Ensign Ewart of the Dragoons, symbolically finished Napoleon's career when he snatched the eagle of the 45th regiment at Waterloo. Yet the exile of Saint Helena left a last-gasp liberalism which had a Scottish tinge. Thomas Reid, Lord Byron, and Walter Scott were as chic in post-war France as paroled French officers were in Scottish burghs.

France's mainly seaport-based industries were destroyed by the British blockade and Napoleon's retaliatory 'continental system'. In Britain what William Cobbett called 'The Thing' rode this out: the National Debt and its bankers in the City of London who included many Scots—Barclay, Coutts, and Drummond. Less fortunate were the highlanders who returned to their straths to find them desolate, and the industrial workers—mainly weavers—who faced increased competition with the 'iron fingers' of power-looms, ex-servicemen and Irish immigrants, and lower wages. Living standards had risen by about a third in the period, 1750–1815. Now they stagnated and, by the 1840s, fell.

'Dundasism' had gone global. Patronage and profit, with occasional touches of the whip, kept wartime Britain in order. Reform impulses had not been completely suppressed. In 1802 a group of young Edinburgh Whig lawyers—Henry Cockburn, Francis Jeffrey, Henry Brougham, Francis Horner—pupils of Dugald Stewart, founded a new publication, The *Edinburgh Review*. This broadcast the principles of a moderate, non-revolutionary liberalism. It also carried the early work of the far-from-Whiggish Walter Scott, an undeviating government supporter. Edinburgh appealed: the *jeunesse dorée*, including Lord John Russell and Lord Palmerston, barred by Napoleon from the Grand Tour, went to the university to study under Dugald Stewart. Sydney Smith and Thomas de Quincey, 'The English Opium Eater', came north to write for journals which paid well, while a useful colony of ex-radicals—Wordsworth, Coleridge, Southey—positioned themselves, and the 'moral heart of England', not too far from the Border, in the Lake District. Everyone marvelled over Byron. Scots urbanization was now occurring at an almost headlong rate, the fastest of any country in Europe, but bourgeois society—ostentatiously patriotic but also demanding recognition—seemed somehow to cope with these alarming statistics.

The war's end meant that economics and politics combined, north and south of the Border, to swell the demand for change. Among the weavers, strikes broke out, and confrontations between reformers and Lord Liverpool's government led to bloodshed. In 1820, a year after the 'slaughter of Peterloo' in Manchester, a combination of government agents provocateur and home-grown radicals led to a brief, tragi-comic revolt of weavers, intent on capturing the Carron Ironworks. Dragoons dispersed them at Bonnymuir, south of Falkirk. Three—Baird, Hardie, and Wilson—were executed, and some transported. The government had moved troops by steamboat to suppress the radicals: the first military use of the new technology. Walter Scott fretted about the combination of mechanization and towns, then in 1822, in a sort of Tory triumphalism, brought George IV in state to Edinburgh. The 'royal jaunt' had an incidental benefit: the rediscovery of the Crown Jewels, 'the Honours of Scotland', in the castle. However, economic boom and slump, 1823–6, destabilized the government. The Tories tried to compromise with organized workers, with the Court of Session fixing minimum wages by law, and in 1826 Whigs and radicals, led by the Montrose MP Joseph Hume, gained the legalizing of some trade union activity. In 1828, Robert Dundas, second Viscount Melville, saw the writing on the wall, and stood down. The managing of Scottish politics was at an end.

ABBOTSFORD, ALTRIVE, AND THE CLEIKUM INN

In 1812 the 41-year-old Walter Scott, famous for his narrative poems, settled at Clarty Hole, between the Borders mill town of Galashiels and the ruins of Melrose Abbey. 'Muddy hole' shortly became Abbotsford: a writer's house which was also a museum of the man, with relics of Scots antiquity and the Stewarts dotted about its rather eclectic baronial frame, and (within a year or so) woodland planted in the pattern of the dispositions of Waterloo. After

12. *Sir Walter Scott painted by Raeburn, 1822, as he would have been found at his country home, Abbotsford. This tradition led directly into the romantic 'Stag at Bay' style (a near-quote from Sir Walter) of Edwin Landseer. There are now (2014) 400,000 deer in Scotland, which can perhaps manage only a fifth of that number.*

only two years at Abbotsford Waverley, *or 'Tis Sixty Years Since emerged, its plot about the 'Forty-Five and its authorship an open secret. Thereafter two or more novels a year appeared until Scottish history from the Reformation (in* The Monastery, *1820) to the present (in* The Antiquary, *1816) had been bodied forth. Juxtaposing tame heroes with graphically realized farmers, herdsmen, burgesses, and servants, and giving an oblique view of the evolution of a commercial society, Scott's novels contributed both to European nationalism and to the 'scientific' analysis of historical change. Allessandro Manzoni, Honoré de Balzac, Adam Mickiewicz, and Theodor Fontane were inspired; Disraeli and Marx drew—rather different—political lessons.*

Scott was sheriff of Selkirk, publishing entrepreneur, and clan chief, with a local following which included James Hogg, John Gibson Lockhart (his son-in-law and biographer), and General Adam Ferguson, son of the sociologist. Created baronet in 1820 and royal favourite, Scott was on his pinnacle, but the swift-flowing but placid river which was his 'Tory romantic, Whig practical' view of progress, was about to turn nasty. He was overwhelmed by the slump of 1826 and fell into debt for £130,000. He fought back and churned out a dozen hefty books, among them the first reliable Life of Napoleon *(1827). None, save some bleak short stories about modern Scotland which John Buchan shrewdly compared with Turgenev, was particularly readable. He also attacked both political reform and attempts to assimilate Scots law and banking practice with the south: 'In place of Canny Saunders, you will have a damned dangerous North British neighbourhood.' In 1831 he became the target of radicals and his own courthouse in Selkirk was besieged, but by then his health was failing, and did not recover, even after a Mediterranean voyage. He died at Abbotsford on 21 September 1832.*

The lonely cottage of Altrive, 24 kilometres up the Yarrow water from Abbotsford, housed the quite different spirit of James Hogg, promoted but also patronized by Scott. Hogg, who had started life as a shepherd, and though self-educated, became folklorist, poet, parodist, and novelist of alarming unconventionality. Libelled by Scott's entourage as a lovable buffoon and always on the edge of more depressing Burns-style bankruptcy, his art contrasted the visionary and the earthly, and in his greatest work, The

Memoirs and Confessions of a Justified Sinner *(1823)—set at the time of the Union of 1707, but timeless in its concerns—dramatized the tensions that dragged the human personality—and particularly the Calvinist personality—apart. Sentimentalized for decades after his death in 1839, Hogg was recognized by André Gide in a more troubled age as writer of world-class talent. He also commented, more than ironically, on the pressures that beset 'improved' Scotland.*

'Meg Dods' was the landlady of the Cleikum Inn in one of Scott's lesser-known novels St Ronan's Well *(1822). Independent-minded, caustic, and a remarkable cook, she took on her own existence in the* Cook and Housewife's Manual *(1826) which anticipated Mrs Beeton by thirty years and ran to eleven editions. This was written by Christian Elizabeth Johnstone, novelist, editor, and feminist. A divorcée (something easier to become in Scotland than in England), Johnstone ran Tait's Edinburgh Magazine until her retirement in 1857. Early feminism in Scotland has rather suffered from an obsession with the metropolitan elite, but Scotland was where Mary Shelley (daughter of Mary Wollstonecraft, and creator of Frankenstein) spent much of a creative life, and from where the pioneer male pro-suffragist John Stuart Mill stemmed. Johnstone—like many of her contemporaries: the novelists Susan Ferrier and Margaret Oliphant, the astronomer Elizabeth Somerville, the explorer Isabella Bird—didn't directly challenge a complacent male elite, but in print was able to undermine its pretensions. Marion Reid's* A Plea for Woman *(1843), the first demand for the suffrage since Wollstonecraft, was warmly welcomed by her, and the next generation would take their places on School Boards (1872) and local councils (1890).*

DISRUPTIONS

In 1822 the *Edinbourgeois* started to build the Parthenon on top of the Calton Hill, to commemorate the war. In 1824, with twelve columns erected, they stopped. A decade later the city was bankrupt, and Tory Scotland at an end. If political change in the late 1820s was radical in the United Kingdom as a whole, it was practically revolutionary in Scotland, borne along not just by a discontent shared by artisan and middle class, but by an industrialization process launched into a new phase by the expansion of the Monklands coalfield and its huge 'blackband' iron reserves: not just two-thirds cheaper than imported ores but yielding a very pure metal for castings.

Earl Grey in the Lords and Lord John Russell responded by adopting electoral reform. The Whigs were accompanied by, and discreetly encouraged, mass organizations—Reform Unions—and demonstrations, some of which got badly out of hand. The Tory Lord Provost of Edinburgh was nearly lynched in 1831. Pointing out the alternative of a revolution (which toppled the reactionary Charles X of France in 1830—he was exiled to Holyrood) the Whigs delivered a sweeping reform. 'Not one jot, not one tittle, of the old system ought to survive,' was Francis Jeffrey's boast as the new Lord Advocate, and in Scotland the result was an increase from 4,500 to 65,000 electors, along with the prompt abolition of the old burgh constitutions and their self-electing councils: 'I had indeed a sore heart when I saw the Whigs and Whiglings coming louping, like the puddocks of Egypt, over among the right hand benches of the House of Commons, greedy as corbies and chattering like pyets.' John Galt's weevil-like Tory Archibald Jobbry captured the dismay of the old gang. The total number of burgh seats rose to twenty-three, giving two each to Edinburgh and Glasgow. Effectively, the once-dominant Tories were knocked out of Scottish politics for half a century. There was, however, no radical or nationalist triumph. Scots workers, soon disillusioned, were to become enthusiastic Chartists after 1838. They demanded the Six Points—universal male suffrage, equal electoral districts, no income qualification for MPs, payment for MPs, the secret ballot, and annual Parliaments. This was essentially a British movement and they tended to be the moderates within it, singing 'Scots Wha Hae!' at their meetings, but then combining Chartism with education, religion, temperance or cooperation, and radical weekly papers; even allying with the Anti-Corn Law League. Working in exporting industries, they were natural free traders.

The period after reform was, instead, to be dominated by religion. Because the influence of the Kirk ran deep into social and cultural life, its control became a struggle between the landlords and the growing middle

13. *The Rev Dr Thomas Chalmers, as influential as an economist and politician as he was a preacher, who split the Kirk in 1843. A Free Church migration to New Zealand named its landfall Port Chalmers. In 1886 the Rev Patrick Murdoch set out from Banff to convert Australia to the Free Kirk, with surprising media consequences.*

class in the burghs and on the land. Initially the three-way fight between 'non-intrusionists', 'seceders', and the Kirk resembled 'Dissent' versus 'Church' in England—enough to mislead English politicians. Between 1833 and 1843—a period known to the Scots as 'the Ten Years' Conflict'—the evangelical clergy and laity, now in the majority in the General Assembly, fought to stop the landowners from 'intruding' their clergy candidates into the parish churches. The evangelical leader was the Revd Thomas Chalmers (1780–1847), once a near-deist, now the preacher of a renewed 'Godly Commonwealth'.

The conflict was complex: between the moderates, increasingly government pensioners, those who, like Chalmers, would settle for a cleansed establishment, and fighters for an entirely voluntary Church system. An arid theological legalism obscures the fact that the battle for the Kirk was a struggle for a national institution with extensive secular powers over the poor law and education: the Kirk's assumption of a special covenanted status implied yet another latter-day 'bond of manrent'. Just as the Reformation of 1560 had seen religious change used to elude French domination and negotiate a new relationship with England, Chalmers's vision of a self-governing Church implied a further renegotiation, distancing Scotland from the English menaces of Benthamite secularism and the Catholic revival. The landlords were backed by the Court of Session; whereupon the Kirk tabled 'The Claim of Right'. But the Whigs had lost office, and the Claim was turned down by Sir Robert Peel's government in 1842. In May of the following year Chalmers led a third of the clergy out of the Kirk.

The 'Disruption' of 1843 was glorified by the new Free Kirk, and commemorated by a series of pioneering photographs of its leaders, by D. O. Hill and Robert Adamson, but was damaging for Scots autonomy. Despite a burst of energy, which produced a notable inflation of religious building—much of it, ironically, in the 'Catholic' Gothic style (Pugin, no less, built Edinburgh's Tolbooth St Johns for the Free Kirk), government rapidly transferred the Kirk's social and educational roles to secular boards and bureaucrats. Within sixty years the Free Kirk's challenge had failed and reunification was on the agenda; it took place in 1929. Only industrialization and urbanization marked nineteenth-century Scotland more than this dispute, though Protestant dissent of the type was frequent in Europe at this time, as indeed was 'liberal Catholicism'.

After 1843 Scottish politics were further disturbed by two things. The crisis over Free Trade in 1846 overthrew Peel and split the Scottish Conservatives for a generation. Scotland benefited as an exporting country with efficient farming. Outside some counties, whose old privileges—'faggot votes'—kept them in, Benjamin Disraeli's Tories scarcely counted in Scottish parliamentary politics, though their exotic leader—imitator of Carlyle as well as Scott in his novels—thought Scots and Jews had a close affinity. The electoral geography of the country remained static until the 1900s. It got more Liberal in the east, though a rather old-fashioned, individualist Liberalism of the sort represented by Duncan MacLaren, MP for Edinburgh, John Bright's dour brother-in-law. The Tories clung on in the south-west and some western burghs, where they were helped by Protestant prejudice against Irish Catholic immigrants. Tory MPs in east-coast burghs were as rare as hens' teeth.

By the second crisis, however, Scots Tories benefited. The appalling living conditions of the growing industrial towns, their lack of water supply and adequate sewers, their tiny, overcrowded flats, provoked epidemic disease. Life expectation for workers was scarcely over thirty years. Cholera struck in 1832, 1848, 1853, and 1865–6 and typhus outbreaks were frequent. The instability of trade also meant that unemployment-generated poverty dramatically increased, far beyond the capacities of the old kirk-based system of relief through collections. In 1840 this covered only 60 per cent of needs, even after Chalmers tried to modernize it through the 'casework' of urban kirk sessions. Against his opposition, a secular poor law was introduced by Sir Robert Peel's government in 1845, organized through parochial boards under a central Board of Supervision in Edinburgh, which got powers over health in 1848. The advocates of such reforms, such as the 'father' of the Scottish poor law, Professor W. P. Alison and his brother, Sheriff Sir Archibald Alison, were often philanthropic Tories, many of whom went on to dominate the administration of an otherwise liberal country.

'A GIANT CAME TO OUR TOWN IN THE NIGHT . . .'

Auld Mouldyburgh fairly was rowed aff its feet,
And naething gat leave to stand still;
They pulled doon the houses, and widened the street,
And biggit a muckle brick mill.
And droves o'new comers, that naebody kent,
Were workin', they kentna at what;
The bodies were just in a perfect ferment,
And didna ken what to be at.

Sic smashin' and chappin' was a'round about,
Sic clankin', sic rattlin', an'din;
Wi' rocks blaun like thunder frae quarries without,
And smiddies an' reeshlin' within;
And wheelbarrows drivin' a' hours of the day,
Wi' Eerishmen swearin' like Turks;
And horses were fetchin' wi' cartfu's o'clay,
And plaister and stanes for the works.

Soon a' kinds o'traders cam flockin' in shoals,
The railway brocht wonders to pass;
Colliers cam howkin' to sair us wi' coals,
And gas-bodies cam to make gas;
And butchers, sae greasy, wi' sheep, beef and pigs,
And schoolmasters cam for the teachin';
And doctors wi' doses, and barbers wi' wigs,
And kirks were ereckit for preachin'.

One of the better poems in an otherwise copycat-Burns anthology *Whistle-Binkie* (1858) shows the suddenness of the industrial impact: 'A giant came to our town in the night', as James Barrie later recollected of Kirriemuir, when in the 1870s the handloom gave way to the linen factory. In 1834–45 the Kirk's General Assembly compiled a second *Statistical Account*. This showed a country in the course of rapid and enveloping change. The shrewd satirist and social commentator John Galt had presented a wry view of politics and society in his two 'theoretical histories' *The Annals of the*

Parish (1820) and *The Provost* (1821); in the recollections of the Revd Micah Balwhidder he saw the old, rather lazy values of a conservative countryside give way to the profit-driven enterprise of *The Wealth of Nations*, and in Provost Pawkie he sketched a local magnate with a lot of Henry Dundas in him. National feeling was limited: radical workers, fortified by the 'unstamped' press, tended to claim a 'British' identity to cope with the 'British' dimensions of industrial change. What impressed most English and foreign commentators was the rasping social critique of Thomas Carlyle (1795–1881) who, starting in the *Edinburgh*, grabbed Britain in general and also the young Marx and Engels with his claim of a mechanical revolution and a 'condition of England question'. Assenting to this was the 'noise and smoky breath' of the country's monster city, Glasgow.

GLASGOW

Glasgow was startling, but it wasn't new. It had been relatively withdrawn from Scotland's turbulent history, proud of the implausible career of its sixth-century patron Kentigern or Mungo, a forerunner of Columba, to whose honour its cathedral was dedicated. On the edge of the Highlands, it had always gone in for trade, building its fine steepled Merchants Hall in 1661–9 and its own harbour—Port Glasgow—on the tidal Clyde near Greenock in 1668. Gaelic was heard far more frequently in its streets than in those of Edinburgh. After the Union, tobacco was the first commodity that the Glasgow merchants started to trade in, dominating the European supply by the mid-eighteenth century, and cutting the Forth and Clyde, a small ship canal, to the centre of the city, then on to Grangemouth and the ironfield of the Monklands between 1760 and 1790. Glaswegians, like Walter Scott's Bailie Nicol Jarvie in Rob Roy *(1817), were independent but alive to the benefits of the Union:*

Let ilka ane roose the ford as they find it. I say, 'Let Glasgow flourish!' whilk is judiciously and elegantly putten round the town's arms by way of bye-word. Now, since St. Mungo catched herrings in the Clyde, what was ever like to gar us flourish like the sugar and tobacco trade? Will ony body tell me that, and grumble at the treaty that opened us a road west-awa yonder?

Sugar, linen, and cotton followed the tobacco boom, the last industry becoming second only to that of Lancashire. Daniel Defoe's 'beautifullest little city', a town as striking as, say, Heidelberg, grouped round its cathedral, bishop's palace, and university, became dwarfed by a grid-iron pattern of sandstone blocks of offices, warehouses, factories, and shops, pale grey at first, then stygian black from the smoke which swept in from the foundries of Govan, the textile mills of Paisley, and the huge smokestack—'Tennant's Stalk'—of the world's largest sulphuric acid works.

Around 50,000 in 1750, the city's population reached 110,000 in 1801, and 345,000 in 1850. In 1911 when it laid claim to being 'the second city' of the empire it was 784,000, and new boundaries in 1912 would take it over the million: a far bigger proportion of its country's population than London ever attained. It reflected Scotland's urban character—concentrated in the narrow 'Central Belt' and its rich coalfield between the estuaries of the Rivers Forth and Clyde, and particularly in the counties of Lanark and Renfrew— drawn from neighbouring counties, the Highlands, Ireland, and latterly Italy and the Baltic. Like other 'railway age' cities, Glasgow had much in common with its Atlantic contemporaries: Cardiff, Barcelona, the Eastern seaboard towns of the USA and—a parallel often invoked—Chicago.

Good government had a standing priority: the possibility of total disaster, through epidemic or disorder, was simply too close. In 1848 there was a wild bread riot in which a mob held the city centre for two days before being broken up by gunfire from a company of veteran soldiers. Four died. A decade later the city fathers were launching massive projects like the supply of water from remote Loch Katrine, inaugurated in 1859, and the Improvement Trust of the 1860s. This was followed by urban tram and underground lines and the detailed supervision of how people lived in their tiny and cramped flats—in 1871 75 per cent of Glasgow families lived in one or two rooms. For the middle classes there was long-distance commuting from small towns on the beautiful Clyde estuary; a tendency to build, knock down, and rebuild; an eye for the European avant-garde. In the slums and workshops swelled a cosmopolitan proletariat. Was it revolutionary, or divided by race and religion? The Glasgow skilled worker—as engineer, shipwright, or boilermaker, the 'second citizen' of the empire—was, the brothers James and Muirhead Bone found, uncompromising:

When his time was served he became a Union man, and thought all the world of his District Delegate. He is a very good workman, who could turn his hand to many things, and 'make a job o' them a'. He is intelligent, and has a clear perception of injustice. But according to his lights he is a reasonable man. He stands up for himself not only against the common enemy, the employer, but also against his comrades in allied trades if they invade his frontiers. He is gruff, intractable and independent, and his latent irritability takes fire if his rights are infringed. Of servility he has not a trace.

Three international exhibitions—in 1888, 1901, and 1911—were held on an almost Parisian scale. The first left the city with cash for an immense red sandstone art gallery in Kelvingrove Park; the city's younger artists campaigned to fill it with the works of advanced artists, pride of place going to the Scots-American James McNeill Whistler's Study in grey and black: Thomas Carlyle (1877), a monument to the great irascible critic of industrial society. Yet the Scotland that the 'Glasgow Boys' (W. Y. MacGregor, John Lavery, Joe Crawhall)—or designers like the remarkable Charles Rennie Mackintosh (1868–1928)—celebrated was essentially a rural community, realized in sober use of colour but still recognizably related to the Kailyard, the folksy never-never land frozen in the sentimental mass-circulation novels and stories of 'Ian MacLaren' (the Revd John Watson) and S. R. Crockett. Only one, underestimated, poet—Alexander Smith—wrote about the industrial city, and only the painter and etcher Sir Muirhead Bone occupied himself with the Clyde, its shipyards and engineering works.

Glasgow's popular culture was one of escape, reassurance, and melodrama rather than confrontation. Escape into history and the rural past; reassurance through sentimental love stories; and the melodrama of the newspaper serial and the cheap working-class theatre on the one hand, and the hell-fire of grim black churches on the other. By the end of the century these had been joined by football. Rangers dates from 1872 and its rival Celtic from 1888. Behind both lay the efforts of churches to order and control the lives of young men—the first mass youth organization, the Boys' Brigade, was founded in Glasgow in 1883. To this was added the attempt of the Catholic community, confined to low-status jobs, to win parity of esteem. With the world's greatest concentration of shipbuilding and marine

engineering, and second-largest locomotive works, Glasgow in 1913 was
flourishing, but on a very specialized industrial base.

The literati of the 'Enlightenment' had wanted to promote a 'balanced' social development based on agriculture and rural industries—in planned villages and factory towns such as New Lanark. This was a 'national' policy in all but name but one which couldn't cope with the huge new facts of 'west Britain'. This rough, competitive, endlessly adaptive co-prosperity zone drew on the capitalist expertise—forged in slaving, tobacco, and cotton— of Liverpool, Manchester, and Glasgow. A classic example of the 'creative chaos' of J. A. Schumpeter's entrepreneur-driven economy, it chased after markets, sources of raw material, and instant returns on investment, using cheap money and such social engineering as came to hand. These amounted to desperate attempts to keep the lid on a low-paid, hard-drinking labour force, penned in tiny flats and increasingly prone to mutiny as the economy became affected by cyclic depression, and even poorer migrants poured in from famine-stricken Ireland on steamers offering sixpenny fares.

In 1842 Britain experienced one of its sharpest slumps. Nowhere was this more severe than in the Scottish cotton capital, Paisley, famous for its India-pattern shawls. Unemployment among the weavers reached over 60 per cent, and the situation was so bad that the Minister of Paisley Abbey, the Revd Patrick Brewster, went Chartist, and the cabinet of Sir Robert Peel stepped in to organize poor relief themselves. Writing in Manchester a couple of years later, Friedrich Engels expected that the next depression would end in revolution; he provided the data for *The Communist Manifesto*, which he and Karl Marx published in 1848; its tone and savage wit came from Carlyle's *Chartism* (1839). Obscure at the time, the *Manifesto* would change the world. But not Britain or Scotland.

Cotton trapped both investors and workers, but profit and new technology liberated. Investment—'blind capital seeking its four per cent'— surged into the capital goods industries, which Scotland was particularly well suited to exploit. In the 1830s boom a railway network was promoted which by the early 1840s linked the chief towns of the central belt. The 'Railway Mania' of 1844–5 extended the system very rapidly, to Aberdeen in

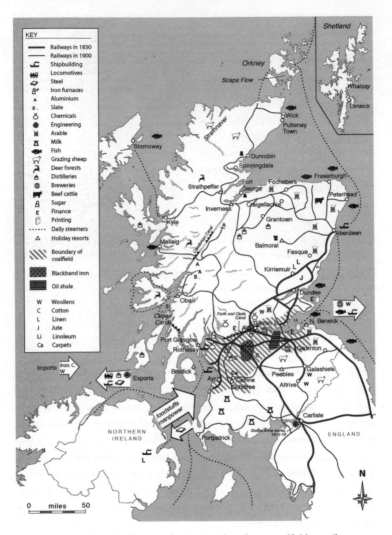

Map 3. *Industrial Scotland, c.1900, showing canals, railways, coalfields, textile areas*

14. *Walter Scott Baronial: Ardverikie House, Kinlochrannoch, 1910. Victoria and Albert's annual autumn migration to Deeside began in the 1840s: good news for railways, builders, and tartan weavers, not so good news for deer. 'Baronial' piles appeared in every glen reproducing, in Osbert Lancaster's words, 'medieval qualities of insulation and sanitation'. Even among these, Ardverikie's architect David Rhind let it rip.*

the north and southwards by two competing lines—the West Coast Caledonian and the East Coast North British—to England. Much of the capital for railway construction came from England, much of the labour from Ireland, but Glasgow and Springburn, in particular, gained a reputation for locomotive building which would make it one of the world's greatest railway centres. The expertise of the city's makers of machinery and steam engines for textile mills and ships gave their partnerships—backed up by helpful joint-stock banks—a broad repertoire. The new market enabled them to extend this to carriages and waggons, rails and structural equipment for bridges and stations.

As dynamic entrepreneurs, consider the Houldsworth family. Derbyshire farmers who in the 1770s went in for cotton and Jamaican plantations, they moved to Manchester, then in the 1800s to Glasgow where James Watt built them a huge mill. In 1832, however, they shifted into iron, buying the

Coltness estate which once belonged to Sir James Steuart, the Jacobite economist. Thereafter its pits and blast furnaces became among the busiest heavy-industrial concentrations in Britain, providing pig iron for rail-rolling works and Glasgow engineers (and for export), later feeding Colvilles' steelworks at Motherwell. As the Coltness measures became worked out, their net was flung further, to Cumberland, the Coventry coalfield, and then north Spain, with balancing investments—in the event of heavy industrial downturns—made in cement and brickworks.

Other English and European businessmen—Alfred Yarrow in ships, Henry Dübs in locomotives, Alfred Nobel in explosives—moved north, while some great landowners in the new industrial areas were Scots—in Wales the Douglas-Pennants, the Cawdors, and above all the marquess of Bute, who owned most of Cardiff. Other Scottish businessmen looked south: the Barclays and Coutts became bankers, and there were publishers galore—Black, Constable, Chambers, Macmillan. Duncan MacLaren's heirs, the lords Aberconway, moved into Welsh shipping and Cornish china clay; the MacConnells started in Manchester cotton, then moved into Welsh slate, the Fairbairns into engine-building, the Cayzers into shipping. Not only did these moves make sense in economic terms, they also activated a Britain-wide interpretation of—and ability to control—economic change.

This success story didn't end with the conquest of the railways. In the 1850s and 1860s Glasgow engine builders set to work to solve the problem of steam at sea, the fact that marine boilers could only produce steam from sea water at low pressures. This made them huge, low-powered, and very inefficient, incapable of competing with the new wood-and-iron-built 'clipper' ships, such as the famous *Cutty Sark* (1869) on the China tea and Australian wool runs. What was needed was a compact, high-pressure engine which would condense its own 'fresh' water. By the 1860s, with the cooperation of the great scientist William Thomson (later Lord Kelvin) at the University, Charles Randolph and John Elder made the breakthrough, and the result, an ordinary-looking Greenock-built screw steamer, the Blue Funnel liner *Agamemnon*, set out in 1865 for the Far East, with enough coal for the trip there and back, and plenty of cargo space. Within twenty years sail had been pushed into the margins of the merchant marine.

This was Scotland's last industrial breakthrough, fortunate in its timing, as America was riven by the Civil War, 1861–5, in which most of its merchant ships were sunk or outflagged, and Germany was plunged in Bismarck's wars of unification. The boost that the Clyde gained lasted until the outbreak of the First World War. Meanwhile the iron industry of Lanarkshire adapted in the 1870s to the age of steel, with Motherwell becoming the Scottish equivalent of the Krupps' Essen.

Scotland, however, wasn't over-specialized—like South Wales, for example, which concentrated on tinplate and coal. British cotton textiles were dominated by Lancashire cotton, but Scotland concentrated on thread, and the woollen, linen, and jute industries were mechanized, respectively in the Borders (tweed) and Ochils (tartans), and Strathmore and Dundee. Together with ships, steel, and engineering they provided an impetus big enough to sustain a wide range of specialized manufacturers of fairly basic consumer goods: linoleum in Kirkcaldy, carpets at Kilmarnock, furniture, crockery, beer and spirits in and around the four cities, paraffin from shale oil in West Lothian. Foodstuffs—tea, coffee, tinned beef, and salmon—were marketed by private chain stores like those of Sir Thomas Lipton or the fast-expanding Co-op societies. In this way Scotland was, up to 1914, a miniature of the UK economy, rather than a specialized division of it.

REVOLUTIONARY EMPIRE

Most of the products of the Clyde's heavy industries were destined for export: ships, railway equipment, structural engineering, processing plant, steam engines, thread, and iron. Where these capital-goods exports went, Scottish engineers, investment managers, and administrators followed. This was a peculiar industrialization, unaccompanied by any large-scale transition to consumer-goods industries, or indeed by much wealth for the Scottish workers. Until 1900 wages were about 10 per cent under the British level, high pay for skilled men being offset by low pay for unskilled immigrants, women, and boys. Yet labour relations were rarely explosive until that time, and Scottish workers seemed to have horizons greater than wage-bargaining. Was there a clue to this in the dependence of the Scots on imperial markets for their goods, imperial investments for their money, and imperial careers for their children?

What Adam Smith called the 'mercantile economy' was an extension of war and diplomacy through trade, for which Scotland was unusually well placed. The expansion of British rule in India, under the patronage of 'John Company', and the Scots on its Board of Control made the 'Nabob' familiar, his wealth gained by taxation, trade, and corruption. This sort of wealth surfaces in Jane Austen, rarely sympathetically. Indian money flowed into lowland estates and, when the Company was forced to reform its operations, into the development of expert government. The Dundases rode that one out, too. Posts in India (and later in the navy) were eagerly taken up and Scottish schools and universities exerted themselves to supply recruits.

They also exported colonists. Many of the Presbyterian borderers who in the seventeenth century were 'planted' in Ulster became, as the 'Scotch-Irish' of America, ruthless fighters, expelling the British from their Thirteen Colonies and the Indians from their land, and furnishing many American Presidents (notably the populist Andrew Jackson). Scots were also prominent 'free settlers' in Australia, New Zealand, and South Africa. 'Sticking together like bricks' as an Australian remarked, they were farmers and gardeners, adept at transplanting and exploiting new crops, and entrepreneurs with skills reinforced by engineering, religion, medicine, and teaching. As J. K. Galbraith found on the Canadian shore of Lake Erie, their devotion to money hinged on the obsessive. Used to moving considerable distances within Scotland and Britain, the Scots—and two million of them left between 1820 and 1914, an extraordinary number for an *industrialized* country—carried with them a sense of identity, built up out of Kirk, Freemasonry, and family, which meant that self-sustaining communities were rapidly created. They migrated, as Sir Charles Dilke, MP noted in the 1860s, 'in calculating contentment'; the very much larger number of Irish 'in desperation and misery'. Yet a radical tradition continued. In Canada in the 1830s William Lyon MacKenzie headed the popular opposition to London-appointed governors, Sir John A. MacDonald became the first Federal premier in 1867, and Scots Lord Mountstephen and Lord Strathcona built the Canadian Pacific Railway, the iron bond of federation. In New Zealand the radical party had a succession of Scots leaders; the first Labour premier of the Commonwealth of Australia in 1910 was a former Ayrshire miner, Andrew Fisher.

More questionable, ethically, was much of their enterprise. Settler democracy tended to be won at the expense of native rights, and 'progress' could take strange forms. Above the village of Lairg in Sutherland an Indian temple stands over the grave of Sir John Matheson, a 'tacksman's' son who became co-founder of Jardine, Matheson and Company, breakers of the East India Company's monopoly and the main supplier of opium from Indian plantations to his China depot in Hong Kong. Lord Palmerston waged war with the Chinese in 1840 to protect this trade, and right up to the end of British rule, in 1997, the acme of Hong Kong society and its Scottish base—in the Royal Bank—were the 'Taipans': the families of Jardine, Matheson, Herries, and Keswick.

Scots—Outram, Napier, Elphinstone—also fronted the expansion of British rule in India, which, following the expulsion of the French, steadily defeated or subordinated native rulers. By the early nineteenth century they replaced the sheer greed of the first Nabobs with philosophical system. Utilitarian reform, preached by disciples of Jeremy Bentham, notably James Mill and his son John Stuart, and the historian, poet, and critic T. B. Macaulay envisaged a modernized and substantially native-run subcontinent. Macaulay's *Minute on Education* (1836) was a key initiative in the Anglicization of India and the missionary leader Alexander Duff was no less important in building up secondary and higher education. This reached a peak of dynamic activity in the governor generalship of the earl of Dalhousie, 1848–56, in which extensive road and railway, administrative, and university schemes were undertaken. But the result of this headlong modernization was to be a violent conservative reaction—the Indian Mutiny of 1857, and the British response to it.

DUNDEE

No town reflected the impact of imperialism on Scotland more than Dundee, at the mouth of the Tay estuary. In an absurd way, this was personified by William MacGonagall, an underemployed Irish weaver and would-be

Shakespearean actor, with a claim to the title of 'the world's worst poet' and a reputation almost as far-flung to match. His doggerel specialized in battles and disasters, and his lines on the Tay Bridge collapse of 1879 are far better known in Britain than Theodor Fontane's classic Die Brücke am Tay:

> Beautiful Railway Bridge of the Silv'ry Tay
> Alas! I am very sorry to say
> That ninety lives have been taken away
> On the last Sabbath day of eighteen hundred and seventy-nine
> Which will be remembered for a very long time.

Dundee really was at the centre of empire. In the mid-nineteenth century it became the jute capital of Europe, processing the fibre, imported from India, into yarn which was woven into sacks, carpets, and linoleum. The jute industry was based on the town's existing involvement in the Arctic whale fishery, a way of getting oil before the invention of paraffin (also a Scots discovery)—the whaler-type survey ship Discovery (1901) is preserved on Dundee quay. Whale oil was used to make the jute fibres flexible, a technology borrowed from the existing linen industry, and between the 1830s and 1870s its production rocketed, the two-kilometre-long tidal quay of the city was crammed with sailing ships from Calcutta, around where the jute was grown and dispatched. In the 1860s about half the town's workers were in the jute mills, and huge fortunes were made by a relatively few 'Jute Barons' from families such as the Baxters, Bonars, and Grimonds. However, these increasingly invested in Calcutta factories (because of the cheapness of their wages) and put their profits into the infrastructure of the United States—railroads, coal mines, real estate—by means of the investment trusts which the city pioneered along with Edinburgh solicitors. The Flemings went from the shop floor to the City in one generation, and to James Bond in three.

Politically, Dundee was radical. In the nineteenth century it created a lively press in which many of the news stories and poems came from working people. It was a centre of Chartism and later in 1906 returned one of Scotland's first Labour MPs, George Wilkie. His Liberal companion was Winston Churchill, then a radical. When Churchill was thrown out, sixteen years later, it was in favour of a prohibitionist, Edwin Scrymgeour, who was *supported by the newly enfranchised women jute workers. Later on the local Labour Party combined with the Indian nationalists to put forward the Indian socialist leader Krishna Menon as its candidate.*

In the 1920s the Liberal newspaper firm of John Leng was taken over by the Conservative Thomson family, whose string of folksy weekly papers and children's comics, notably the Beano *and* Dandy *reached practically every Scottish, and many British, homes. What kid didn't know Lord Snooty, Dennis the Menace, Roy of the Rovers? Even today Oor Wullie and the Broons in the* Sunday Post *preserve a Scottish urban lifestyle of eighty years ago: Grandpaw, Paw (for a description see the Bone brothers on the Clydeside craftsman) Maw, and in order of age Hen (21), Joe, Daphne, Maggie, Horace, the twins, and the bairn (2). Strongly anti-union, Thomson's papers still supplied one of the best journalistic trainings, reflected in the disproportionate number of Scots to be found working in London's Fleet Street. James Cameron, the humanitarian and socialist, effectively the obituarist of the old empire, was its greatest graduate.*

The 1850s, intellectually lively with some remarkable history being written, but in politics a critical, disquieting decade, almost took its cue from Carlyle's dark *Latter-Day Pamphlets* (1850): pessimistic about greed, sloganizing, and maladministration. Some of these concerns were echoed by the Society for the Vindication of Scottish Rights, a Conservative-Radical patriotic alliance, launched in 1854, only to be sidelined by the Crimean War (1854–6) and the Indian Mutiny. The first saw the bravery of the soldiers— the 'Thin Red Line' of the highlanders at Balaclava—betrayed by incompetent generals, while the violence of the mutineers and the revenge of the British subverted the modernization of India by the utilitarians. It also fanned a racism, anti-coloured and anti-Irish, generated in lowland Scotland by the likes of Professor Robert Knox—the anatomist who was supplied by Burke and Hare—and the Tory home ruler the Revd James Begg. Setbacks abroad would weaken and distract Britain and give Bismarck his chance in Europe, but the decade also saw imperialism reinforced by one of the country's most heroic, if ultimately quixotic enterprises: the golden age of the African explorer-missionaries.

This stemmed from the split in the Kirk, imperial expansion, and the anti-slavery cause. While the old 'moderates' had regarded missionaries as dangerous fanatics and Africans as primitives, mid-Victorian Whigs saw the Churches, on balance, as aids to colonial government. The movement's pre-eminent hero was David Livingstone (1813–73), son of a cotton-spinner from the Lanarkshire mill village of Blantyre, who trained as a doctor at the Andersonian University in Glasgow, and explored (successfully) and evangelized (unsuccessfully) for years in Africa, tracking the course of the Zambesi River and discovering the central African lakes. After his death the Shire highlands above Lake Nyasa virtually became a Scots colony, with the Free Kirk established at Blantyre and the Church of Scotland at Livingstonia.

In the 1880s a new, more imperially minded generation of missionaries, whose ideologue was the charismatic scientist-theologian Henry Drummond (1851–97), linked their work to British expansion and the 'partition of Africa' decided by the Berlin Conference of 1884–5—something graven on the public mind by the martyrdom of General Gordon (engineer, evangelical, of Scots descent) at Khartoum. As a result of foreign investment, career structures, missionary activity, and even Gladstone's notion of 'International Public Right', Liberal Imperialism became a keynote of late Victorian Scottish politics, exemplified by the glamorous aristocrat the earl of Rosebery (1847–1929), briefly and unsuccessfully prime minister in 1894, and the energetic Bismarckian state-socialist R. B. Haldane (1856–1928), who preached the gospel of 'national efficiency' as the basis of a new consensus. Rosebery briefly flirted with 'home rule all round' in the 1880s, as the first stage of imperial federation. Haldane was a Fabian-style centralizer who feared a coming European confrontation and prepared the British army for it; his schemes for scientific development and higher education later led him into the Labour Party. Out of this phase came the Boys' Brigade, with its icons of Bible and rifle—and later, more successfully and permanently, Bible and football.

VICTORIAN VALUES

With the exception of the religious issue, Scottish politics between 1832 and the 1880s was stable, even dull. In some counties, notably in the Borders and

Highlands, a few great landed families still exercised power, with farmers only beginning to elect MPs after the 1867 Reform Act and the 1872 act which gave the secret ballot. In an echo of the eighteenth century, the duke of Argyll 'MacCailein Mor', 'Great Son of Colin' still sat in two of Gladstone's cabinets. Queen Victoria's daughter married his son. In the burghs (most of which were still 'grouped' together, voting separately from the surrounding counties) conflicts between Free Churchmen, Dissenters (United Presbyterians), and the Auld Kirk made for many contests *between* Liberals. Macaulay sat for Edinburgh, but was thought unsound on disestablishment, so the Dissenters, headed by Duncan MacLaren, brother-in-law of the English free trader John Bright, threw him out in 1847. In the burghs (usually 'grouped' together) working-class male householders got the vote in 1867, but in the counties they had to wait until 1884.

'BARBIE'—A VICTORIAN SMALL BURGH

In 1901 a young Scots journalist, George Douglas Brown, wrote a brilliant, bitter novel, with the structure of a Greek tragedy, called The House with the Green Shutters. *It chronicled the downfall of John Gourlay, carter, of 'Barbie' (said to be based on Brown's home town of Ochiltree in Ayrshire). But it could stand for many 'small burghs' of between 3,000 and 7,000 in population, in an age when standardization was fast increasing. The nature and divisions of Scottish society were reflected in these 175 communities, self-governing since the Middle Ages, which could have as few as 800 or 900 inhabitants, while some industrial 'villages' like Bellshill had over 12,000.*

Set in a landscape of large fields and farms, and built of local stone, mainly red or cream sandstone, but with black lava stone in the Borders and granite in the north-east, roofed in slate from Ballachulish or Easdale, most of their buildings were new. The timber and plaster thatched cottages of the medieval burghs had vanished, brick-building was rare. Perhaps a school or church existed from the eighteenth century, in classical style, surrounded by rows of solid one- or two-storey houses and shops, in which domestic industries such as 'fancy' weaving, shoemaking, and tailoring were still carried on. The town house for the provost, bailies (magistrates), and council, elected by the ratepayers after the 1833 act, was often modern and 'baronial' in style, with offices also for the parish board (1845, reformed in 1896) and school board (1872). These were also the agents for central government. Unlike a German or French town, there was no government office—sous-prefecture or Regierungspräsidium. Its tower and battlements challenged (at least) six churches—Kirk, Free Kirk, United Presbyterian (voluntary), Secession, Episcopalian (the 'Piskies' had once been Jacobites but were now favoured by the English and the upper classes), and a Roman Catholic chapel. There would be a Masonic Lodge and a Volunteer hall, because the Scots were pioneer Masons and after the Volunteer Act of 1859, enthusiastic amateur soldiers. West Scottish burghs had Orange Halls, and the din of flute and drum.

A road would wind to where, often some distance out of town, stood the railway station (five trains a day), of one of the five Scots companies, with warehouses for agricultural goods, a coal depot, perhaps an auction mart and foundry and a gasworks, owned often by the burgh council, and a neat row of cottages for the 'railway folk'. In town there would be courthouse, police station, post-and-telegraph office, hotel (respectable), half-a-dozen alehouses (not respectable), usually two printers and newspaper offices (Liberal and Conservative), a branch or branches of the seven main Scottish banks (the country was notoriously 'over-banked'), a library donated by Andrew Carnegie, and a solemn, well-tended cemetery, replete with obelisks, table tombs, and, after the 1850s, Celtic crosses. Fin-de-siècle innovations were the cottage hospital, a local co-op society catering for the well-doing working class, a bicycle repairer for Dunlop and Fleming's pneumatic-tyred safety bikes, of which there would be a hundred or so, the water turbine which provided some villas with flickering electricity, Alessandro Macari's fish restaurant and ice-cream parlour, and the young laird's three-ton Argyll touring car, built at Alexandria in the Vale of Leven.

Open street markets were unusual in Scotland (the weather was unhelpful and there were no small tenant farmers to supply them) but there were usually many small shops, butchers and fishmongers, seedsmen, smiths, carriers. Horses everywhere would make for a smelly main street, noisy, too, with the clatter of hooves, iron tyres, and tackety boots. The local elite, for George Douglas Brown these were 'the bodies': provost, Auld Kirk minister,

doctor, lawyer, headmaster, were more private now, but could be seen in the
bigger local stores which sold 'luxury' goods—coffee, wine, their own blends
of whisky—to the surrounding large farms and mansion houses. A public
park, with well-trimmed lawns, a cast-iron fountain (celebrating the water
supply drawn from a local loch in the 1860s) and children's swings
(padlocked on Sundays) often a clock tower or mercat cross, and statue to
some local notable, completed the scene. On the fringes of the town were the
sandstone villas, in Italianate, classical, or 'baronial' styles, of the local
middle class, along with many who had made money abroad and retired to
their native district. Set back from the road in its 'policies' would be the 'big
hoose' of the laird, unornamented and probably eighteenth-century classical,
though perhaps incorporating an earlier tower, with its walled garden and
greenhouses, stables, 'mains' or home farm, and rows of 'steading' cottages.

Downwind of the town, near its factory—for wool or linen, or maybe
paper or leather—were the closer-packed ranks of workers' cottages: one- or
two-roomed or flats with the upper floor accessible by outside stairs and
served by outside toilets, standing in dusty open spaces and drying greens
where bairns played football. Some might be 'model' dwellings in which the
foreman or skilled workers lived, others, older and smaller, suffered from
damp and dirt, and housed unskilled workers and immigrants, often from
the Highlands and Ireland. (Only in the 1960s would these be cleared in their
entirety; council houses—for the well-doing working class, postmen, railway
and council employees, came in the 1920s.) Private estates of rather small
semi-detached or terrace houses started at that time but really date from the
'motor age' of the 1970s. Outside the town there would be for the better-off
tennis-courts and a curling rink, and in any town of more than 3,000, the
well-kept turf of a golf course. Not usually visible from these was (sometimes)
a rudimentary sewage farm, and the grim barrack of the local Poorhouse,
where such of the workers as lasted to their sixties would end up.

The controllers of this new wealth were unsentimental about the past.
The dukes of Hamilton allowed mining entrepreneurs to scoop the coal out
from under their classical palace at Hamilton, with the result that subsidence made it uninhabitable and it had to be demolished in the 1920s, its

only relic a huge, echoing mausoleum. Glasgow University shifted in the 1860s from its Scots Renaissance quadrangle—one of the finest works of the period—in the crumbling medieval High Street to Sir Gilbert Scott's Belgian-Gothic pile in the more salubrious West End. The old college was flattened to make way for a railway goods yard.

To many observers, particularly the English, the culture of Victorian Scotland was unobtrusive, crushed under money-making and fundamentalist Calvinism. In his influential study *The History of Civilisation in England* (1861), H. T. Buckle accused his Scots contemporaries of submitting to a near-medieval theocracy—and many of the latter agreed, clearing off to the opportunities of London, whom they provided with many journalists as well as politicians and publishers. Hadn't Carlyle called journalists 'the priests of our new church'? Critics such as E. S. Dallas, David Masson, George Gilfillan, and Robertson Nicoll altered the shape of English literature. But they didn't write it. In the age of Trollope, Thackeray, Dickens, and George Eliot the Scots were marginalized, even though they produced some strange, disturbing talents like the fantasist-moralist George MacDonald and the grim atheists James Thomson ('B V' was the pseudonym he used) and John Davidson, whose art reflected the strains of their native society.

In fact, the 1860s was probably the closest Scotland came to becoming 'North Britain', after the nationalist revival of the 1850s petered out. John Stuart Mill, Scots by descent but moulded by Bentham, Wordsworth, and Coleridge, landed a devastating critique of the Scots common-sense tradition in his *Examination of Sir William Hamilton's Philosophy* (1864); Matthew Arnold's *Celtic Literature* (1867) praised the other-worldliness of the Celts, their 'revolt against the monstrous despotism of fact', which sounded retrospective and condescending. Walter Bagehot's *English Constitution* and the more radical *Essays on Reform* (both 1867) by young dons, often from a Scottish background, such as James Bryce and Leslie Stephen, took British political homogeneity for inevitable and desirable. Radicals north and south of the border united in agitating for the 1867 Second Reform Act and the legalization of trade unions. David Livingstone was a 'British' figure, as was his contemporary Alexander MacDonald, an iron miner who rose by the same educational route to become, in 1874, the first trade union MP—for Stafford. When the Education (Scotland) Act was carried in 1872, it seemed only to reflect the English measure of the previous year, the work of W. E. Forster of Bradford, Carlyle's friend, and Arnold's brother-in-law.

Yet assimilation was undermined by the way Scots legislation was handled in Westminster (it would be a foolhardy English MP who would try to interfere), the energetic life of the Scottish daily and weekly press, a radical taste in painting (first the Barbizon school, then the Impressionists, then the innovations of the 'Glasgow Boys' and the 'Scottish Colourists'), and an architecture which bellowed its originality—literally—from the rooftops. One of its spiritual fathers, the international lawyer and university reformer Professor James Lorimer, condemned the 'Cockney' takeover of Britain, restored Scots castles, and in 1884 proposed a European federation intended to promote regional diversity instead of great power conflict. What Englishman would have dared do that?

ROTHESAY: TOURIST SCOTLAND

'A pretty little town, built round a fine bay, with hills in the distance, and a fine harbour.' With Queen Victoria, what you saw was what you got. She sailed into Rothesay in 1847. It was just coming to the end of a phase as a textile and fisheries centre; much further back it had been a royal burgh (in 1400) and the site of a powerful moated castle, built by the Viking ruler Magnus Barefoot in 1098. The title duke of Rothesay was after 1398 that of the heir to the Scottish throne.

The town's real career began shortly after the queen's visit: as Scotland's premier holiday resort. It started respectably, with hydropathic hotels erected in the German manner. The esplanade was created in 1869–70, a tramway and swimming baths built in 1882, a pier in 1884: fountains and bandstands followed. The population went up from 4,100 in 1821 to 9,108 in 1891, but this was nothing to the thousands who flocked into the town during the summer and in particular at the 'Glasgow Fair' at the end of July. Rothesay was on one side genteel and rather rich, the marquess of Bute, in his huge Florentine-Gothic castle at Mountstuart, and the yachtsmen at the Royal Northern Club. On the other it was proletarian and blowsy, with

Glasgow 'Keelies' flooding down-river 'on the boats' for a couple of days in the open air—or in one of the town's numerous pubs. It wasn't the only resort—Helensburgh, Largs, Dunoon, Ayr, and Troon also set out to cater for holiday-makers. Nor was it on the scale of Blackpool, Morecambe, Llandudno, or Scarborough.

Tourism and holiday-making in Scotland advanced in parallel with industrialization and urbanization. The new townspeople demanded access to the 'green lungs' of the central belt. For the winners, the villages on the fringes of the growing cities became a refuge from the pollution and disease of the centres. Families would migrate to places like Edinburgh's Colinton or Balerno on the Pentland hills, in much the same way as Italians moved in summer from city to villa; Glasgow had the Firth of Clyde. Henry Bell's pioneer steamer the Comet (1812) was the enterprise of a Helensburgh hotel owner, and the summer migration was also encouraged by the building of turnpike roads and later railways.

These catered for English and foreign visitors. Travellers to and through Scotland in the eighteenth century—such as Dr Samuel Johnson and James Boswell in 1771—were still curiosities, but the 'Scots tour' was stimulated by interest in Macpherson's Ossian; later the wars with France checked visits to continental spas and the Grand Tour, while Scott's novels advertised the place: particularly after 1848, when the Anglo-Scottish railways were built. There was also a north–south trend, with tens of thousands of Scots visiting London for the Crystal Palace in 1851. Samuel Smiles rejoiced at this fulfilment of the Union, as at Berwick he saw the endless excursion trains cross the Royal Border Bridge, and the main organizer of this, Thomas Cook and Son, built up a big excursion business to Scotland from London and the English midlands. Steamers multiplied, serving the Clyde and the Hebrides; and along their main routes, chiefly 'the Royal Route to the Isles' developed by David MacBrayne—Glasgow via Rothesay to Oban, Fort William, and Inverness—settlements of hotels and boarding houses grew up. The population of Oban went up from 600 in 1791 to 5,000 in 1891, and Inverness from 5,000 to 20,000.

For the workers summer holidays only came in the 1850s. There were works excursions—implying huge numbers, special trains, and intense respectability. Paddle steamers—cheaper, less controlled, with unlimited

15. *The PS Waverley, built in 1947, is now the last surviving seagoing paddler, at the end of a history that started in Port Glasgow, 1812, with the launch of Henry Bell's 'Comet'. Since she entered service 'doon the watter' Clyde shipyards have fallen from thirty to three.*

capacity for drink and getting rid of it—were more traumatic, given weather, weans (children), drink, and so on:

> One Friday morn at the Glesca Fair
> There was me, masel, an' several mair.
> We a' resolved to go a share,
> An' spend the day in Rothesay O'.
>
> We wandered doon the Broomielaw
> In wind an' rain an' sleet an' snaw
> An' at forty minutes efter twa,
> We got the length o' Rothesay O'.

As ever, the middle classes did better, with sports like tennis, yachting, bowls, and above all golf. Towns had their own municipal links, which went far to make it a 'democratic' game, but also one which brought in the visitors. By 1900 not only was St Andrews, with its Royal and Ancient Club, golf capital of the world, but the railways were promoting huge golfing hotels, and North

> *Berwick in particular—with premiers Rosebery, Balfour, and Asquith*
> *regularly holidaying—had become a British equivalent of Biarritz or*
> *Deauville.*

BRITISH SCOTS

C. P. Snow once observed that most British traditions dated from the last quarter of the nineteenth century. Indeed, much of the character of modern Scotland was created by Victorians whose Scots identity was to say the least part of a complex weave, in which national identity and ambitions were tangled up with English and imperial relationships. At its apex was Queen Victoria, the first reigning royal to take an active interest in the place since 1603. She discovered Scotland in the course of visits with Prince Albert in 1842, 1844, and 1847. The Deeside initiative seems to have been Albert's, as he thought its dense pine forests resembled his native Thuringia, and the artist who did most to popularize the 'Royal Highlands' as a subject was the Englishman Edwin Landseer. In the revolutionary year of 1848 the royal family settled at Balmoral, about 80 kilometres inland from Aberdeen, for the late summer and Albert and a local architect designed a grandiose granite castle which was completed in 1855. The prince of Wales was sent in 1859 as a private pupil to Dr Schmitz, rector of Edinburgh's High School. Albert enjoyed Balmoral for only six years, but then the queen kept it up as a memorial (she visited Ireland and Wales only twice), published *Our Life in the Highlands* (1868), and broke away from her obsessive widowhood only when in the company of her Scottish retainers, notably the ghillie John Brown, to whom rumour had it she was married.

Balmoral's building coincided with the brief flurry of 1850s nationalism, and effectively produced a docile, Britain-friendly version of it: tartan (mightily strengthened by aniline dyes, invented in that decade), tourism, and the cult of field sports, highland games, and country dancing, when aristos old and new would fraternize with the less menacing members of the proletariat. In the Highlands the royals could live a life which was 'simple' and Scots, rather than political and English: different from the formality of Windsor and London. Statesmen had to endure highland autumns, but nowhere was the queen more plausible as Bagehot's 'dignified part of the constitution', lauded by an aristocratic Tory establishment—the Knights of the Thistle, the Royal Company of Archers, Heralds and Limners and Historiographers-Royal. English Tories could find this tartan Ruritania absurd. 'If I gave that man the Thistle, he'd probably eat it,' Disraeli remarked of a dim Scottish duke. But if Victoria did little for any democratic expression of Scottish nationality, for a long time—well into the twentieth century—the Scots didn't seem to notice. If Scottish Liberalism had an embodiment, however, it was a man whom she loathed with a venom worthy of her grandson, the German Emperor Wilhelm II.

The great hero of Scottish politics holidayed only 80 kilometres south of Balmoral, on the family estate of Fasque, near Montrose. He thought, however, when on his deathbed in 1898, only of his first and last loves, the University of Oxford and the Church of England. William Ewart Gladstone (1809–98) was of all transferred nationalists the most complex. He was completely Scots, combining Gaelic and lowland blood. His father was a Leith merchant who like many Scots traded out of Liverpool, yet his education was that of a member of the English upper classes, trained at Eton and Christ Church for a Tory political career.

A High Churchman, and through his friendship with John Henry Newman and James Hope-Scott, inheritor of Abbotsford, almost a Catholic convert, Gladstone shared the seriousness of his Scots fellow countrymen, and the Disruption affected an intellect which was basically theological. He followed Sir Robert Peel out of the Tories when the latter adopted Free Trade in 1846, and as chancellor in the early 1850s carried out the modernization of Britain's public finances and bureaucracy. The notion that politics was a projection of individual morality helped convert him in the 1860s to democracy, and in turn the concession in 1867 of the vote to urban householders created a public for his combination of high principle and thoroughly modern manipulation of the mass media. Carried into Downing Street in 1868, he proceeded to disestablish the Irish Church, pass the Education Act (1871 in England, 1872 in Scotland) quasi-legalize trade unions, and introduce the secret ballot. In 1879–80 he returned to Scotland in triumph by contesting the Tory seat of Midlothian as part of his campaign against Disraeli's imperialistic foreign policy and in defence of the Balkan Christians—a campaign aided by whistle-stop train tours and blanket press coverage. His subsequent crusade, to give land reform and self-government to Ireland, was taken by many younger Liberals as an implicit promise of the same status for Scotland.

At this point Gladstone became enigmatic. The restoration of the Scottish Secretaryship (carried by consensus in 1885, in answer to protests about delays in Scots legislation) and a Highland Land Act, giving crofters security of tenure (they had just got the vote and were using it to good effect) were as far as he would go. Both were intended to inhibit any growth of the unbudgeable discontent the Irish were showing. In fact most of his successors were strong if moralistic imperialists, thirled to (committed to) the historic Anglo-Scottish partnership, and most Scottish voters, after Gladstone's withdrawal from public life in 1893, backed them or even voted for Unionists (most of whom were ex-Liberals rather than Tories). Deferential Scotland seemed a great reservoir of safe seats for Liberal and Tory leaders, and much less radical than it had once been. Even so, the shadow of 'the People's William' as a democratic liberator lay long. In the 1920s the socialist leader of the Miners Union, Bob Smillie, asked to name the greatest influence on him, said without hesitation 'Gladstone'.

Yet within the radical movement the leaven of another Anglo-Scot was working away: the 'Graduate of Oxford', John Ruskin. The son of the sherry shipper who with his partners Telford and Domecq established fortified wine as *the* British taste (which lasted until the late twentieth century), Ruskin was, like his friends Carlyle and Gladstone, 'a Scot of Scots'. He started as an art critic in *Modern Painters* (1843), then annexed Carlyle's social critique and in writings like *Unto this Last* (1862), broadened it into an environmental and aesthetic one. Britain came to be seen in terms far different from mid-Victorian complacency. 'If you will tell me what you ultimately intend Bradford to be, perhaps I can tell you what Bradford can ultimately produce.' With this phrase Ruskin launched into an attack on a Britain quarried and built over into a coal-pit and slum, because of the absence of any criteria other than profit and loss. While Carlyle burned himself out with his huge biography *Frederick the Great*, Ruskin (for much of the time on the edge of sanity) formulated a critique of capitalism which became the basis of much of twentieth-century social democracy, both in itself and through its influence on such as William Morris, Patrick Geddes, Leo Tolstoy, Mohandas Gandhi, and J. A. Hobson. Ruskin's influence was worldwide (and perhaps more significant today than ever before) but carried forward into many fields the social concerns of the Scots Enlightenment. Impossible to pin down as a democrat, his support of home rule distanced himself from the otherwise triumphal imperial radicalism of his day. Comparing Tyre, Venice, and Britain, he was not sanguine: 'Of the First of these great powers only the memory remains; of the Second the ruins; the Third which inherits their greatness, if it forget their example, may be led through prouder eminence to less pitied destruction.'

That challenge was, if anything, more relevant in *fin-de-siècle* Scotland, and was echoed in much of the literature, art, and architecture of the time, in the buildings of Charles Rennie Mackintosh, the social teaching of the philosophers Edward Caird and Henry Jones and the economist William Smart, the programmes of the municipal socialists of Glasgow, and the patronage of collectors, philanthropists, and educators such as Sir William Burrell, Sir Daniel Stevenson, and Andrew Carnegie. Patrick Geddes, Ruskinian, sociologist, and town-planning polymath, identified a 'Scottish Renaissance' in the 1890s. He had some grounds for doing so: the decade saw much literary energy from the likes of 'Fiona MacLeod', Neil Munro, the young John Buchan, and George Douglas Brown (though this was overlaid by the commercialized nostalgia of the 'Kailyard'); and in painting and architecture the country was travelling far from the academic sentimentalism and baronial revivalism of the mid-Victorians. The 'Glasgow Boys' and such architects as Robert Lorimer, Baillie Scott, and Sir J. J. Burnet, as well as Mackintosh, were winning European reputations for the subtle interplay of tradition and technical innovation.

Who did the Victorian Scots actually believe they were? The question isn't straightforward. The capitalist bourgeoisie thought internationally: as shipbuilders, engineers, iron and coal merchants, investment managers. Their culture moulded itself round this framework: their openness to French painting, Norwegian and Russian drama, German philosophy. Scots were translators of Ibsen (William Archer), Nietzsche (Thomas Common), Proust (C. K. Scott-Moncrieff), and Freud (James Strachey). Below them, the middling levels were ostentatiously Scots in the way that appalled the likes of Hugh MacDiarmid: 'Burns-night Scottishness' starts in the 1880s: partly for imperial consumption under the patronage of the egregious Lord Rosebery but equally welcome in Britain, where many stalwarts of literary patriotism tended to be the 'tally men' or credit drapers, whom some regarded as 'worse than the Jews'.

Much local distinctiveness was already dying out through railways, newspapers, and elementary schools. Scots were predominantly urban, something that led to 'civics', sounded by Geddes, Carnegie, and many 'progressive' councillors, rather than 'nation'. Occupation and its hierarchies, in a five-and-a-half-day week, counted; sociologists have noted that egalitarian but 'aspiring' societies socialize less than inegalitarian but stable ones, so preparation for 'getting on by getting out' inhibited the sort of national identity European states projected: a schools curriculum, male conscription, and language-based cultures. Even the popular culture of England was less divided. But urbanization left lots of connections with life on the land or in small towns: the local paper arriving each week, the network of friends, the church or pub which catered for Lewis folk or Borderers. If Scots were profoundly class-conscious, this was more 'of a class' than 'for a class', as Marx and Engels found. Something similar applied to their nationalism. In this sense *fin-de-siècle* Scotland was imperial, but it was also—far more than England—European.

Around 1910 the future art collector and perceptive editor of *Ruskin Today* (1954), the young Kenneth Clark, was cruising with his parents on the Mediterranean in the family steam yacht, a thousand tons of cream-buff-and-gilt elegance built out of the profits of Paisley thread. At Monte Carlo, a Paris retailer came to dine, and was so impressed that she made Clark's father an offer. Clark Senior accepted, put the family into the local grand hotel. He cabled for a replacement, then he changed his mind, and cabled for Scots workers to build him a villa instead, which they did. In under a decade, the steam yacht would be as passé as the coracle . . .

6 | JOURNEY TO THE FRONTIER?
1906–2003

O Scotland is
The barren fig.
Up, carles, up,
And round it jig!
A miracle's
Oor only chance.
Up, carles, up
And let us dance!

(HUGH MACDIARMID, 1926)

WORK AS IF YOU LIVE IN THE EARLY DAYS OF A BETTER NATION.

(DENNIS LEE, quoted by Alisdair Gray, 1985)

HIGH TIDE AND ARMAGEDDON

Arthur Balfour, languid laird of Whittinghame, led his Unionist government to catastrophe in 1906. He observed that he was the victim of a tide of radicalism sweeping Europe: revolution in Russia, anticlerical radicalism in France, socialist advance in Germany. Scotland's version was a Liberal triumph. There was a short but severe slump in 1906–8—a taste of what was to come—but the economy boomed until it reached record production in 1913–14, and these years were to prove the apogee of the Liberals. They held fifty-seven out of the country's seventy-two seats and provided the prime minister, Sir Henry Campbell-Bannerman, a genial old-fashioned radical—his statue on Castle Hill still surveys Stirling, his constituency. His commitment to free trade, in a country which lived by it (mining, iron and steel, shipbuilding, and engineering were over a third of output) overcame a Unionist party split by Joe Chamberlain's programme of protection.

The Liberal Party, since Gladstone's day the conscience of Scotland, was impressive yet rather inert: it dominated the burghs and counties of east Scotland, but was weaker in the west, where it had been squeezed by Unionists and militant Protestants. After years of electing 'carpet-bagging' MPs, who were often English, its new generation, the anti-imperial, nationalistic 'Young Scots', were getting restive. Organized Labour was also making its presence felt: the success of Glasgow's weekly *Forward*, founded by Tom Johnston in 1906, reminded voters that the founders of the Labour Party in 1900 were Scots: James Keir Hardie and Ramsay MacDonald. But continuing issues of land reform and church disestablishment, and Irish backing for the Liberals over home rule, checked Labour's growth so much that Hardie and MacDonald both sat for southern constituencies.

Liberal leadership passed in 1908 to H. H. Asquith, MP for East Fife since 1886, and married into the Tennant chemical clan. He was theoretically committed to 'home rule all round' (which got some formal support in Commons debates) as were his mighty associates Lloyd George and Winston Churchill; but they were also working on the foundations of the welfare state: labour exchanges, legal freedom for trade unions, old-age pensions, unemployment, and health insurance. Along with the Dreadnought race with Germany, this had a de facto centralizing tendency.

In 1909, however, the European revolution caught up. British politics was gripped by the controversy over Lloyd George's radical Budget and the attempt of the House of Lords to defeat it. Perhaps because there were only sixteen Scots representative peers, Scotland was less affected by the resistance of the Tory 'last ditchers', salient in England, where Asquith would lose his overall majority. Tom Johnston lashed the landed order furiously in 'Our Scots Noble Families' which sold 100,000 copies as a *Forward* special. Scotland remained Liberal in the two 1910 elections, although among fast-increasing trade unionists, the miners were now affiliated to Labour, and the railwaymen and dockers were getting militant. Seventy years later, the Glasgow engineer and radical Harry McShane would remember how the speakers on Glasgow Green, once dominated by religion, went political. And also went female; Scotswomen like Helen Crawfurd, Flora Drummond, and Elsie Inglis provided some of the most energetic of the suffrage campaigners who harried the government. The approach of home rule for Ireland, however, meant that Unionist activity—under the Scots-Canadian iron dealer Andrew Bonar Law—was increasing by 1914, with Ulster's Protestants and their leaders invoking the Covenant of 1638, and threatening civil war. After 28 June, and the shots of Sarajevo, everything changed.

Enlistment in Kitchener's 'New Army' was high—partly to avenge 'poor little Belgium', after the Congo scandals an imperfect martyr, partly because of a fear of unemployment when the war hit the exporting industries. Propaganda, whether 'documentary' like Viscount Bryce's report on German atrocities (many fabricated) in Belgium, or fictional, like 'Ian Hay's' *The First Hundred Thousand* and John Buchan's *The Thirty-nine Steps* (all 1915), was sharp, persuasive, and Scots. Half a million would serve as infantry in France in the 'Big Pushes' that followed the Battle of Loos in October 1915, notably on the Somme in July–November 1916. Douglas Haig, Commander-in-Chief from December 1915, was Scots, but could only offer to out-produce and out-slaughter the Central Powers. By the time the Scottish National War Memorial, by the great arts and crafts architect Sir Robert Lorimer, was rising in Edinburgh Castle, 1924–7, Haig's reputation was crumbling. The admirals fared no better. After the indecisive clash of battlefleets off Jutland in May 1916, they were terrified of a German

16. *A standard 'Scotch Goods' engine designed by William Holmes, outshopped from Springburn Works in 1891 and in its brand-new grey livery. Thousands were built but each one seemed to have its own character—and complicated tool kit. 'Maude' as she was called after World War I service, survives on the Bo'ness and Kinneill Railway.*

breakout, and tried to retain destroyer and cruiser escorts around their huge, obsolescent Dreadnoughts. Lloyd George and the politicians forced them to break up the 'fleet in being' to provide convoys for merchantmen, otherwise being sunk in hundreds by German submarines.

Weapons unforeseen—submarines, machine guns, radio, tanks, aircraft (some 55,000 had been built by 1918, many in Scotland)—and millions of high-explosive shells placed immense demands on UK industry. Liberals were placed in a quandary. Their traditional peaceability was broken by Lloyd George's drive as Minister of Munitions, intervening in the sulphurous labour relations of the Clyde, to convert its engineering works to war production. Clydeside magnates got 'dilution'—the replacement of skilled men with women and the unskilled—along with the jailing of trade unionists and radical agitators like the Marxist teacher John MacLean, but also the regulating of rents in late 1915, which sharply collectivized Scots urban society. Forced into coalition with the Unionists in May 1915, Asquith and the Liberals were deserted by Lloyd George in December 1916 for a war cabinet which was really a five-man Committee of Public Safety.* In 1917, when the French ground to a standstill after the catastrophic Nivelle offensives, and the Russians reversed into revolution, liberating German troops for the Western front, a certain *outré* Scottish originality outfaced even the grim competence of Field Marshal Ludendorff.

John Buchan sent the US press off in the tracks of a small, strange Anglo-Irishman who was beating hell out of the Turks in the Negev desert. The promises made to Major Lawrence didn't quite square with those Balfour made to a biochemist in Manchester who was indispensable to shell manufacture, Dr Chaim Weizmann: of a national home for the Jews. Viscount Bryce and his young semi-pacifist allies managed to sell to President Woodrow Wilson (by descent a Galloway Scot) the idea of a Covenant of the League of Nations. This eased the USA's entry in April 1917. The 'damned little Welsh attorney's' Scottish industrial allies took the dominant role in organizing the British war economy: 'men of push and go' like Sir Joseph Maclay, shipping controller, Sir Eric Geddes, transport minister, Sir James Lithgow in the shipyards, Lord Beaverbrook and John Buchan in propaganda, and William Weir in the rapidly expanding aircraft business: all of them under the dour but competent rebel-turned-Chancellor, Bonar Law.

In May 1918 Haig stopped the last German offensive. At the second battle of Amiens on 8 August thousands of tanks powered a counter-attack which shattered German morale. Ordered to sea, the High Seas fleet mutinied in its harbours, and the Kaiser abdicated. Within months, a Europe which in 1914 had only three republics—France, Switzerland, and San Marino—acquired a further nine, where Russia, Austria, and Turkey had once ruled. Lenin made John MacLean Soviet Consul in Scotland, hoping for support from the Red Clyde. It didn't come.

Liberal horizons narrowed even more when the electorate, as the result of the Reform Act of 1918, expanded threefold not just by enfranchising women over 30 but non-householder men. Only the unions could organize

---

* Its members reflected 'Atlantic Britain'. Only two were born in England. The trade unionist Arthur Henderson was Scots, Bonar Law Scots-Canadian, Viscount Milner was the son of my predecessor as English professor in Tübingen. The Marquess Curzon was a genuine Anglo-Norman aristocrat, but Lloyd George, though born in Manchester, was monoglot Welsh until he went to school.

them. 'Home rule all round' hove into view again, as part of attempts to settle the Irish situation, increasingly tense since the Easter Rising of 1916, but it was dwarfed by the problem of demobilization. The Scottish Secretary, Robert Munro, panicked about a 'bolshevik-type rising' in Glasgow in early 1919 when the Trades Council called a strike for the Forty Hour Week: troops and tanks were sent north by train. But the disturbances fizzled out, and Munro, through buying off the Scots Hierarchy with his Education Act of 1918, which incorporated its schools in the state system, detached the Catholics.

This didn't stop some aid to the IRA passing through Glasgow, but Scotland remained unmilitant and only intellectuals wanted to emulate the Irish Free State, declared in 1921. When the Irish went, the home rule interest at Westminster went with them. Instead, for the troops returning from the war, the deciding issue was housing—whose horrors had been exposed by a Royal Commission, appointed in 1913, which reported in 1917. The key group in electoral politics was no longer made up of Liberal lawyers like Munro. Even the industrialists (particularly in shipping, railways, and banking) were selling up and moving south. The trade unionists kept their numbers and were joined by many Labour councillors. They would shortly take centre stage.

SLUMP AND RENAISSANCE

By November 1922 the political landscape had utterly changed. 'Red Clydeside', disillusion with the Lloyd George coalition over Ireland, and sheer growth in voters, sent Labour's vote from 3.6 per cent in 1910 to 32 per cent, and its MPs from three to twenty-nine, among them a notable group of left-wingers—the 'Clydesiders'. They were led by two contrasting figures. James Maxton, the cadaverous, lank-haired former teacher, 'didn't just preach the revolution, he looked it'. Brilliant orator and fervent humanitarian, he was no strategist, and would cost his Independent Labour Party dear. John Wheatley had strategy in his bones: a tubby Irish miner who went successfully into business and won the Catholic vote for Labour. As Minister of Health in the 1924 Labour Cabinet (a third of which was Scots) he created Britain's social housing policy, of central government subsidies for local authority building and letting. It lasted until Mrs Thatcher's day.

Wheatley shared the proto-Keynesian 'underconsumptionist' ideas of J. A. Hobson—until the workers were paid decently, a demand-led revival was fantasy. Ideas were needed, for 1921 also saw a catastrophic and continuing economic recession. Once wartime sinkings were made good, shipping orders dried up and the Clyde yards fell idle, by now linked into huge vertical monopolies which extended from shipping lines through shipyards and steelworks to coal and iron mines. Demand for capital goods collapsed; competition from oil and electricity grew. The results were felt all along the line; over 20 per cent were unemployed, and looked likely to remain so. Labour, in office in 1924 and 1929–31—its Scottish Secretary on both occasions was the Fife miners' leader Wullie Adamson whose dull exterior concealed a duller intellect—could do little for the Scots economy, because of its commitment to free-trading orthodoxy.

Eric Geddes had offered the Scots their own railway system in 1922. They turned him down, fearing (rightly) that it would be uneconomic. The associated problems of the coal industry touched off the General Strike of 3–12 May 1926, the great moment of the Scottish left in the inter-war years, and the hinge of two radical masterpieces, Hugh MacDiarmid's 'A Drunk Man Looks at the Thistle' (1926) and Lewis Grassic Gibbon's *Cloud Howe* (1933). But this moment was one of heartbreaking failure. The solidarity of dockers and railwaymen across the country with the locked-out miners

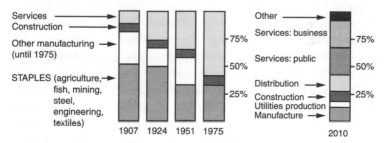

17. *Trends in the main Scottish economic sectors, 1907–2010.*
After 1980 offshore (UK Shelf) oil and gas production could add up to 25% of Scottish GDP.

was ended by a timid TUC: in MacDiarmid's words 'the thistle like a rocket soared I an' cam doon like the stick'. The strike ended twenty years' challenge by 'direct action'. The road forward was through local government or Parliament—or through the expert committee, as Tom Johnston, Labour's ideas man, was finding out on the Empire Marketing Board. (The Board produced the deeply unimperial figure of John Grierson, film maker and enthusiast for Soviet Agitprop, who even got Rudyard Kipling applauding Eisenstein!) In fact, Scottish policy—after 1926 in the hands of civil service departments, which replaced the old semi-representative boards—was scarcely discussed in Cabinet until the Second World War, and so paralysed was the second MacDonald government by the Wall Street slump that Labour was nearly obliterated when he deserted it to form the 'National Government' in 1931. Of thirty-six Labour MPs in 1929 only seven survived, four of whom then flounced off with Maxton and the ILP. Scotland's 'red' reputation belied a predominant Unionism, which would last (apart from 1945–51) to the late 1950s. Why was this?

Labour's rise was sudden, linked to rent control and the Irish alliance. As a result Liberals and Conservatives fused at a city level, and were reinforced by a Protestant working class susceptible to Unionist propaganda, government intervention and an anti-Catholicism which was often explicitly racist. The left was, in contrast, fragmented. Small though it was, away from the 'Little Moscows' of the Fife coalfield, the Communist Party of Great Britain, founded 1920, could call on Scottish stalwarts such as Willie Gallacher (MP for West Fife, 1935–55), Harry McShane, and Abe Moffat. By the mid-1930s it would displace the ILP. Also competing was, after 1928, the National Party of Scotland, formed mainly by dissident members of the ILP. Swamped in the rightwards trend of 1931, it reorganized itself into the Scottish National Party three years later. More dramatic was the rise of militant Protestant parties in Glasgow and Edinburgh in the early 1930s, a Scottish variant of the far right which choked off any Scottish fascism because it regarded it as a Catholic conspiracy. Labour made municipal progress, taking over most big-town councils (save Edinburgh) in the 1930s, but after the 1935 election it still had only twenty MPs to the Unionists' fifty.

During the 1930s the vogue was for cross-party collaboration, to secure industrial diversification, arms orders, and in 1935 the completion of the great Cunard liner *Queen Mary*. 'Small-n-nationalism', in the shape of the Scottish National Development Council, the Saltire Society, the Scottish Council for Social Service, and the National Trust for Scotland, was encouraged by two leading politicians Tom Johnston and Walter Elliot. Johnston was out of Parliament until 1935. Elliot was a leftish Unionist whose ideas had much in common with his socialist rival. A scientist and wit, whose friends included James Bridie the playwright, John Grierson, and John Boyd-Orr the nutritionist, his modus operandi was once described as 'discussing things drunk and deciding them sober'. Scottish Under-Secretary, 1924–9, Minister of Agriculture, 1932–6, Elliot as Secretary of State, 1936–8, organized further Keynesian-influenced planning groups, such as the Scottish Economic Committee, Films of Scotland, and the Scottish Special Housing Association, and above all Glasgow's successful Empire Exhibition in 1938.

MOTHERWELL

The Burgh of Motherwell and Wishaw was the writing on Scotland's wall. So thought the poet Edwin Muir, who started his doleful Scottish Journey there in 1935. The town had over 40 per cent unemployed.

Motherwell lies across the main Glasgow–Carlisle railway 20 kilometres south-east of Glasgow. Before 1848, when the line opened, it was completely rural, a hilly plateau forming a penisula above the deep valleys of the Rivers Clyde and Calder. A hundred or so cottages housed linen-weavers, who hunted with their dogs, and still acted Allan Ramsay's The Gentle Shepherd annually. The railway changed all that, as Motherwell became the junction between the Caledonian Railway from Glasgow to England and the lines to the north of Scotland. So, the 'Caley' rapidly set up its locomotive and carriage works, and a wrought-iron works followed, the first of many which subsequently lined the railway for 6 kilometres to Motherwell's twin town of Wishaw. Under the leadership of a local family, the Colvilles, Motherwell became after 1870 the centre of the Scottish steel industry, using German Siemens open-hearth furnaces to convert pig iron from neighbouring blast furnaces. Around the steelworks settled works for alloys, railway waggons, cranes, bridges, colliery machinery, and tramcars.

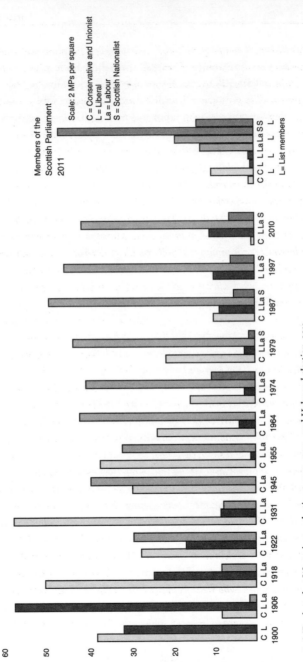

18. *MPs elected at Westminster elections, 1900–2010, and Holyrood election, 2011.*

Motherwell's 400 people in 1850 grew to 50,000 in Motherwell and Wishaw in 1911, with a workforce elite which was prosperous, Liberal-voting, and sustained Scotland's second-biggest co-operative society. The new community—'frontier town' was a phrase often used of a very American-like phenomenon—had to cope with subsidence from the omnipresent collieries, overcrowding, pollution, and a tangle of not very representative local authorities—two parish councils for the poor and health (1845), town council (1866) for building, lighting, drainage, roads, two school boards (1872), Lanark county council (1889). Less favoured were minorities—gastarbeiters—from Ireland and Lithuania, who moved in to do the hard, ill-paid manual work. Motherwell became Scotland's largest Catholic diocese, and one of the few signs of hope that Muir found was the grotto that unemployed Catholic miners had built, on the pattern of Lourdes, at Carfin. All were cheered up by the fish-and-chip shops and ice-cream parlours of the town's Italians, which after the First World War came to replace the pubs, as alcohol consumption fell by two-thirds.

After 1921 Motherwell's economy collapsed. Unemployment surged to nearly 40 per cent and would have been even higher had not many emigrated. (In 1934 the steel firm of Stewarts and Lloyds moved its works and workforce from nearby Mossend to Corby, 480 kilometres south in Northamptonshire: to this day the Corby accent is Scots.) This produced reactions as various as Britain's first Communist MP in 1922–3, an independent Orange MP in 1923–4, and in 1945 the first ever Scottish National Party MP. Another way out of this crisis was via religion, education, culture, and sport, generated in the town's twenty-odd churches, five cinemas, and big Carnegie library. Motherwell produced notable Calvinist and Catholic clergy, from Professor William Barclay to Cardinal Thomas Winning, historians and writers such as Professor Tom Devine and Liz Lochhead, Olympic-winner swimmers and footballers: Cathie Gibson, Nancy Riach, Ian St John, and—perhaps less predictably—Scotland's greatest post-war musician, Sir Alexander Gibson. (The intensity of a commitment to their society as much as to their sport would be seen in three monumental figures who went from the Lanarkshire coalfield into British football: Matt Busby, Bill Shankly, and Jock Stein.) Things started to look up with rearmament in 1935, and after the war, with Motherwell's works in a *seller's market, the place was prosperous as never before, though small-scale rentier-capitalism had all but vanished: in the 1970s 96 per cent of households rented from the Council.*

Even in the uncertainties of the 1960s the town got a second wind of heavy industry, when the Macmillan government subsidized Colvilles to build Ravenscraig: a steelworks and strip-mill for the sort of steel the new Scottish motor industry required. Always an uncertain prospect (its ore supplies had to be trans-shipped first at Glasgow, later at Hunterston on the Clyde) Ravenscraig was forced into total eclipse with that industry's closure in the 1980s. In 1992 it was shut down by privatized British Steel and in 1996 only a hole in the ground remained. The future for its better-doing inhabitants was one of commuting—the railway to Glasgow had been electrified since 1960—and for the others, survival in some of the most 'excluded' housing schemes in Britain. Would a 'new Ravenscraig'—shops, sports complexes, science park—announced in 2001, revitalize the district, or suck out of it such vitality as remained?

Scots industrialists tried to diversify into consumer goods—the nation's notorious sweet tooth was further rotted by such delights as mass-produced biscuits, sweets, and fizzy drinks like 'Irn Bru'; but it was a struggle to get Motherwell a factory making electric fires. In 1934 the National Government created a Scottish Regional Commissioner, dealing with Fife, Ayrshire, and Lanarkshire (outside Glasgow) who tried various job-creation ploys, and eventually ended up by pioneering, jointly with the Scottish Office, economic planning. But the real regenerator was Adolf Hitler, in power in January 1933, and the collapse of the Disarmament Conference at Geneva. The government ploughed funds into four new battleships, two aircraft carriers, cruisers, destroyers, and submarines, with much of the work going to the Clyde. A huge air armament programme—under the direction of William Weir—brought Rolls Royce to Glasgow's new Hillington industrial estate, building the aero-engines for Spitfires and Hurricanes. Hills sprouted the twin timber towers of Robert Watson-Watt's radar beacons, which would launch the fighters at oncoming bombers. After the *Queen Mary* took the Blue Riband in 1936,

John Brown's laid down the *Queen Elizabeth*, patently a troopship as much as a liner.

In 1939 new government offices, St Andrews House (a tour de force by Tommy Tait, modernist creator of the Empire Exhibition, replacing a hideous scheme for a London-designed slab) opened on a ledge of the Calton Hill. This was an Elliot coup, perhaps his greatest. Scotland was now physically governed from Edinburgh, not from Whitehall. How important this was would shortly be seen.

A NEW SCOTLAND

Many of Patrick Geddes's schemes perished in the First World War. His 'Cities' exhibition was sunk by the German cruiser *Emden* en route to India; his visionary scheme for an Arab–Jewish University of Jerusalem, though backed by Weizmann, went down to sectarianism. But his vision of a 'Scottish Renaissance' got real, in the politicized Scots revivalism headed by the poet and critic Christopher Grieve 'Hugh MacDiarmid' in the 1920s. The paradox was that the work of this energetic cultural stage manager was known to only a tiny percentage of Scots: the 'nationalist writer' label was more likely to be pinned on successful London performers such as Compton Mackenzie or Eric Linklater. Even MacDiarmid's friend Lewis Grassic Gibbon, whose *Scots Quair* (1932–4) was the movement's equivalent of the *Waverley Novels*, shared little of the former's nationalism. But the *Quair* was—compellingly—written in the vernacular, emphasizing the most significant difference from the 1890s: the revival of the Scots tongue, pushed out of the mainstream since the Union of the Crowns in 1603. To this was added politics, with the creation of the National Party of Scotland in 1928. The party took over three decades to establish itself, but a 'Condition of Scotland Question' became fundamental. In some ways this repeated Carlyle's concerns, but focused on the depression; behind rather feverish parallels made between Scotland and the Irish Free State was the need for institutions which could discuss the country's future and cope with a distorted economy and ill-housed society.

Intellectually the Renaissance was archaic. Its ambitions were democratic, internationalist, scientific, and socialist, but at a time when

19. *Alexander Moffatt,* Poets' Pub. *Of the poets of the 'literary renaissance' shown here, in the 1960s, 'Hugh MacDiarmid' and 'Robert Garioch' wrote in the Doric, Norman MacCaig in an elegant metaphysical English, and Iain Crichton Smith in both English and Gaelic. Sorley MacLean was the greatest Gaelic poet since the eighteenth century.*

urbanization and mass culture—housing, industrial change, cinema, and radio—was determining a new politics, it was actually less urban than Hume, Smith, Ferguson, and the literati had been; its ambitions utopian and remote from modern Scotland. The 'Kirriemuir career'—after J. M. Barrie—of success in Scottish small towns, and then emigration, rather than city life, seemed typical: to Neil Gunn or Edwin Muir the city meant the 'fall'. MacDiarmid wanted to recapture Gaelic Scotland as 'scientific': to return to a minutely observed, unromanticized nature derived from the praise-poetry of the bards. Grassic Gibbon took his Mearns folk into urban Scotland, but they took to it about as much as they took to clothes. The contradictions and frustrations were such that exile seemed almost the only outcome: to Fitzrovia or Fleet Street or Canada.

CORSTORPHINE

One of the few hundred passengers a year who took to the air in Captain Gandar-Dower's Avro Ansons or De Havilland Rapides from Turnhouse aerodrome would spot, 5 kilometres out from Edinburgh on the Glasgow road, the ex-village of Corstorphine. There, one of Scotland's finest late-medieval parish churches was no longer alone with its cottages. Since the railway had come in 1902—eleven minutes from Waverley—it had grown up as a middle-class suburb, served by electric tram from 1923 (Edinburgh trams had been cable-hauled until then). In 1900 Edinburgh Zoo was designed by Patrick Geddes and built on Corstorphine Hill. To the east, across the golf links and allotments, loomed the middle-class temples of Murrayfield rugby stadium and indoor curling rink.

In the inter-war years Corstorphine resembled London's 'Metroland', with suburbanites working in Edinburgh's banks, lawyers' chambers, department stores—Jenners, Binns, Patrick Thomsons—and government offices. The houses which invaded the grounds of demolished villas and former farms, however, were bungalows rather than semis. The Scots bungalow—3 bed., 2 recep.—was brick-built and harled, set in a garden, with the spaciousness and all-on-one-floor convenience of the flat its owners had previously tenanted. Within it were a new generation of household goods—electric cookers, irons, kettles and fires, early fridges, hoovers, and washing machines, a few of which were made in Scotland. Shops were dominated by chain stores such as Coopers, Edinburgh and Dumfriesshire Dairies, and St Cuthbert's Co-op and the inevitable bank branches. Primary schools and churches followed, and garages to serve the growing car population: assembly-line Fords, Austins, Standards, as the grand Scots names of Argyll and Arroll-Johnston had gone in the 1920s.

Youngsters had to take the tram into town and to the Plaza or Palais to dance, or to the football at Tynecastle (Hearts) and Easter Road (Hibs). A talkie cinema started in 1931, and a big art-deco roadhouse, the Maybury, rose where after 1937 the No. 26 tram stopped and the 'Boulevard' began—the three-lane A8 to Glasgow, modernized in 1930–3. South-east, at nearby Saughton, Corporation buses ran to a new industrial estate and one of Edinburgh's first council-housing schemes: solid stone-built terraces for *'labour aristocrats' such as council workmen, printers, and foremen. Life was quiet, save for the occasional plane heading to or from Turnhouse and— until the 1980s (!)—the clip-clop of the Co-op's milk floats. Just the sort of place from which 'girls, little girls' in their gym-slips and blazers, would go by cycle and tram to fee-paying secondary schools (Edinburgh had a dozen, and they weren't expensive) where the likes of Jean Brodie—of the first post-suffrage generation—presided over 'la crème de la crème'.*

Did the Renaissance matter to ordinary Scots? They might read Link-later, Mackenzie, and A. J. Cronin, or read about them in Beaverbrook's *Scottish Daily Express.* They were glad enough to have a job—more of them now in the service industries, in chain stores or garages, restaurants or cinemas—and a house with a bathroom. They were living longer (a boy born in 1870 could expect to live to 41, his grandson, born in 1950, to 64)

20. *A big Gorbals family snapped by Oscar Marzaroli in the 1960s. Notice how big sister is bossing the wee yins. Tragically both Marzaroli and the painter Joan Eardley, who captured these survival artists, died young.*

because the childhood killer diseases were now being eliminated, and a rudimentary health service of district nurses and 'panel patients' who got free treatment was being created. They were better taught in more modern schools: the Scots spent 40 per cent more on education than the UK, and had 50 per cent more at secondary schools. Teachers might squirm as record levels of cinema-going and enthusiasm for 'the dancing' were added to football, but their pupils were also climbing and walking, swimming in new public baths, going to cafés instead of having to choose between church and pub (the latter was hard-hit by severe new licensing laws), and having a more relaxed private life.

The Scots doctor Marie Stopes had started the sexual revolution with her *Married Love* in 1918.* Naomi Mitchison and Rebecca West politicized it and carried it south, and writers and campaigners such as Catherine Carswell, Marion MacNeill, Wendy Wood, Agnes Mure MacKenzie, and Helen Cruikshank countered the macho tendencies of the national movement. The middle classes encountered Freud and Jung (Scotland had a high count of psychoanalytic pioneers: A. J. Brock, Maurice Nicoll, Ronald Fairbairn, Jock Sutherland, R. D. Laing) as well as D. H. Lawrence, Hugh MacDiarmid, and the young W. H. Auden, in the teacher-journalist-artist sort of bohemia—dirndls and corduroys, studio flats and beards—so deftly captured by Muriel Spark in *The Prime of Miss Jean Brodie* (1955).

WAR AND WELFARE

Nationalism was muted in Scots politics in the 1930s, not least because of its unfortunate European connotations. The fact that Scottish nationalism was left-wing and democratic didn't protect it from being identified by its enemies with authoritarian regimes like those in Italy after 1922, Germany after 1933, and Spain after the Civil War of 1936–9. To a writer sympathetic to the Renaissance like Edwin Muir, the priority was the struggle against fascism, and many young Scots went as volunteers to Spain to fight and die in the bid to stop Franco. Fascism had some noisy adherents—Captain

* With the same *praefervidium ingenium Scotorum* as James Mill writing six volumes on India without ever going there, Dr Stopes wrote this paean to sexuality while still a virgin.

Maule Ramsay, MP, Professors Charles Sarolea and A. P. Laurie; more discreet was the support given by important sections of Scottish businessmen and aristocrats to it, through participation in chemical and cotton cartels which were active in Germany and Italy. Rudolf Hess's flight to try to make contact with the duke of Hamilton in May 1941 wasn't utterly quixotic.

'No more war' sentiment peaked in the mid-1930s. The Peace Pledge Union's Canon Dick Sheppard was elected Rector of Glasgow University in 1936, although much of the city's returning prosperity was based on arms orders. Guilty relief greeted Chamberlain's Munich Agreement in 1938, followed by acceptance of inevitable hostilities. After 3 September 1939, involvement in war would penetrate Scots society for nearly two decades, intensifying as the USA and Russia entered the conflict in 1941. The country's vital strategic position, commanding both the shortest transatlantic route and the gate to the northern seas made Prestwick the world's busiest airport, with bomber after bomber arriving from the USA, and in the western sea lochs the convoys were assembled which would fight their way through hellish conditions to Archangel or Murmansk. The war of 1939–45 was a complex, intellectually demanding one which exploited a well-educated society in nuclear research, code-cracking, and black propaganda at Bletchley Park, involvement with partisans, along with a sideways glance at neutral Ireland, and a memory of the betrayal of 'reconstruction' after 1918. Many of a trained generation would die in Libya, before Monte Cassino, in Malaya and Burma, over Berlin, or off Murmansk, though it took years for the scale of this loss to be realized.

Churchill supplanted Chamberlain in May 1940. In February 1941 he produced, at last, the political correlate of the Scottish Renaissance. Faced with the prospect of the same industrial trouble that had plagued the Clydeside Munitions area in 1915–16, he put in a poacher-turned-gamekeeper: Tom Johnston, former editor of *Forward*, critical nationalist, and a socialist who understood how bureaucracies worked. Johnston argued for, and got, a 'Council of State on Post-War Problems' (a meeting of all the ex-Scottish Secretaries) to discuss and settle consensually on policy. 'Post-war' was interpreted flexibly: the country got its fair share of munitions works, an early version of the National Health Service hospitals forecast by the Beveridge Report of 1942, and in 1943 a commitment to build hydro-electric plants all over the Highlands. Johnston would, if frustrated, mutter ominously about 'a Sinn Fein movement coming up' and (for a small and fissile party) the SNP did rather well, winning Motherwell in the war's closing months. At a time when Scotland's MPs and press were overwhelmingly Tory, Johnston had pulled off a remarkable coup. Henceforth Scottish politics would (after a wobble in 1950–9) shift to the left, with small 'n' nationalism waiting attentively in the wings.

Johnston's successors, Joe Westwood and Arthur Woodburn, were timid, and Labour's Scottishness went into abeyance as its majority soared in July 1945. Though post-war culture had its moments—the founding of the Edinburgh Festival in 1947, with Tyrone Guthrie and Robert Kemp's enthralling revival in 1948, after nearly four centuries, of Sir David Lindsay's *The Three Estates*—in comparison with the 1930s the scene was dull. There was a brief flourishing of Scots-interest films, including Sandy Mackendrick's sharp satires *Whisky Galore* and *The Maggie*, but the BBC under Melville Dinwiddie—Reith's inhibitions without Reith's genius—squashed originality for a generation, and until 1955 Tory editors dominated the press. In education the 'Kirriemuir career' functioned—kicking its products unerringly south. Alasdair Gray, whose career started in this decade, may have got it right in *1982 Janine* (1984) when he represented Scotland by a product of the 1950s, Jock MacLeish, a precariously reformed alcoholic, bent double with a burden of frustrated world-changing ideas. One route out was simply that: 282,000 emigrated in the period 1951–61.

The unity created by war and Attlee's socialist reconstruction lasted until the late 1950s, reinforced by the nationalization of transport, power and steel, welfare reform, and in 1948 the creation of the National Health Service. All but 5 per cent of the Scots electors voted Labour or Conservative; the latter even got a narrow majority of seats and votes in 1955. The Liberals under the Orkney MP Jo Grimond gradually revived; they favoured home rule in principle, but represented areas such as the Northern Isles or the Borders, which were mortally suspicious of it. The SNP didn't sustain its 1945 success and remained a tiny grouping with only a few local authority seats.

This conservative and intimidating landscape was conveyed by novels like J. D. Scott's *The End of an Old Song* (1955), in which a lad o' pairts burns down the family castle and with it (he hopes) the spirit of Scotland past, or the paralysed militarism of James Kennaway's *Tunes of Glory* (1962). Returning from a trip to Italy was, for the young Iain Crichton Smith,

> Like leaving a warm flat
> For a lonely castle,
> Hissing with ghosts.

But this may have been because people were 'going private', after a couple of decades of compulsion (national service lasted from 1939 to 1961), austerity, and often danger; trying to get on with their own lives: a job, a house with 'all mod. cons. and gdn.', a decent education for the kids, somewhere warm for the holidays. Some people reached this modest utopia sooner than others.

NEW TOWN

Bill Forsyth's film Gregory's Girl *(1980) has our teenage hero come out of his parents' new house in Cumbernauld and pick his way carefully through a garden and pedestrian walkway crawling with babies. This highlighted one aspect of the places where 200,000 Scots lived by 1980: a lot of people grew up there at the same time. The new town principle wasn't new, it had eighteenth-century precedents, but the scale of development was.*

After the Second World War, the Labour government embarked— Britain-wide—on a programme of new town building. This was modelled on projects like Letchworth (1903) and Welwyn Garden City (1920), where (of all places!) Lewis Grassic Gibbon wrote his Scots Quair *in 1932–4. The 1940s new towns were aimed at decanting workers from the cities, allowing better housing to 'trickle down' to slum dwellers, and to house labour near new coalfields. Labour's first two new towns were East Kilbride (1947) and Glenrothes (1948). East Kilbride drew in many electric and consumer goods factories, around the state-owned National Engineering Laboratory. Only 11 kilometres south of Glasgow and intended for former tenement dwellers, its houses were on the whole terrace-style and low-density, but transport was still based on buses (at this time there was only one car per ten Scots). The same pattern applied to Glenrothes, but its development was almost ended*

21. *Cumbernauld from the air, late 1960s. The new towns were a success and even now can charm, with their parks, footpath networks, and sculptures. But they were designed for buses not cars, and neither the quality of Scottish housing, nor its affordability, has improved since.*

when the new Rothes colliery was killed by a series of geological faults. By the time of Cumbernauld (1955) with its futuristic town centre on stilts, attention had switched to providing for 100 per cent car ownership, but segregating people and cars; this principle also extended to Livingston (1962) and Irvine (1969). A further project at Tweedbank near Galashiels was never more than a village (the absence of the Borders railway, 1969–2015, didn't help). Yet they proved, with their low-density housing, parkland, and walkways, pleasant places to grow up in: without the technical and social disasters which befell the high-rise blocks of the inner cities. They would, in the 1970s and 1980s, provide land and labour for Silicon Glen.

Churchill returned to office in 1951 and trundled along in low gear until 1955. His wife Clemmie was Scots, he sat for Dundee, 1906–22, and he used to drop the hard stuff once a year for a tea party with Maxton & Co. He could make devolutionary sounds convincing enough to encourage, or at least baffle, bodies like John MacCormick's Scottish Covenant Movement in the late 1940s, but went no further than administrative decentralization of a consensual welfare state that was really the only major change from his first days as an MP. The Wheatley act gradually improved housing, though half of Scots households in 1951 still occupied two rooms or less, heated by coal brought, like most long distance freight, by steam train.

Churchill was loyally regretted, not least by his old trusty James Stuart, Secretary of State. At the 1955 election the success of Sir Anthony Eden was down to an enduring Protestant unionism and Liberal weakness and division; but the Union proved dependent on Britain's imperial pretensions and the institutions they had upheld. The first shock came in 1956 with the abortive Suez invasion. This had a threefold impact: provoking a lasting slump—particularly severe in Scotland, accelerating the 'scramble from Africa', and creating a demand for giant tankers which the Clyde couldn't build. In the 1959 election the Tories started to lose in Scotland; although they were led 1957–63 by the great-grandson of an Arran crofter, Harold Macmillan, and decolonization was carried through by another Gael, the colonial secretary Iain MacLeod. In the popular fiction of the time, the guardian of empire moved from the decencies of Buchan to the sex-sadism-and-snobbery of Ian Fleming's James Bond. In print this had an elegaic quality; on screen Sean Connery made Bond sharper and ironic. Connery *was* patriotic: but for Scotland, not for Britain.

WHITE HEAT, DULL GLOW, BLACK, BLACK OIL

Macmillan was progressive and Keynesian—he published him, after all—and his economic adviser was a Keynesian lad o' pairts, Sir Alec Cairncross. The Scottish Office didn't exactly glitter under his Secretaries of State, John Maclay and Michael Noble, but Downing Street and some unusual allies—notably Lord Polwarth of the Scottish Council: Development and Industry and George Middleton, boss of the STUC—got the idea of planning up and running. The Conservatives commissioned the semi-official Toothill Report into 'Scotland's Industrial Future' in 1961. But the voters were mutinous, and didn't get any less so when in 1963 Sir Alec Douglas-Home was 'evolved' into the premiership: a lurch back to 'grouse moor' politics. Labour didn't have it on a plate. The Liberals were doing well in the Highlands and Borders, partly out of protest against the railway closures demanded by the Beeching Plan, and in 1962 William Wolfe, a West Lothian manufacturer (and part-time poet, mystic, and pacifist) began an SNP revival. This emerged as a fitful challenger to the Labour Party of Harold Wilson, its dogma of centralized planning given a 'white heat of technology' sheen, and represented in Scotland, after Wilson's October 1964 victory, by the fiercely unionist Secretary of State Willie Ross, whose dominie (school masterish) style was summed up in an oft-deployed phrase 'Ye'll dae whit ye're telt!'

The 1960s, however, passed beyond conventional control. An apparently benign science wasn't just churning out inventions—transistors, artificial fibres and plastics, pharmaceuticals—but coupling these with social change to give revolutionary outcomes: in entertainment, transport, sexuality. BBC TV started only in 1952, Scottish Television, regarded by its boss, the Canadian Roy Thompson, as 'a licence to print money' in 1955: hardly a house lacked the box by 1960. One car per seven Scots in 1960 became one per five in 1978 (and one per two in 1996) and the folk who could afford a car could usually afford a summer charter flight to the sun. Had Chris Guthrie—'Chris Caledonia' of *A Scots Quair*—been born in 1950, and had Grassic Gibbon been around to record her, she would have passed from Edwardian chastity via sexual liberation to socialist feminism by 1975: a steep learning-curve for a 'new woman'.

Scotland's catching-up process, which had continuity between Macmillan and Wilson, concentrated on shifting the economy from capital goods to consumer goods, providing new housing, new roads, and new town centres crammed with fridges, washing machines, and TVs, which people hoped would be manufactured in Scotland. The old industries didn't need much prompting to disappear: they had been living on borrowed time since the later 1940s, while Germany and Japan re-equipped their shipyards and engineering works. By the early 1960s locomotives had almost gone and shipbuilding was fading fast. Ravenscraig steelworks was supposed to feed strip steel to the Rootes assembly line at Linwood, Paisley, and a British Motor Corporation works at Bathgate, though the economics of both were doubtful.

Labour's strategy was ambitious, beginning with its Highlands and Islands Development Board and National Plan of 1965, along with a major inquiry into local government under Lord Wheatley, and the comprehensivization of nearly all of state secondary education, but few of the new industrial developments ever ran at full capacity. Mine closures continued, as electric generation (1,900 megawatts in 1939, 10,400 in 1978) saw coal giving way to oil and increasingly to nuclear energy, and regional policy was used to set up more manufacturing industry to use the power: a pulp mill at Corpach, and an aluminium smelter at Invergordon. An experimental reactor at Chapelcross (1955) was followed by another at Dounreay, a Magnox plant at Hunterston, and then two Advanced Gas-Cooled reactors at Hunterston B (1976) and Torness (1988). Nuclear power, providing 60 per cent in 2002, was under 40 per cent in 2012, while renewables—hydro and wind—reached 35 per cent. New semi-skilled jobs replaced most of those lost; supermarkets, light engineering, and tourism gave good openings for women. But the shrinking of the skilled trades— whether of shipwright, miner, ploughman or engineer—would have profound social implications.

In 1970 Edward Heath and the Tories unexpectedly won the election on a platform of industrial rationalization: a government memorandum menaced the future of shipbuilding on Clydeside. The Upper Clyde 'work-in' led by the glamorous and eloquent Communists Jimmie Reid and Jimmie Airlie gained world publicity and prefaced a radical decade in which Alasdair Gray's 'Scottish Cooperative Wholesale Republic' seemed a possibility. But the real area of job growth was in the service industries, of which the most spectacular element was tourism.

22. *Alasdair Gray, Central Scotland, from* Lanark, 1982. *Gray wasn't just the remarkable creator of* Lanark *but a gifted and witty black-and-white artist. His image of central Scotland not only shows its headlong modernization in the 1960s, but the politics behind this, in the conning towers of nuclear submarines and the massive power-wielding figure of Thomas Hobbes's Leviathan in the background.*

AVIEMORE: www.visitscotland.com

In the heart of the Grampians, Aviemore straggled along the banks of the River Spey on the A9 from Perth to Inverness. In the 1870s it became an important junction on the Highland Railway, the route south for whisky coming by rail from the Spey valley, but with the Beeching Report of 1961 this role was threatened. That year, however, the Conservatives were persuaded by a senior Scottish civil servant, George Pottinger, and the department store 'takeover king', Sir Hugh Fraser, to build an ambitious tourist centre there. This was intended to cater both for summer tourists and—something quite new—winter skiers. It was controversial from the first: its sawn-off skyscrapers were unloved, and their architect, the Yorkshireman John Poulson was, with Pottinger, jailed for corruption in 1974.

Aviemore responded to a real problem. In the 1950s and 1960s Scots traditional resorts were declining so rapidly that people wondered why Ayr or Troon, Leven or Prestonpans had ever attracted anyone. Numbers of boarding-houses slumped, along with what remained of tourist facilities, like the Clyde excursion steamers, which were replaced by prosaic car ferries and scrapped. But journeys into the Highlands increased, aided by subsidies from the new Highland and Islands Development Board (1965) and the building of double-track roads, along with the electricity of the Hydro Board.

Was tourism the big earner? Americans, the bulk of foreign tourists, were often attracted to a fantastic Brigadoon (Vincente Minnelli thought about shooting on location, decided that Scotland didn't look Scottish enough, and stayed in Hollywood). Later, increasing numbers of European tourists and Inter-railers came; some fell for the country and stayed. This owed much to higher education, summer schools, and above all the Edinburgh Festival, long regarded as an alien transplant but by the 1970s seen as a major earner. Income from tourism was about £2.5 billion in 2000 but barely matched what Scots spent abroad, particularly in Spain and the United States. Aviemore came to stand for mediocre international facilities, and whisky, bagpipes, kilts, and the Loch Ness Monster. Glasgow in 1990 determined to restyle itself as 'European City of Culture' responding to a European Union initiative launched by the Greek actress and socialist Commissioner Melina Mercouri. With three world-class museums, it succeeded—for a time. But when this became a strategy pursued Europe-wide by failing industrial areas—the Basque Country or the Saarland—it had diminishing returns. Glasgow's Merchant City, or Culture City, extended only to where real hopelessness started on decayed, drug-ridden housing schemes.

Scotland's tourism was under 10 per cent of the business attracted by London and the south-east. Why? The answer seemed to lie in the quality of communications and in hotel investment. London and Scottish airports' passenger movements went up by roughly a third between 2002–12 to 133 and 20 millions respectively, but could Scotland get close to her population entitlement, let alone exceed it? Or did the answer lie at sea? By 1999 both the Forth and Clyde ports were again catering for passengers from cruise liners, but a passenger/freight ro-ro service to Zeebrugge only lasted from 2002–10, and the outlook for freight wasn't bright. The Forth and Clyde Canal, ineptly abandoned in 1962 just as inland cruising was beginning to boom, was being revived as a Millennium project funded by the National Lottery, but was it part of a tourist strategy? Near Aviemore £9 million had been spent on a Swiss-built funicular up the Cairngorms—a matter of endless controversy—yet the future of the highland rail system remained problematic.

The reputation of Scotland was mixed, from stunning scenery and outstanding cooking in small country hotels to unpredictable, often terrible weather, little for bored kids to do during it, dangerous fried food and glum towns, gutted by shopping malls. Could this combat remoteness and—alas—the Scots' worsening command of foreign languages? The first coalition (1999–2003) had to cope with a soaring pound and falling visitor numbers. Salmond wanted a 50% increase 2007–15, but growth was near imperceptible. He captured the 2014 Commonwealth Games but was trumped by the 2012 London Olympics.

Between 1964 and 1970 Labour promised much and didn't deliver. The *Plan for Scotland* (1966) was terminated by the economic crisis of 1967. The Cullingworth inquiry showed the appalling state of Scottish housing, but plans for reform were either pigeon-holed, or (in the case of councillors' infatuation with 'high-rise' buildings) run away with. The voters, their expectations aroused and then frustrated, took revenge at by-elections and local elections. Tories and Liberals initially profited, but then the highly professional organization of the SNP started to count. Following Plaid Cymru's 1966 success at Carmarthen, Winifred Ewing in November 1967 won a by-election at Hamilton, and the nationalist challenge became such that Edward Heath sold his party a mild scheme of devolution, and Wilson (hoping to kick the whole thing into the long grass) announced the Crowther (later Kilbrandon) Commission on the Constitution.

'Events, dear boy, events' disrupted things, not least the Tory victory and Heath's entry into the European Economic Community, accomplished in 1973 and confirmed by referendum in 1975. The Scots were less enthusiastic than the English south-east. When, after a leisurely process, Lord Kilbrandon reported in November 1973, the discovery of North Sea oil and its coincidence with a tenfold increase in oil prices reanimated the SNP. Willie Ross clumsily denounced the Kilbrandon Report as the 'Kill-devolution Report', only to see one of Labour's safest seats, Glasgow Govan, fall within days to a formidable 'new woman', Margo MacDonald of the SNP. But the main challenge to the two 'English' parties, as the General Elections of February and October 1974 showed, would come from the other end of Scotland, the north-east.

ABERDEEN AND BUCHAN

American oil men who in the 1970s encountered Maitland Mackie, County Convener of Aberdeenshire, expected some couthy backwoodsman. Instead, they found a shrewd international wheeler-dealer with a leading Labour and a leading Liberal for brothers and a Texan wife. In that decade the north-east wasn't in any sense remote, but the centre of Scotland's economic life, to which it had always contributed disproportionately, though often in surprising ways: strange to think of Aberdeen as a centre of the Renaissance, the Enlightenment, and the socialist movement, all of which it had been. From Dundee to Aberdeen is a long stretch of bleak country, not at first glance looking all that different from what Agricola's legionaries must have seen as they marched towards Mons Graupius. And at the end of the run was the broad Dee, 213,000 people, and a glittering-granite, boat-, gull-, and fish-packed city.

Aberdeen was remote, which was why its development had been at once local and European. Its fish merchants supplied the Baltic ports with salted herring, and the Scottish market with haddock and cod; its farmers the lean Aberdeen Angus beef, bulls of fabulous price and potency, and much of the barley for the distilleries of Speyside and the islands. This wasn't, however, traditional: Buchan pioneered both agri-capitalism in its 'muckle ferms' and in the partnerships which from the 1870s ran steam drifters and steam trawlers from great harbours such as Fraserburgh and Peterhead. Aberdeen had two universities—Bishop Elphinstone's Kings College of 1494, next to St Machar's Cathedral (1357), and Marischal College (1593) in the town centre—when England had the same number. Even Fraserburgh had one, for a time. Strathmore and the Mearns to the south and Buchan to the north were famous for 'lads o' pairts', encouraged by local bursaries; they produced J. M. Barrie and A. S. Neill, and the novelists George MacDonald and Grassic Gibbon, and the fiddle-and-accordion bands to be found at every local dance. They also had a dialect as remote from English as Swabian is from German, and were the last great centre of the oral tradition of the Scottish ballad, codified in the 1850s by the Bostonian professor Francis Child, and spectacularly reborn in Hamish Henderson's recording of the tinker singer Jeannie Robertson in the 1940s.

The politics of the region were radical, in the old-fashioned Liberal sense, though there were pockets of Labour activists strung out along the fishing towns and the communities served or created by the Great North of Scotland Railway: paradoxically, this helped the Tories as it divided the leftish vote. As the working class declined with rail and factory closures in the 1960s, the region's rural politics changed to Liberal and SNP. Because of its nearness to the oilfields, much of the oil and gas was piped ashore at Cruden Bay and St Fergus, and Aberdeen became the major junction and business centre of the enterprise, from where the rigs and production platforms, or the more remote outposts of the Shetlands, were supplied. Did this benefit local industry? Yes: but it stopped being local. The high wages offered offshore destroyed many north-east businesses, and the fluctuations in the oil price (in 1983 it was almost $40 a barrel, in 1986 $10; in mid-1999

*$10, by late 2013 $110) meant that Scots-owned start-ups supplying rigs,
warehousing, and divers nearly all had to merge with multinational
concerns.*

Oil looked marginal in 1970. Deep-sea drilling, remoteness, and awful
weather made for frontier conditions, only overcome by new technology,
chiefly computers and satellites. But the Arab annexation of the black stuff
after the Yom Kippur War in the autumn of 1973 made it viable. The Seven
Sisters—the great oil multinationals—steamed into most east-coast ports,
reversing the post-Union pattern of Atlantic-led growth, and reversing, too,
the old imperial paradigm: instead of Scots as exploiters, they were now the
exploited, forced to submit to huge economic changes, while denied any say
in them. The shrewd manipulation of the oil issue by the SNP under Wolfe
and Gordon Wilson MP, arguing along these lines and with the positive
example of Norway and its fine-tuned social-democratic policies of ownership and control in mind, had dramatic electoral effects in the two elections
of 1974. Seven SNP MPs were elected in February, eleven in October, and
with the party biting at Labour's heels in a further thirty-six seats, Harold
Wilson was glad he had forced Labour into support for devolution in the
summer. A White Paper outlined a limited Scots Assembly, denounced not
only by the Nationalists, but by a Labour rebel group under the effervescent
Jim Sillars, and an articulate far left whose great artistic achievement were
John McGrath's ceilidh-cum-morality *The Cheviot, the Stag and the Black,
Black Oil* (1973), and Gordon Brown's *The Red Paper on Scotland* (1975).
Could devolution be made to stick—particularly once the SNP menace
declined, which it did after 1977?

The politics of the 1970s resembled the children's game of musical
chairs; whoever was sitting on the right chair would inherit the bounty of
the oil. In 1978 James Callaghan's Labour lost its nerve and suffered for
it. Labour's left resented the way the IMF had dictated policy to Callaghan
in 1976; it also had a major success in Tony Benn's management of the oil
business. But it could not keep its own supporters or lower-paid trade
unionists under discipline, and it stumbled over the protracted and unpopular cause of devolution. The Scotland and Wales Bill—for assemblies

23. *Margaret Thatcher visits an oil platform, early 1980s. Without the riches of the North Sea she would have been bankrupt very soon; Thatcher (married to oilman Dennis) never let on about it. But Britain's apparent free-market success in the 1980s would be influential on 'liberated' east Europe.*

with strictly limited powers, with two members per Westminster seat, elected on the traditional first-past-the-post system—was defeated in 1977 because of common action between Conservatives and Labour's articulate unionists. Reintroduced in 1978, it passed, but on condition of a referendum which showed over 40 per cent of the entire electorate voting 'Yes'. In constitutional practice this could only be advisory. Such was the weakness of Callaghan's government that it became critical.

UNDER THE HANDBAG, 1979–1990

Westminster won this round. The Referendum of 1 March 1979 showed only a bare majority of 32 per cent to 31 per cent of Scots backing devolution, and failed to meet parliament's conditions. The Welsh outcome was a total disaster. But the once rock-like certainties of British government were crumbling. The response—Mrs Margaret Thatcher—was centralized and disastrous. A shift to monetarist economics captivated her Conservative government, which was centre-right rather than extremist; its outcome was a collapse in production as high interest rates and oil at $40 a barrel (on account of the Gulf crisis) drove the pound through the ceiling and destroyed about 20 per cent of manufacturing industry.

ORKNEY AND SHETLAND

The North Sea discoveries concentrated the Scots' attention on the Northern Isles, and their semi-detached relationship to the rest of the country. One of the oilfields, Piper, had a pipeline to the Orkney island of Flotta, while the great Brent Field was connected with Sullom Voe on Shetland, which would become after 1979 Britain's fourth port in terms of tonnage handled. The islanders looked enviously at their one-time rulers, the Norwegians, who became one of Europe's wealthiest nations on the basis of their oil wealth, and state intervention.

The treeless, whalebacked islands—a dispersed pattern in Orkney, a long winding land mass in Shetland—were remote from the Scottish mainland, involving an expensive flight from Inverness or Aberdeen, or a ferry trip overnight to Shetland. But they had been Norwegian until 1469, and stood on a major trading route. In Kirkwall the handsome 'Early English' cathedral was built after 1137 by the same masons who built Trondheim in Norway and Durham in northern England. Midsummer in the early eighteenth century would see 2,000 Dutch herring 'busses' off Lerwick. Land tenure in the islands, had once been based on Scandinavian 'Udal law', simpler and more democratic than on the mainland, enabling tenants to pass on their holdings, and Orkney farms were larger and more fertile than highland crofts.

Still, the decline of the Hanse trade and the Reformation, coupled with the dominance of the seventeenth-century Stewart earls, (descended from King James V, and bastards in every sense of the word) meant two centuries of relative isolation. Both archipelagos recovered through trade, fishing, and crofting. Shetlanders smuggled, and Orkney supplied trappers and fur traders to the Hudson Bay Company. Victorian Shetlanders were organized by their dynamic local MP, Alexander Anderson, as the seamen of the Peninsular and Oriental Steam Navigation Company and even on one occasion of the Brazilian navy. Strategic use of the islands also increased in the First World War, when Orkney's nearly enclosed Scapa Flow became a major British naval base. In 1918–19 it was the scene of the internment of the German High Seas fleet, and its self-destruction; in 1939 a solitary U-boat penetrated its defences to sink the elderly battleship Royal Oak, with huge loss of life. Scalloway in Shetland became a major centre of the Norwegian resistance.

Though remote, the islands always echoed Scotland's cultural ambitions. In the 1930s Hugh MacDiarmid exiled himself to Whalsay in Shetland; his contemporary Edwin Muir's deeply negative critique of industrial Scotland was based on his 'fall' from the edenic Orkney island of Wyre on which he was brought up. Orkney's first successful modern writer, Eric Linklater, imitated Byron and travelled widely, while George Mackay Brown scarcely left the islands at all. Only travelling to Lothian to go to Newbattle Abbey college to study under Muir, and then to Edinburgh University, he spent the rest of his life in Stromness, becoming—after the launch of the Orkney Festival in 1976, with the composer Peter Maxwell Davies—the 'geist' of the islands.

Before Sullom Voe was commissioned, Zetland County Council under an inspired Chief Executive, Ian Clark, promoted their own act which enabled them to take a substantial slice of the oil income. In the devolution controversy of the late 1970s this even brought their relationship to the rest of Scotland into question. Under Holyrood (in which their LibDem MSP Jim Wallace was Deputy First Minister, 1999–2007) their future could be uncertain, though they are well placed for marine renewables.

The paradox thereafter was that, as Thatcher returned to economic orthodoxy, her government got more and more right-wing. Trying to behave as if they were still living in the 1970s, the Scots' disaffection increased; regional and district councils attempted to run their own socialist republics, which the government stymied by rate-capping and withholding grants. Effective though this was, Thatcherism was viewed from outside, with a tendency to favour her opponents, whether Argentinians (Scots dissented strongly from the consensus which favoured the Falklands War) or miners, whose struggle in 1984–5 *against* their Scottish boss, Ian Macgregor, gained the same sort of support that the Clyde shipbuilders had enjoyed in 1971.

Thatcher projected purposive individualism. In reality she was pragmatic—and for many years very lucky. A cult of personality (was this the work of 'damned mischievous North Britons' such as the St Andrews economists and Rupert Murdoch?) transformed her into a prophet of global marketism, which she was not. Yet the shift in the British economy to high-value-added services both cushioned her negative impact where it mattered—in the English south-east—and projected her as 'radical'. In fact, much of this boom owed its existence to huge capital transfers from the Middle East, and their management or consumption in London. In Scotland she wrecked much of the 'Fordist' economy which had been expensively created or conserved in the 1960s—car-making, and much of the aluminium and shipbuilding industries closed down in the 'sado-monetarist' slump—but an individualist ethos didn't replace collectivism. She attracted inward investment by throwing subsidies at it, and her negative impact was qualified by the extent to which the Edinburgh area emulated the success of the English south-east, managing the savings of the minority who were doing well.

The long boom of 1983–8 was nurtured by North Sea oil, which reached its peak production, amounting to 5 per cent of UK GNP, in 1986. Some of the money went to enrich the middle class, who saw their favourite sport, speculating in housing, yield returns of over 300 per cent over the decade, or to expand the welfare budget, to prevent the disaffected from taking to the streets. Unemployment spending rose in real terms, with the ironic effect that public expenditure was the same after Thatcher in 1990 as it had been before her. What was being stripped away was the state's participation in generating wealth, something which, in the longer term, weakened the whole process of corporate economic management.

In Scotland this management was initially handled, quite expertly, by the Secretary of State, George Younger, a former brewer and one of the old governing elite. But Thatcher was upset by Younger's failure to win the 1983 election and municipal contests, and this feeling approached panic as the oil price collapsed after 1986. In Wales, after the 1979 debacle, the Tories' concession in 1981 of the S4C Welsh-language television channel boosted them in the 1983 election, and made Labour look fragile. Their Scottish colleagues had only the consolation that the SNP had fallen from eleven to two MPs, so the crisis of the 1970s didn't look as if it would repeat itself. Tories seemed reasonably secure in their rural and suburban seats, but greater reliance on local taxation hit their less wealthy supporters, and local elections results, if projected nationally, threatened a wipe-out. So in 1987 economic 'radicals' sold Thatcher a 'Poll Tax'—a flat-rate charge. This became a UK policy, and a fateful one for her.

What was happening to Scottish society? The year 1981 had been marked by violent confrontation in English cities—riots and house burnings—but Scotland remained quiet. The increase in unemployment was greeted not with resistance, save in the case of the miners, but with resignation. A process of divide and rule seemed to be effective; the numbers in poverty steeply increased, from 10 per cent to over 30 per cent, but many of the well-doing within the working class bought themselves out of 'servitude' to local authorities, the owner-occupied proportion of housing rising from a third to two-thirds, 1986–96. Thatcher was initially cool on council-house sales, but later claimed them as a personal initiative. She may have been right in the first place; they did her party no good. Scots still moved out in search of better jobs; the population gently declined during the 1980s, and when it rose in the early 1990s, this was due to immigration by retired people from the south. The folk were ageing and unhealthy; in fact, in terms of heart disease they reached east-European levels of morbidity. Mid-1990s Scots exercised little, smoked and drank too much, walked less and motored more than the English. An 'excluded' Scotland—perhaps 30 per cent—existed on neglected housing schemes, but poverty wasn't the full explanation: rather the substantial and growing class of 'insecure Scots', whose situation could be deduced from the economic landscape.

CHARLOTTE SQUARE AND SILICON GLEN

Few tourists ever spare more than a second glance at the pastel-coloured sheds that surround airports, unless they happen to be overnighting in one. Warehouses, factories, call-centres, universities: the sheds could be any of these. The retailing sheds—Toys 'R Us, IKEA, B&Q—are the more intrusive. Yet this was Scotland in the 1990s for most of its people. Silicon Glen stretched from Prestwick Airport, north of Ayr, to around Dundee: its sheds were producing many of Europe's desktop computers, mobile phones, and cash dispensers. Charlotte Square, Robert Adam's masterpiece of 1811 in central Edinburgh, once the centre of the finance sector, was in fact reverting to politics and gentility—the Scottish Executive met in Bute House. The name meant in reality more sheds: the headquarters buildings, in the west Edinburgh suburban sprawl, of the banks, insurance companies, and fund managers who handled some £250 billion of the world's wealth.

In 1918 the Marxist pedagogue John MacLean spoke of Scotland being 'in the rapids of revolution'; he may have been echoing Walter Scott in Waverley, but in the 1970s and 1980s the rapidity of the flow increased, and the Scots—in particular the Scots business class—lost the means of checking it. Only one major Scots oil-related firm, the Wood group of Aberdeen, survived the North Sea oil boom. Following on the closures of 1981–2, about two-thirds of Scottish manufacturing was sold south in 1985–6, a process which climaxed spectacularly in the Guinness takeover of Distillers in 1986, an episode so crooked that several of the Guinness elite were jailed. No less spectacular was the rise and fall of Robert Maxwell, publisher, helicopter operator, would-be politician, elective Scot, and fraud. These were only the tips of processes which left Scots small businessmen and white-collar employees increasingly uncertain about what their prospects were, or even who was employing them.

Over a century earlier, Scots manufacturers (notably those of Dundee) had invested abroad rather than in home industry, laying the foundations of international financial markets. Now this became part of a global pattern in which Scots trusts invested in America and the Far East on behalf of life insurance clients, while American and Far Eastern concerns increasingly (though selectively) invested in Scotland as an information-technology manufacturing centre. Scotland provided global finance both with its foot soldiers and a good part of its general staff, but without much in between. The growth both of Silicon Glen and Charlotte Square was spectacular, but narrowly based. Most Scottish hi-tech plants were 'screwdriver' concerns, importing all but 5 per cent of their material.

The high-value-added business of software or headquarters development didn't obey the rules of 'critical mass' and move in. It went to Ireland, the 'Celtic Tiger', instead. The Irish government, with a GDP 60 per cent that of Scotland in 1976 had coordinated its virtuoso handling of European Union grants with a strategic concentration on pharmaceuticals and software, and a favourable demographic structure: two-thirds of its population were under 30. By 2000 its output had drawn level.

Scotland's financial sector was also narrowly based, mainly on the Royal Bank (Britain's second largest by 2000), which only just escaped takeover in 1980, and the life assurance houses, which badly overreached themselves selling 'portable pensions' in the early 1990s. As devolution took effect in 1999, a further 'revolution' was under way, with the demutualization of big insurance houses and the merger of the Bank of Scotland with the Halifax, England's biggest building society, which had become a bank. Was there any longer a Scottish financial sector as such? Or did a less secure future lie in the mushrooming of call centres, from Wick to Greenock. This low-tech frontage of the communications revolution *increased its employees from 20,000 to nearly 45,000 in five years. But were these jobs tolerable, and how long would they last?*

Insecurity provided a diffused undercurrent in Scottish politics after 1986. Hardly any institutions showed the permanence and resilience which would have been visible in the 1950s and 1960s. The churches, Presbyterian and Catholic, were haemorrhaging members: a collective culture of hymns and psalms, consolation and solidarity, was being surrendered. Divorce proved the terminus of a third of marriages (and fewer couples were getting legally married anyway). Education had a good conceit of itself. Theoretically schools were almost 100 per cent comprehensive, but their standards varied from over 60 per cent of pupils getting university entrance in middle-class burghs to about 25 per cent of 'slum schools' where anyone doing highers was a rarity. Teachers had lost status since the 1960s, visible in their salaries, and in a drift away from the classroom into higher and further education, or into early retirement. Strongly unionized, they were fair game for right-wing commentators, but they had had a hard task holding out against a barrage of sport-sex-and-gambling from Scotland's tabloid mass media.

Much of this unsettlement showed up in the enigma of the *soi-disant* 'culture industries'. The Edinburgh Festival-and-Fringe was a huge money-spinner, but the collapse of institutionalized left-wing culture took with it much of a serious-minded, autodidact public in and around the trade unions and the Communist Party. 'Culture-as-industry' realized the capital which an earlier age had built up through collections, museums, galleries, and urban architecture, as with 'Glasgow: City of Culture' in 1990. But the strength of 'native' production in art and literature could easily give way to the new lingua franca of shopping and brand names.

It was, in part, the sense of an ill-divided world which prompted a remarkable shift in the arts during the 1980s. Scotland's painters and poets like W. G. Gillies, or Elizabeth Blackadder, Norman MacCaig or Sorley MacLean had remained, like the 'Renaissance Men' ruralist in their inspiration. But now the post-industrial urban predicament stimulated new voices and re-awoke older ones, more class-conscious and cosmopolitan in their outlook: expressionist-influenced painters like Ken Currie and Peter Howson, writers like Alasdair Gray and James Kelman, Liz Lochhead and William McIlvanney. Taboos about subject matter, scandalously broken by such as Alex Trocchi in the 1960s, no longer counted. A younger generation exploited these bridgeheads with—at least—acumen. The advances that Irvine Welsh got for 'books for people who don't read books'—the habitués of the burgeoning dance-and-drug culture of 1990s 'yoof'—probably totalled everything that every Scottish author had received in the twentieth century, but was he anything to do with literature? The English writer, Edinburgh-based J. K. Rowling, bundled together everything children had ever wanted to read about—school stories, fantasies, epics, monsters— made £37 million out of *Harry Potter*, and was talked about as the first billionaire author. The Scottish Arts Council baulked at paying £90,000 a year to keep the country's literary reviews alive.

At the turn of the millennium the traditional industries clung on to life with their fingernails. There was one locomotive works at Kilmarnock, and the last deep coal mine, at Longannet, closed in March 2002. Three shipyards (Yarrows, Ferguson, and Govan) were left on the Clyde; a single rolling mill at Motherwell was all that remained of steel. In 1999–2000 massive redundancies hit the Ardersier and Nigg oil platform yards, farming incomes plummeted by over 40 per cent in two years, imperilling family farms throughout the country, and fishing faced drastic quota cuts in order to save species like cod which had become endangered. More species of fish than salmon (which had gone from king of the river to broiler chicken status in a couple of decades) were farmed, in a £350 million industry, but problems of infestation and effluent grew acute, perhaps fatal.

The Executive in 2000 chopped a project for a Harris superquarry, which some claimed would bring jobs, and others environmental disaster. Environmental disaster did indeed bring jobs to remote Dounreay, where it would take thirty years and upwards of £2 billion to sort out the mess that Britain's stab at building a fast breeder reactor had left. Scottish Natural Heritage had high ambitions, and gained a creditable record in conserving the Highlands. Performance in areas like recycling household waste (under 10 per cent in 2002, and Europe's worst) rose to 40 per cent by 2010.

POLL TAX TO PARLIAMENT

The Poll Tax was where Thatcher's pragmatism and luck deserted her. She got keen on the idea because the urban poor wouldn't vote, and the ex-ratepayers would vote for her. But the sense that Scotland was being experimented on, plus the inequity of the Tax, led to defiance at all social levels and concerted tactical voting in the 1987 election. The Tory vote fell by only 4 per cent but the party lost over half of its MPs. From then on Scottish politics took on its own momentum, only occasionally understood in the south. The confrontation renewed Labour's commitment to devolution, and aligned it with the Campaign for a Scottish Assembly's programme of a Scottish Constitutional Convention. This was reinforced by a by-election in November 1988 which saw Jim Sillars, ex-Labour MP and one of the SNP's most charismatic publicists, beat Labour in Govan. Labour's Shadow Secretary of State, Donald Dewar, agreed to abide by the Convention's scheme, which centred on a 129-member Parliament of seventy-three constituencies (as for Westminster, plus Orkney) plus fifty-six members in eight regional lists, elected by proportional representation and with promises of female parity (women had hitherto done very badly in Scottish elections). This really implied a Labour–Liberal pact, as the SNP left the Convention early on. But by 1991, as the Conservatives plunged into a messy internal conflict, the momentum of Devolution seemed unstoppable.

Until, in the 1992 election, it stopped. Preaching the defence of the Union, John Major's Conservatives slightly increased their vote and even captured an extra seat. The anti-Tory vote was divided between Labour and a reviving SNP, under a sharp young leader, Alex Salmond, and suffered from poll-tax rebels falling off the register. This was a false reassurance for Major. By September, with Britain's ejection from the European Monetary System, it was downhill all the way. Labour, led by John Smith and then by his memory, won council by-election after by-election, often beating the Tories into fourth place. Substantial devolution demonstrations in Glasgow and Edinburgh isolated them even more. A gerrymandered local government 'reform' in 1995, intended to secure them a few bases, failed; so too did the 'return of the Stone'. Divided over Europe, and riven by scandals, they were attacked by further tactical voting in May 1997, and in Scotland wiped out altogether.

The constitutional issue scarcely registered on Major, who moaned about 'the end of a thousand years of history', but was too mired in party conflict to have any effect. Of Labour leaders, only John Smith was really committed; Neil Kinnock and Tony Blair regarded devolution as regrettable if necessary. Blair's commitment in 1996 to a preliminary referendum caused near-mutiny in Scottish Labour's ranks—his new Shadow Secretary, George Robertson, was put in an impossible position—but in fact continued a line started by Smith. Blair wanted to make the Scots responsible for any extra tax powers, allowing him to remain a low-tax man. But the referendum also committed him to early action and he had plenty of Scots in his Cabinet—Chancellor Brown, Foreign Minister Cook, Lord Chancellor Irvine—to remind him of this. The referendum took place on 12 September 1997. It was interrupted by the death of Diana Princess of Wales (the Scots were reserved in their emotions) but, with all the home rule parties working together, the voters came out two to one (64–36 per cent) in favour of a Parliament with tax-raising powers. Legislation managed by Dewar, now Secretary of State, followed with the Westminster stages being completed by September 1998. MPs of all parties save the SNP took little interest, and indeed only six Labour MPs announced they would go north.

Labour squabbled over candidate selection, and got embroiled in scandals in its west of Scotland fortresses, so the SNP seemed well placed for the first Scottish general election on 6 May 1999. Labour's answer was to ship in 'spin-doctors' from London and to campaign under the powerful Chancellor Gordon Brown, rather than Dewar or Blair. Alex Salmond miscalculated with a foreign policy démarche—opposing the bombing of Serbia—which, if diplomatically respectable, put him in the tabloids' crossfire. 'Carrying the war to Slobbo' through the agency of Foreign Minister Cook and NATO General Secretary George Robertson could and did fit snugly with 'Taking a baseball bat to the Nats'. Bombing eliminated the 'body-bag' risk for Whitehall as well as Washington, and as for the costs of a severed Danube waterway and the economic collapse of south-east Europe.

On 1 July 1997 pipes screamed, drums beat, and the British left Hong Kong. 'Empire Made' had been an old joke, but now the place became the pivot of a campaign which swept much of British manufacture away. It helped Scotland's carbon footprint to fall, but if you factored in Chinese and freighter pollution the global impact remained the same.

But with her parliament Scotland reappeared as a piece on the political chessboard she had quit at Câteau-Cambrésis in 1559. In the 1999 election Labour got fifty-six seats and the SNP thirty-five. First Minister Dewar had to coalesce with the Liberal Democrats at seventeen. The Scottish Tories re-entered UK politics with eighteen, and three microparties (Greens, Scottish Socialists, Independent Labour) had one characterful MSP each.

Though called Holyrood, the parliament actually convened from 1999 to 2004 in the Assembly Hall of the Kirk above Edinburgh's Mound. Dewar faced tensions over the size of the block grant and the powers of Whitehall's Scotland Secretary. The latter waned, but Dewar's coalition got an annual 5 per cent increase until 2007. Of 129 MSPs, 37 per cent were women: as a comparison, only 19 women had got to Westminster in the period from 1918 to 1998. A commitment to equality, not fees, marked early higher education reform, where the Cubie Committee settled on a system of loans and grants, but trouble soon started. Holyrood building costs rose twofold. A mischievous English editor on the Labour tabloid *Record* attacked Dewar's attempt to repeal Thatcher's anti-gay legislation by provoking opposition from two likely SNP allies, Brian Souter and Cardinal Thomas Winning. Where Blair spun, Dewar stumbled. The *Record* ran a hostile referendum with 34 per cent voting, and got a majority. But revelations of clerical abuse quietened Winning, who died unexpectedly in 2004, the first of many blows to his Church, while newspaper circulation would more than halve by 2013. Dewar had restored his reputation by summer 2000, when his heart problems spread and rendered a fall on 12 October fatal. The grief that followed betrayed his enemies' immaturity.

Polls showed Holyrood catching Westminster up, even before MPs were demeaned by Blair's behaviour over Iraq in 2002–3 and the expenses scandals. Holyrood's open style of government took advantage of computers and new media; its petitions system gained a world reputation. The place was sober and party discipline loose, a consensus which bored Alex Salmond, who returned to Westminster in autumn 2000. In September 2001the new First Minister, Henry McLeish, supposedly a Gordon Brown ally, was felled by a minor scandal, and Jack McConnell took over with a cabinet reflecting Labour's western fortresses. Though McConnell depended on Blair and was ignored by Brown, the SNP's John Swinney couldn't dislodge him. In the May 2003 election both big parties lost to the Greens (7) and the Scottish Socialists (6), whose leader Tommy Sheridan got warrant sales (compulsory auctions of debtors' goods) banned and even stirred Sean Connery. Of three independents, Margo MacDonald beat the Edinburgh SNP machine and made herself the only real—and ruthless—debater in the place.

24. *A Scottish Parliament committee in session in one of the six striking committee rooms, from which the general public is excluded on only a few occasions. All parts of the building are accessible to wheelchairs, hours are family-friendly, and the agenda has confounded those who thought the Scots illiberal. In 2014 two party leaders – Green and Tory – are gay.*

GLASGOW CALTON AND 'ALBYN PARK'

Glasgow's high-rises had gone the way of her tenements, succeeded by dinky new terraces. Yet the economically inactive nudged 30 per cent, and the life expectation of a man in the East End's Calton Ward (population 22,000, 90 per cent white and Scots) was 54 years in 2006, well below the Gaza Strip (70.5 years). Fast food marinated in fat, cheap alcohol, fags, and drugs pulled down children whose chances were poor from birth. In Calton's heart was the 'Barras', a market turning over £1 billion in fake goods a year. A nearby street had, in 200 yards, four bookies and sixteen 'bandits': electronic gaming machines; Scots put £4 billion a year into them, of which 3 per cent stuck with the operators. Calton wasn't typical, but its facts denied Adam Smith's 'sympathy': it didn't show the London East End synergy of migrant enterprise, but excision from a society whose competitive values excluded moral sense. Failing industry had to sustain a complex social superstructure; upward cash transfers—those 3-percenters—meant absolute losers. So Calton, where the biggest cause of under-thirty death was violence, became 'it'. West Scottish mores propelled Scots crime-writing into 'tartan noir', which paid: meditative fiction did not. James Kelman, Glasgow's Dostoevski, said he earned on average £15,000 a year; Ian Rankin made £1 million a book.

'Manicured lawns, swimming pools, security systems . . . nearby Ryder Cup golf course' was PR-speak for Scotland's 'millionaire's rows'. Such places as 'Albyn Park' irrupted on the northern and southern fringes of the central belt, their houses 'the colour of dead skin' in the journalist Iain MacWhirter's vivid phrase. Nods to decent architects—Adam or Mackintosh—covered quick geld: white goods, luxury, recreation, and above all big 4x4 cars. Building quality? Scottish housing, even expensive stuff, scraped grade C of the European thermal standard. Most German houses got B.

Where did the money come from? Was this 'moral hazard' land, with bankers stashing rip-off bonuses or laundering dodgy cash from the badlands of the West? In 2006 high-end property sold for up to £7 million:

not later. Albyn folk didn't give much away . . . when they were around.
They had other places with better weather to cruise to or play golf at—
Marbella, Florida, the Algarve. The richest 100 (20 per cent from oil, 10 per
cent from construction, 10 per cent from property) weren't liked much,
except when they played good football (few did) or won the lottery: brash
Donald Trump went from hero to zero with an overblown Aberdeen golf
course. Still, grandees from the councils, quangos, or the police rarely
turned down a charity bash in Country Clubland. Where did the law figure
in this? Its corporate power seemed to protect bankers after the collapse of
2008 and the subsequent revelations. Not one got investigated, let alone
jailed. When Scotland's only Leonardo vanished from the Duke of
Buccleuch's Drumlanrig Castle in August 2003 (it returned to Glasgow in
March 2010, via a Liverpool lawyer and a Glasgow cop), no-one was put on
trial. 'A big boy did it and ran away . . .?'

7 | 'DEVO-MAX' OR INDEPENDENCE?
2003–2014

Open the doors! Light of the day, shine in; light of the mind, shine out!
We have a building which is more than a building.
There is a commerce between inner and outer, between brightness and
*   shadow, between the world and those who think about the world.*
Is it not a mystery? The parts cohere, they come together like petals of a flower,
*   yet they also send their tongues outward to feel and taste the teeming earth.*
Did you want classic columns and predictable pediments? A growl of old
*   Gothic grandeur? A blissfully boring box?*
Not here, no thanks! No icon, no IKEA, no iceberg, but curves and caverns,
*   nooks and niches, huddles and heavens, syncopations and surprises.*
*   Leave symmetry to the cemetery.*
But bring together slate and stainless steel, black granite and grey granite,
*   seasoned oak and sycamore, concrete blond and smooth as silk – the mix*
*   is lmost alive – it breathes and beckons – imperial marble it is not!*

When you convene you will be reconvening, with a sense of not wholly the
*   power, not yet wholly the power, but a good sense of what was once in*
*   the honour of your grasp.*
All right. Forget, or don't forget, the past. Trumpets and robes are fine, but
*   in the resent and the future you will need something more.*
What is it? We, the people, cannot tell you yet, but you will know about it
*   when we do tell you.*
We give you our consent to govern, don't pocket it and ride away.
We give you our deepest dearest wish to govern well, don't say we have no
*   mandate to be so bold.*
We give you this great building, don't let your work and hope be other than
*   great when you enter and begin.*
So now begin. Open the doors and begin.

(EDWIN MORGAN, 'Opening the Scottish Parliament',
Holyrood, 9 October 2004)

THE WEATHER IN THE STREETS

In 1981 IBM introduced its desktop computer, some of its floppy-disc development coming from Burroughs at its Glenrothes factory. By 2006 the cyberclearances had emptied Silicon Glen, once the desktop's habitat, and Burroughs had shut, but by then handhelds from the Orient had revolutionised finance, entertainment, and publishing, and brought pervasive problems of surveillance and sabotage. Could people and their values—let alone societies—keep up? 'Social media' was affecting the function and even formation of the brain itself. Young people texted rather than argued, made split-second financial decisions, overstretched the basic inputs. New technology as well as social change brought to the 'estates' of education, religion, law, local government, journalism, broadcasting, and sport, a series of distinct crises, while electricity demand in Scotland went up 30 per cent between 1976 and 2013.

'The others talk about politics, we talk about the weather.' A German Green slogan seemed apt after 2000. The North Atlantic 'jetstream' became erratic, with poor summers and severe winters. Then 2009/10 and 2010/11 brought record-breaking cold, followed in July 2013 by broiling heat. Rain increased fresh water, otherwise a diminishing 3 per cent of the world's blue stuff, and 'weather'—waves, wind, tides, and currents—hosted energy equivalent of 12,000 *million* tons of coal every year: the basis of a 'Saudi Arabia of Renewables' potentially supplying 25 per cent of the EU's electricity. The downside was that Arctic icecap-melt foreboded not just coastal flooding but oceanic acidity and threatened the subsea currents that brought the Gulf Stream north. Could Scotland become a new Labrador?

Human nature didn't help. Scots were elderly, frail, and poor, and second only to Americans in fatness. The population rose to 5.3 million only because of immigration, mainly from 'new' EU countries, notably Poland, and an acceptance of this unusual in the UK as a whole. In a 2013 labour force of 2.75 million, the part-time or self-employed were 35 per cent and growing, while wages in the contact-centres of the 'information economy' in which 137,000 Scots (5%) worked were £300 a week—half what had once been earned in the mines. Scots coal died in 2013. North Sea oil peaked in 1999, when a barrel cost only $10. It then declined, with only 30 per cent of reserves supposedly remaining by 2010, but barrel-price climbed to over $100 and stayed put.

This encouraged Alex Salmond, who returned to the SNP leadership in 2004 and won the Holyrood election on 3 May 2007. The national issue strode centre-stage, with energy—oil, renewables, conservation—its ticket for revival, but in a complex socio-political environment which overshadowed Westminster MPs. Would it last?

The SNP had 47 out of 129 seats. A coalition with the LibDems was expected, but foundered on Salmond's commitment to an independence referendum. The result was a minority government: rare in the UK though frequent in Europe. Veterans compared the FM to Harold Wilson, surviving on a tiny majority in 1964–6, but his pawky *bonhomie* owed more to John Smith, or to the literary-minded Walter Scott's Bailie Nicoll Jarvie. He liked horse-racing (which helped beguile the Queen) and gambled that taking over the civil service was better than sharing a parliamentary majority. John Swinney as Finance Secretary approached the 32 local authorities (nearly all run by coalitions under a new 'single transferable vote' PR system), and quickly gained an 'historic compromise' on powers and finance. Both deals lasted.

Salmond followed Ireland's Eamon de Valera, arguing for 'external association' with the UK rather than becoming a Canadian-style fixer, steering the Union, like Alberta's Peter Lougheed in the 1970s. He held on to the fixed poll date of 5 May 2011, when he won 69 of 129 seats, and slated an independence referendum for 18 September 2014. But in office he had to promote a proto- nation while running a European region whose manufacturing had sunk to 12 per cent of GDP.

'He never writes, he never phones.' Cole Porter gave Salmond his view of life with Tony Blair. On 27 June 2007 Gordon Brown took over at Downing Street. Relations with him were better than McConnell's had been, but Salmond lost the constitutionalist Prof Neil MacCormick to cancer: a loss for a regime stronger on tactics than strategy. Still, Edinburgh was a finance *metropole* in an 'arc of opportunity'—from Finland via Norway, Ireland, Iceland to Portugal—of 'boutique' economies doing better in GDP per capita than Italy and Spain. The prospect of carbon-free power was a bonus to this security. So it looked in early 2008.

CABINET-MAKING

The Lib-Lab coalitions of 1999–2007 had used ministries to reward the faithful. Of their 73 MSPs, 38 would hold office. Salmond chose only 14 out of the SNP's 47 between 2007–11. The Law Officers became non-political, ending a partisanship older than the Union. Five Cabinet Secretaries handled finance, environment, health, education, and justice. These squared the various sections of his party (well-disciplined, anyway). Orthodoxy prevailed under Swinney at Finance, and Nicola Sturgeon knew the labyrinthine NHS mind. Salmond created a Council of Economic Advisers (CEA) to critique policy, as in Roosevelt's USA in the 1920a, but this was pre-empted by a friendly civil service under Sir John Elvidge and Sir Peter Housden, both English.

UK premiers traditionally played off 'supply' against 'spending' ministers. In Scotland, whose block grant increase fell from 5 per cent to 1.8 per cent, the contest was instead between 'talky' and 'silent' ministries. Environment, Culture, and Education spawned argumentative *fora*, but manufacture was now so marginal that quangos like Scottish Enterprise (SE) tended to speak for it; by contrast, rural affairs, agriculture, and local government had well-funded lobbies like the National Farmers Union, the Scottish Fishermen's' Federation, and COSLA. 'He/she knows where the bodies are buried' was a line often applied to this oligarchy, whose economics were obscure and little questioned by a declining press.

Salmond and Swinney had come from Edinburgh finance. The merged Halifax Bank of Scotland dominated the UK mortgage business, and the Royal Bank of Scotland (Salmond was its oil economist, 1982–8) took over the larger National Westminster Bank in 2000. In 2007 its £9.2 billion surplus made up a third of the profits of Scotland's bigger companies. Aided by computers and privatization, notably of the railways in 1997, both banks became hyper-inventive, responding to a takeover fever generated by hedge funds, private equity, and 'structured investment vehicles' (SIVs) whose debt expanded to reduce tax liability. In January 2008 RBS beat Barclays to acquire the Dutch ABN Amro, making it Europe's second-largest bank. Could banks finance renewables as they had boosted oil? Maybe. But their dealers kept a low profile, in bonus-bought country houses.

CASH TO THE PEOPLE

The 32 new Councils were all coalitions save in Labour's fortresses around Glasgow. Swinney 'horse-traded', taking cash from Scottish Enterprise and its Highland counterpart. Council tax (the 20 per cent that the councils raised) was frozen, small businesses granted rate relief, and ring-fenced government grants replaced by agreements to devolve policy choices to councils. But the 1995 single-tier bodies were fragile and unloved. Their Private Finance Initiative (PFI) contracts kept costing, even when sold on and managed from tax havens, though building workers were a stable 6 per cent of the labour force compared to manufacturing. Council professionals stayed with golden handcuffs—or went with golden handshakes when police and fire services were centralized in 2013. Labour's rule was shaken: its Scottish leader, the bright Wendy Alexander, couldn't check Salmond, neither could five successive Scotland Secretaries in Whitehall. On 26 June 2008 the SNP won Glasgow East, Labour's second safest Westminster seat.

Then came the finance earthquake. Chancellor Gordon Brown had replaced his earlier hostility to mergers by enthusiasm for 'light touch regulation'. Dealers inspired by Chicago-school Nobel Prizewinners underwrote 'loaning billions to Homer Simpson'—*the* 'sub-primer' with the self-declared income—while shovelling their bonuses into land, property, or tax havens. But from mid-2007 the 'mortgage banks', starting with Northern Rock, hit liquidity problems. These spread in 2008 to 'monoline insurers' like the giant American AIG. George W. Bush's Treasury saved it, but let Lehman Brothers sink on 16 September that year. The wholesale capital market then dried up, aggravated by illegal 'libor' rate-fixing by bankers. This hit HBoS, then RBS, then the Dunfermline Building Society. Brown's October 2008 innovation of 'quantitative easing' (devaluation) rescued the City, but the Scottish, Irish, and Icelandic finance booms were now exposed as add-ons to the Ponzi-like operations which Big Finance had undertaken through 'regulatory capture'. Some of those responsible—RBS's Fred Goodwin, HBoS's Andy Hornby—were summoned before John McFall's Treasury Select Committee at Westminster. They appeared, apologised and—still uninvestigated—scuttled off with cash denied to their employees and shareholders. Salmond now looked credulous, and a by-election victory at Glenrothes on 6 November saved Brown. The coupling of Scottish finance to Scottish power—in every sense—could not survive this pinstripe Darien.

BLACK FISH TO CHINESE KILTS

Ecological ambitions remained, discussed at Copenhagen (December 2009) and Cancun (November 2010). Yet when a freeze-up promptly closed central belt roads, motorist grievances forced out the transport and climate change minister. His colleagues' car-miles faced a target cut of 21 per cent between 2007 and 2011, but managed only 3 per cent. In Europe and London commuters increasingly used bus, tram, or train, but Scots drove an average 7,000 miles a year. Of Stirling Council's *urban* office-workers only 10 per cent walked or cycled, compared with 39 per cent in Copenhagen. Towns were ringed by giant supermarkets, mail-order firms, call-centres, and retail parks. These brought councils 'development gain', but sapped local shops and suppliers. Dumfries, regarded by Strathclyde University in 1993 as the UK's best small town, seemed 'Tesco'd to death'—and typical—by 2010.

Targets continued to be problematic. By 2010 Edinburgh's attempt at a tram from Leith to the Airport became the EU's worst-managed transport scheme—though it would eventually open in 2014. Peak Oil would overtake the second Forth Road Bridge: 'iconic' for Swinney, it looked obsolete while still on the drawing-board. At its northern landfall, the 65,000 ton 'carcase' of the aircraft-carrier HMS 'Queen Elizabeth' was being assembled at Rosyth. David Cameron, Coalition-Tory PM from May 2010, found that completing it cost less than ending BAe's contract.

In 2007 at Fraserburgh Harbour, on the 'oil coast', two trawlers the size of warships contrasted with stories of skippers burning wooden drifters on the beach because of the Common Fisheries Policy. The Scots liked the EU to annoy the English: UKIP got nowhere in the north. But fishing was sacrosanct, even though aquaculture (£367million) was gaining on traditional catches (£443 million). In 2011–12 some Shetland skippers were convicted of landing at least £37 million worth of 'black fish' at Lerwick, winked at by the industry and unaffected by government supervision. The North Sea was showing signs of near-fatal overfishing.

City-driven 'Mergers and Acquisitions' (2004–7) shadowed the land. In 2005 BP sold its Grangemouth petro-chemical complex to private equity group INEOS; by 2012 it was 50% Chinese-controlled and looking shaky. Scottish & Newcastle was taken over by Carlsberg-Heineken in 2007. S&N had replaced its Scottish breweries with its headquarters; now that closed. The other pillar of 'food-and-drink', Diageo, closed its Kilmarnock and Glasgow sites in 2009 in favour of Fife, where a plant like an oil refinery churned out Smirnoff Vodka *and* Gordon's Gin, *and* grain spirit for blends, *and* alcopops for Scottish teenies. The biggest meat processor, Hall's, sold to Dutch Vion in 2008 (thanks to HBoS bankers), closed in 2012 with the loss of over 2,000 jobs. Scotland had 28 per cent of UK energy jobs; wages at Grangemouth refinery were about £30,000; but in growth areas like online retail, Amazon's huge warehouses paid £200 a week to employees—and little or no tax . . .

The Salmond style was patriotic. Kilts—often in unusual tartans of purple, yellow, black—were near-compulsory at rugby matches and weddings. At odds with 'quality tourism', Chinese-made tartanry was piled high and sold cheap, notably by hard-working Sikhs in the Royal Mile in Edinburgh. 'Homecoming' in 2009 aimed to celebrate 250 years since Burns's birth, revive culture, and meet a 30 per cent growth target, yet the Gathered Clans caused trouble. The weather held up, but the fest didn't pay: small firms ran into debt, recriminations dragged on, and income flat-lined. Burns was the toast of the elderly, while cheap supermarket drink and the smoking ban emptied the village howff as quickly as the kirk; 30 per cent closed between 2007–12.

Social media was inserted in every youthful ear, but reading was a struggle. Primary bairns were cheery and imaginative, but 50 per cent of teenage boys never opened a book for pleasure. The education system was talky but its Curriculum for Excellence didn't challenge: the Modern Studies Association website seemed tied to Wikipedia. At a Holyrood seminar on the '45 only one *teacher* had read Robert Louis Stevenson's *Kidnapped*. Had Holyrood, its services and lobbies, become too attractive an alternative? Yet the Nationalist Club at St Andrews, cradle of the FM himself, had only three members in 2010. The writing was on the skin. Tattooing boomed. From a single studio in 1985 in Glasgow, and 13 in 2005, there were 38 in 2011. The Picti were back.

BOOZE, DRUGS, AND CRIME

Crime fell, but not the view of it—partly through the tabloids, which reached almost 60 per cent of a fast-dwindling market. Soaps, footie, and sex were salted with European records for drugs and drunkenness. In 1975 the Scottish Home Department, sensing the onset of such problems, had funded John Mack and H.-J. Kerner to research *The Crime Industry*—the area between 'moral hazard' and mafia, created by computers, tax havens, and multinationals. Industrial society once balanced the physical effort of the hewer, wright, or horseman with conviviality and political or religious discipline. Its 'service' replacement had at its lower end a complex black economy, perhaps 5 per cent of GDP, which also owed something to the nearby Ulster ghettos. Justice Secretary MacAskill continued Labour's legalism, though drug control and treatment of its victims might have severed a flow which irrigated 'stuff in the West': bankrolling taxis, tanning studios, takeaways, even nurseries.

MacAskill then 'became the story'. On 21 August 2009 he released Abdelbaset al-Megrahi—found guilty in 2001 of the Lockerbie bombing in December 1988—to return to Libya, as his death from prostate cancer seemed imminent. After Whitehall outrage the story emerged of Blair colluding in this to 'turn' Colonel Gaddafi. Holyrood Labour condemned MacAskill, though many held that al-Megrahi had been framed, through shady deals with Middle Eastern terrorists as well as Libya. Al-Megrahi died in May 2012. Gaddafi had been lynched the previous October, in an 'Arab Spring' which soon turned stormy.

Elsewhere Glasgow's 'rest-and-recreation' lifestyle carried off its Labour leader, Stephen Purcell, in late 2009, and far-left matador Tommy Sheridan in 2011. A society which barely paid carers, writers, and inventors blew millions on mysterious football finance, yet matched only 1 per cent of English clubs' TV income. Celtic's millionaires were thrashed *twice* by the amateurs of Ross County. Rangers went down to the Third Division—and the Inland Revenue—in 2012.

THE RENEWABLES CHALLENGE

Scotland's energy role in the 2010s was potentially even bigger than in the oil-rich 1970s, despite manufacturing decline. The new challenge lay in five emerging fields. First, though 30 billion barrels had been extracted by 2011, perhaps 24 billion remained. New extractive technologies could be employed, notably 'Carbon Capture and Storage' (CCS) pumping carbon dioxide from European power stations into existing fields; a two-way gain. Second, low-carbon power could be drawn from the North Sea and Atlantic through wind, wave, and tidal generation. Third, housing could be 'greened' by combining heating by decentralizing generation, or building 'passive' houses which needed minimal heating. Fourth, marine transport through the 'North-East Passage' north of Siberia would cut 7,000 km off the sea-route to Japan and China, and create break-bulk ports in the Orkneys and Shetlands. Finally, this technical momentum could enable Scotland-based engineers to tackle the consequences of sea level rises that would by 2050 threaten half of the world's people. Through offshore engineering and coordinated research, Scotland was uniquely placed to combine such technologies.

But was this reflected in government *organization*? Energy was partly a 'reserved subject' and shared between four Scots ministries. Salmond had yet to build up its financial, training, diplomatic, and legal structure. Germany had pulled round from post-unity strains to refinance manufacture at over 20 per cent of GDP, twice the level of Scotland, where 'offshore' or 'defence' sucked in trained manpower; allowing for population, there were five German engineers to every Scottish one.

Scottish businessmen in summer 2012 ran branch plants and were pessimistic. HBoS, now Lloyds, and RBS, nationalised, went south but stayed feral. The City of London was revived by Olympic Year. Brussels and Paris were scarcely two hours away by Eurostar; elaborate, subsidised public transport linked airports by tube and rapid transit to the lifts of Canary Wharf. Against this, car-dominated central Scotland faced Peak

Oil. 'Europe's Greater Springfield' was back-office, low-wage country, easy pickings for rationalization.

TOWARDS THE REFERENDUM

Labour failed to check Salmond by using the Scotland Office, so it linked with Holyrood Tories and LibDems to promote the Calman Commission (April 2008-June 2009). This offered some new powers over finance, then vanished. But the broadly Scots/social-democrat Liberal leadership ended when Nick Clegg replaced Menzies Campbell as Liberal Democrat leader in 2007, and the downfall of the banks penalised Salmond. In the May 2010 election he was barred from the UK leaders' TV debates. Brown won back his by-election losses (the SNP expected a repeat of May 2007, with 33 per cent and 21 seats; in the end it got only 19 per cent and 6 seats). Campbell continued as MP but vanished from politics.

Holyrood Labour exchanged Wendy Alexander for dour Iain Gray, and late 2010 polls put him 15 points ahead of the SNP. But Cameron's pro-nuclear line and social spending cuts alienated, and on 5 May 2011 the coalition's Scottish vote fell from 33 per cent to 20 per cent. The LibDems, now running the Scotland Office, fell from 14 to 5 MSPs, and saw their 'alternative vote' drop dead UK-wide. Salmond's bid for freedom now defied a Westminster whose Scots' accent faded. Michael Gove, Liam Fox, and Malcolm Rifkind might serve Cameron as English MPs, but Labour's front-bench Scots fell from nine in 2000 to three.

'Independence' got about 30 per cent in the polls, but 'Better Together' didn't describe the Lib-Lab-Tory bearpit. Denying that Scotland would get EU membership, while toying with EU withdrawal? Proposing standing orders to stop Scots MPs (already obscure) voting on English issues? Some Scots Tories even touted federation, a LibDem notion, as doomed in England as the 'alternative vote'. But confederation (a Scandinavian-style association of states) did exist in embryo in the British-Irish Agreement of 1998 . . .

Takeovers and 'reserved' powers sapped Scotland's industry, and in the EU she ran into 'nation-state' hostility to autonomy for Catalonia and

Flanders. There was a long game to play before September 2014. Salmond's economic argument remained: fast-forwarding renewables, in association with such 'non-nuclear' economies as Scandinavia and Germany; copying maritime Norway's case for freedom from agrarian Sweden in 1905. Was he now *aided* by the institutional weakness of the UK itself? Solidarities other than the banks crumbling showed in 2013. The Churches mourned the fallible Cardinal O'Brien; the Murdoch press's phone-tapping embarrassed the Cameron government and the police, and mocked privacy. The BBC's lapses in scrutiny and transparency would have troubled Lord Reith. Among public bodies it was not alone. Coffee chains fiddled their tax; supermarkets flogged dead horses.

Salmond needed a concerted economic case, but took issues one at a time. In 2012 he moved Sturgeon from Health to Infrastructure; his Commons leader Angus Robertson stole Labour's pro-NATO clothes—only just—at the SNP's October conference. Independence still lagged, but the SNP was ahead in the Holyrood polls, and UKIP (now formidable in England) still got nowhere. 'Better Together's unity would inevitably wane as the 7 May 2015 election—*the first date ever to be fixed*—approached. In the referendum 16-year-olds would vote: if you were 16 in 1979 you would remember Welsh devolution going down 20 per cent to 79 per cent on 1 March, but squeaking through in 1997. And if you were a girl? Carol Ann Duffy revived the Poet Laureateship, and Kathleen Jamie gave dash and wit to the environmental critique pioneered by Christopher Smout. Women headed the Tory and Labour parties at Holyrood, while too much of male Scotland, overweight, slumped before the football screen. For how much longer?

Consider the '2014' timetable: European Parliament elections, 5–8 June; Bannockburn 700, 24 June; Scott's *Waverley* 200, 7 July; Glasgow Commonwealth Games, 23 July–3 August; Great War 100, 4 August; Referendum: 'Should Scotland be an independent country?', 18 September; 40th Ryder Cup, Gleneagles, 26–8 September. Such sequences fall rarely. But in a world full of tectonic jolts and tsunamis, Arab springs becoming storms, and rogue finance mocking the law, would any victor treasure power?

ENVOI

Review the *longue durée* of Scotland's history. First, its land-mass— 'wet desert', water-penetrated—was easy to invade but difficult to dominate. Second, this underlay its early-medieval evolution as a multi-ethnic kingdom—Irish, Welsh, Pict, Inglis, Norse—a unity created by negotiation and fairly minimal force. Third, internal balance was secured by external links, whether with England, Europe, or the papacy. Fourth, power was internally devolved to local 'estates' clans, or 'political families' on the land, religious orders which also governed land and education, burghs with their trade, taxation and foreign staples, and courts of law. Fifth, the 'energetic intellect' that was product of such balance became a kind of culture-good, internationally tradable: George Buchanan's *'praefervidum ingenium Scotorum'*.

The downside was a marketism that devalued its product: a tendency to compromise ideals and pursue ambition, a male aggression, most obvious in industry, politics, and sport. *The Red Paper on Scotland*, valuable in 1975, hadn't a woman among its 28 contributors. The insight into the 'thin line between civilisation and barbarism' also scarred. Patrick Geddes's 'Paleotechnics' or carbon-power corroded Scots institutions, alienating the people—chiefly women—whose structure was 'housekeeping'. By 2014 the golf club or football crowd—or the media corps—could often mean Scotsmen behaving badly.

Yet paradoxically, the old industrial skills were demanded as much as the internet, parliament, or care ethic. The new energy sources that lay off

Scotland's shores needed them; the Middle East crisis continued, so more young men would go soldiering. But new networks also became necessary, with a world metropolis on the doorstep, an unrelenting communications revolution, and climate challenge. If Andrew Fletcher saw 'hydrocephalous' London as the nemesis of patriotism in 1707, what had changed?

Christopher Smout, Scotland's most original historian, was an Englishman from the Fens, an artificial land when you thought about it, and his optimism about a future covenant with nature—if severely qualified—was something he shared with the Orcadian Edwin Muir. 'The Horses' symbolised a battle that had to be won:

> . . . Yet they waited,
> Stubborn and shy, as if they had been sent
> By an old command to find our whereabouts,
> And that long-lost archaic companionship.
> In the first moment we had never a thought
> That they were creatures to be owned and used.
> Among them were some half-a-dozen colts
> Dropped in some wilderness of the broken world,
> Yet new as if they had come from their own Eden.
> Since then they have pulled our ploughs and borne our loads,
> But that free servitude still can pierce our hearts.
> Our life is changed. Their coming our beginning.

TIMELINES: 186 DATES IN SCOTTISH HISTORY

1263 Battle of Largs, followed by Scots takeover of Norse possessions, save Orkney and Shetland

1282–3 Edward I conquers Wales

1286 Death of Alexander III

1290 Treaty of Birgham-on-Tweed, giving regnal union with England; abrogated when Margaret of Norway dies

1295–6 'Auld Alliance' with France commences; Edward I invades

1297 Wallace's victory at Stirling Bridge

1305 Wallace executed; Edward's 'Ordinances' for his rule in Scotland

1306 Enthronement of Robert Bruce

1314 Battle of Bannockburn: defeat of Edward II

1320 Declaration of Arbroath sent to Pope

1327–8 Death of Edward II; Treaty of Northampton

1337 Hundred Years War begins between England and France

1349 Black Death strikes for first time

1380 Scots pound no longer linked to English pound

1388 Battle of Otterburn

1400–10 Glendower's rebellion in Wales

1406 Succession, and capture, of James I

1411 Foundation of St Andrews University

1437 Murder of James I

1451 Foundation of Glasgow University

1449–55 James II crushes the Douglases

1460 James II killed by exploding cannon at Roxburgh

1469 Norway cedes Orkney and Shetland to Scots crown

1485 Henry Tudor wins at Bosworth, becomes Henry VII

1488 James IV gains throne after conspiracy against father

1492 Columbus voyages to West Indies

1503 James marries Margaret of England ('Union of Hearts')

1508 Chepman and Myllar's printing press, Edinburgh

1513 Battle of Flodden: defeat and death of James IV

1529–30 James V 'pacifies' Borders

1532 Court of Session

1534 Henry VIII's Act of Supremacy; breach with Rome complete

1707	Act of Union
1712	Patronage Act restoring Landlords' rights to appoint ministers
1714–15	Death of Anne and accession of George I; Jacobite revolt ends at Sherriffmuir
1720	South Sea Bubble
1722	First Scottish railway opened from Cockenzie to Tranent
1728	Trustees for Manufactures and Fisherys
1745–6	Jacobite Rising, ending with battle of Culloden; Scottish Secretaryship abolished
1756–63	Seven Years War with France
1760–1	George III
1762	Ministry of earl of Bute; James Macpherson, *Ossian*
1769	Watt's steam engine patent; Adam Ferguson, *History of Civil Society*
1771	*First Arkwright textile factories in England*
1776	American Colonies revolt; Adam Smith, *Wealth of Nations*
1786	New Lanark Mills opened; Robert Burns, *Poems chiefly in the Scottish Dialect*
1789	*French Revolution*
1791	Sir John Sinclair, *First Statistical Account* (to 1799)
1793	War with France; Burns writes 'Scots wha hae'
1799	Serfdom in Scottish mines and saltworks abolished
1801–3	Peace of Amiens; *Charlotte Dundas* steam-tug on Forth and Clyde Canal; Union with Ireland; first official census
1812	Henry Bell's *Comet*, first European commercial steamer, on Clyde
1814	Sir Walter Scott, *Waverley*
1815	End of French Wars at Waterloo; industrial depression; Corn Law carried
1820	George IV; 'Radical War' climaxes at battle of Bonnymuir
1825–6	Economic slump; partial legalization of trade unions
1828	End of Scottish 'management' by Dundas family
1831	Garnkirk and Glasgow Railway, first steam-operated railway in Scotland
1832	Reform Act; cholera epidemic

1904 *Anglo-French Entente*

1906 Liberal landslide; Sir Henry Campbell-Bannerman premier

1910 George V; constitutional crisis over Budget; two elections; Parliament Act limits power of Lords; industrial unrest in mines, railways, docks increases

1914 Irish Home Rule crisis; First World War breaks out (4 August)

1915–16 'Red Clyde' strikes and disturbances around Glasgow; battles of Jutland and the Sommel; Lloyd George prime minister

1917 *Soviet Revolution in Russia; America enters war*

1918 Reform Act: votes for women over 30; electorate trebled in size; Armistice (11 November)

1920 End of post-war boom; unemployment rises to over 20 per cent

1922 Fall of Lloyd George, Labour breakthrough in elections

1924 First Labour Government under Ramsay MacDonald; Wheatley's Housing Act

1926 General Strike 3–12 May; MacDiarmid's 'A Drunk Man Looks at the Thistle'; BBC gets Charter

1928 National Party of Scotland formed; votes for women over 21

1929 Labour Government; Wall Street Crash; Local Government (Scotland) Act abolishes parish councils and education authorities; United Free Church rejoins Kirk

1931 'National Government' under Ramsay MacDonald

1934 Scottish National Party formed; Scottish Commissioner appointed; Grassic Gibbon completes *A Scots Quair*

1935 *Queen Mary* completed at Clydebank

1938 Empire Exhibition, Glasgow; Munich crisis

1939 Outbreak of Second World War (3 September); Scottish Office moved to Edinburgh; Churchill heads coalition, 10 May

1941 Blitz on British cities; Tom Johnston Secretary of State; USA and Russia enter war

1945 End of war in Europe (8 May); Labour victory; atomic bombs dropped on Japan end war in Far East, 15 August

1946–8 Nationalization of power, gas, transport; creation of National Health Service

1949–51 Korean War; Scottish Covenant movement; Churchill back in
power

1956 Suez Invasion; economic slump cripples heavy industries

1957 *Treaty of Rome sets up European Economic Community*

1961 *Toothill Report* on Scots economy; decolonization

1963–4 *Beeching Report*; Labour in power under Harold Wilso

1966 'A Plan for Scotland'; election; economic slump

1967 Pound devalued; Winnie Ewing, SNP, wins Hamilton

1968 Disturbances in Europe and Ulster; Crowther /Kilbrandon
Commission on the Constitution convened

1969–70 Oil found in North Sea; Neil Armstrong—Langholm man on
moon; Edward Heath in power

1973–4 UK enters EEC; oil-driven crisis; Kilbrandon Report; SNP
successes in February and October elections force devolution
on Labour

1979 Referendum on devolution fails, 1 March; Thatcher wins, 3 May

1984–6 Miners' strike; oil price falls $30 to $10 a barrel; takeover mania;
Guinness scandal; Gorbachev's *perestroika*

1987–8 Tory MPs fall to 10/73; Constitutional Convention; Lockerbie

1989–90 Poll tax; Cold War ends; Thatcher replaced by Major

1997–9 May: Tony Blair's New Labour landslide; July: Hong Kong
handover; devolution referenda: Scotland 74–26%, Wales
50–48%

1998–9 Scotland Act creates 129 MSP parliament; May 1999: Lib-Lab
ministry; Donald Dewar (to Sept. 2000), Henry McLeish FM

2001–3 9/11 crisis; Afghan war, Iraq invasion; economic slump; Jack
McConnell FM, 2001–7

2004 Holyrood parliament building opened; 'light touch' boom

2006 local government: PR voting reform

2007 May: SNP government under Alex Salmond 47/129; Brown PM

2008 October: collapse of Royal Bank of Scotland; Megrahi case

2010–11 May '10: Cameron PM; May '11: Salmond wins Holyrood 69/129

2014 June, Bannockburn 700; July-August: Commonwealth games,
Glasgow; 18 September: Referendum on Scottish Independence.

2015 7 May UK General Election

BIBLIOGRAPHICAL ESSAY

This has to do two things: indicate—admittedly in very general terms—where I got my facts and arguments from, and where the reader can find out more. The stress will be on debates about interpretation, and books with up-to-date bibliographies. Novels and poetry have already been dealt with in the main text, but I have included a brief section on films. Place of publication is London, unless otherwise noted.

GENERAL WORKS

Marinell Ash, in *The Strange Death of Scottish History* (Edinburgh, 1980), argued that Scotland's historians deserted the national cause in the eighteenth and nineteenth centuries, and Colin Kidd, *Subverting Scotland's Past* (Oxford, 1993), blames the Enlightenment Whigs. I don't find this negativity about the Victorians justified. See the work of the 1850s (p. 11), Hume Brown, *History of Scotland* (Cambridge, 1899–1910) and above all W. F. Skene, *Celtic Scotland* (Edinburgh, 1876–81). Is it not more important to relate Scotland to the transnational interpretations of such as Fernand Braudel, *A History of Civilisations* (1987), which were pioneered in Scotland by Adam Ferguson. His *Essay on the History of Civil Society* (1767) has in its 1966 edition a good introduction by Duncan Forbes; his successor was Patrick Geddes; see Helen Meller, *Patrick Geddes: Social Evolutionist and City Planner* (1990).

The raw material is profuse: through the record of digs and finds in the *Proceedings of the Scottish Society of Antiquaries* and reports of the *Ancient Monuments Commission*. The *Old and the New Statistical Accounts* (see pp. 122, 154) and the two Victorian *Ordnance Gazetteers of Scotland* (1860s and 1890s) have much historical material. The *Third Statistical Account* (Edinburgh, 1950–90) is more variable. For current statistical/social data see the various branches of **www.gov.scotland.uk**. The *Encyclopaedia Britannica* (Edinburgh, 1769) had in its 'British' editions, up to the twelfth

(1922) much on Scotland, as did these two late-Victorian monuments the *Dictionary of National Biography* and the *Oxford English Dictionary*, now supplemented by the *Dictionary of Scottish Business Biography* (Aberdeen, 1990) and Michael Lynch, ed., *The Oxford Companion to Scottish History* (Oxford, 2001). Relevant periodicals include *The Scottish History Review* (1910–28, 1947–), *The Innes Review, Scottish Economic and Social History, Scottish Labour History Journal, The Yearbook of Scottish Affairs* (1975–1993), and *Scottish Affairs* (1993–).

Of general histories Rab Houston and Bill Knox, eds., *The New Penguin History of Scotland* (2001) is the latest. James Halliday, *Scotland: A Concise History* (Edinburgh, 1990) comes from a nationalist standpoint, Michael Lynch, *Scotland: A New History* (1991) is strong on religion and politics. J. D. Mackie, *History of Scotland* (1964; Harmondsworth, 1978) has proved robust, though sketchier after 1745. The *Edinburgh History of Scotland* (Archie Duncan, *The Making of the Kingdom*, 1975; Ranald Nicholson, *The Later Middle Ages*, 1974; Gordon Donaldson, *James V-VII*, 1965, and William Ferguson, *1689 to the Present*, 1968) remain basic, though there is much new material in the eight volumes of the *New History of Scotland*, particularly on the earlier and later periods. Whatley and Donnachie, eds., *The Manufacture of Scottish History* (Edinburgh, 1992) unpicks some of the key controversies. On Anglo-Scottish history even a good British account, Kenneth O. Morgan, ed., *The Oxford Illustrated History of Britain* (Oxford, 1984), is variable about Scotland, but fits it into the politics of the British Isles, as does Sandy Grant and Keith Stringer, eds., *Uniting the Kingdom* (1998).

Chalmers Clapperton, *Scotland: A New Study* (Newton Abbot, 1983) contributes studies from physical and human geography. For the arts see Cairns Craig, ed., *A Literary History of Scotland* (4 vols., Aberdeen, 1988–90), Duncan Macmillan, *Scottish Art, 1460–1990* (Edinburgh, 1989) and John Purser, *Scotland's Music* (1992). Glendinning, MacInnes, and MacKenzie, *A History of Scottish Architecture* (Edinburgh, 1996) and Douglas Gifford and Dorothy McMillan, eds., *A History of Scottish Women's Writing* (Edinburgh, 1997). Useful editions of primary sources include Gordon Donaldson, *Scottish Historical Documents* (Edinburgh, 1970), Christopher Smout and Sydney Wood, *Scottish Voices, 1745–1960* (1990), and Louise Yeoman, *Reportage Scotland* (Edinburgh, 2000).

CHAPTER 1

Gordon Menzies, *Who Are the Scots?* (1971), with sections by Stuart Piggett and others, usefully resumes Scottish prehistory, thanks to new technology a burgeoning area of research, for which news stories are often the best record. Barry Cunliffe's *Facing the Ocean* (Oxford, 2000) is magisterial, but I still find myself convinced by Alexander Thom's argument for Stone Age observations in *Megalithic Sites in Britain* (Oxford, 1967), and I largely accept his thesis. Peter Salway, *Roman Britain* (Oxford, 1981), and J. N. L. Myres, *The English Settlements* (Oxford, 1986) have recently been supplemented by Fiona Watson's *In Search of Scotland* (BBC-TV series and book, edited by Gordon Menzies, Edinburgh, 2001). Forget about Simon Schama, whose eye rarely travels north of Watford, but see or read John Davies on *The Celts* (2000); Lloyd and Jenny Laing, *Picts and Scots* (Stroud, 1993) has valuable illustrations. In the *New History* Alfred P. Smyth, *Warlords and Holy Men: Scotland 80–1000* (1984), tackles the 'heroic age', and see David M Wilson, *The Vikings and their Origins* (1970). Dauvit Broun, *The Irish Identity of the Kingdom of the Scots* (1999) sorts out the accounts of the origin of the nation, and D. A. Binchy, *Anglo-Saxon and Celtic Kingship* (Oxford, 1970) supplies comparisons. Robert Bartlett, *The Making of Europe* (1993) is a challenging recent survey which along with C. M. Cipolla, *Before the Industrial Revolution, 1000–1700* (1976) contextualizes the material in Gordon Donaldson, *Scottish Kings* (1967) and Geoffrey Barrow, *The Anglo-Norman Era in Scottish History* (Oxford, 1980).

CHAPTER 2

Geoffrey Barrow, *Kingship and Unity: Scotland, 1000–1306* (1981) deals with the long Anglo-Scottish peace, Sandy Grant, *Independence and Nationhood, 1306–1469* (1984) with its breakdown. It is usefully seen against Bartlett, *England under the Norman and Angevin Kings, 1075–1225* (Oxford, 2000), and Rees Davies, ed., *The British Isles, 1100–1500* (Edinburgh, 1988). Michael Prestwich, *Edward I* (1988) and Fiona Watson, *Under the Hammer* (Phantassie, 1999) set out Edward's invasion and Barrow, *Robert Bruce and the Community of the Realm* (Edinburgh, 1988) the Scots response. Jennifer M. Brown, ed., *Scottish Society in the Fifteenth Century* (1977) can be supplemented by

Michael Brown, *James I* (Edinburgh, 1994) from the series *The Scottish Kings*. For background see J. A. Dwyer, ed., *New Perspectives on the Politics and Culture of Early Modern Scotland* (Edinburgh, 1982), and the earlier essays in Norman MacDougall, ed., *Church, Politics and Society: Scotland 1408–1929* (Edinburgh, 1983). T. C. Smout, ed., *Scotland and Europe 1200–1850* (Edinburgh, 1986) covers external relations. There are still many lacunae, not least for the plagues, trade, and taxation. S. G. E. Lythe and John Butt, *An Economic History of Scotland* (Glasgow, 1995) has a little pre-Reformation material, as does Rosalind K. Marshall, *Virgins and Viragos* (1983) on women in Scotland. See also Spearman and Lynch, eds., *The Scottish Medieval Town* (Edinburgh, 1988) and Peter Yeoman, *Medieval Scotland* (1995) for the urban and rural landscape. Jenny Wormald, *Lords and Men in Scotland: Bonds of Manrent 1442–1603* (Edinburgh, 1985) absorbingly explores the link between feudalism and the age of contract.

CHAPTER 3

To balance Angus Calder, *Revolutionary Empire* (1980) and Christopher Smout's still-striking, *A History of the Scottish People, 1560–1830* (1969) is to get an overview of the 'general crisis' period, much clarified by Grant and Stringer. Christopher Hill, *Reformation to Industrial Revolution, 1530–1780* (1969) summates the Marxian interpretations, while Jenny Wormold, *Court, Kirk and Community, 1470–1625* (1981), Rosalind Mitchison, *Lordship to Patronage, 1603–1745* (1993), and Rab Houston, ed., *Scottish Society, 1500–1800* (Cambridge, 1989) supplement it. Smout has also been controverted by essays in *People and Society in Scotland* (3 vols., Edinburgh, 1988–92), and Tom Devine, *The Scottish Nation, 1680–2000* (1999). There is as yet no Scottish equivalent to Anne Laurence, *Women in England, 1500–1760* (1994), but its sociological approach is valuable.

Roger A. Mason, *Kingship and the Commonwealth* (Phantassie, 1998) and David Stevenson, *The Covenanters* (Edinburgh, 1988) cover the complexities of Scottish religious politics, as does Terry Brotherstone, ed., *Covenant, Charter and Party* (Aberdeen, 1990). Christopher Whatley, *Bought and Sold for English Gold?* (Edinburgh, 1994) provides a compact entrée into the debates on the Union; with three of the worthies of the period vignetted in Antoin E. Murphy, *John Law* (Oxford, 1997), David Daiches, ed., *Fletcher of Saltoun: Writings and Speeches* (Edinburgh, 1979), and John Prebble, *The Darien Disaster* (1968).

CHAPTER 4

Devine, *Scottish Nation*, has its strength in demography, agriculture, and urbanization. In the debate on the Enlightenment George Elder Davie in *The Scottish Enlightenment* (Edinburgh, 1991) confronts Nicholas Phillipson in J. N. Wolfe, ed., *Government and Nationalism in Scotland* (Edinburgh, 1969) and in Mitchison and Phillipson, eds., *Scotland in the Age of Improvement* (Edinburgh, 1970). Campbell and Skinner, eds., *The Origins and Nature of the Scottish Enlightenment* (Edinburgh, 1982) and John Robertson, *The Scottish Enlightenment and the Militia Issue* (Edinburgh, 1985) raise a key aspects of ideology while Carter and Pittock, eds., *Aberdeen and the Enlightenment* (Aberdeen, 1987) shows the regional nature of 'improvement'. Andrew Hook has edited *The History of Scottish Literature*, vol. ii: *1660–1800* (Aberdeen, 1987) and written *From Goosecreek to Gandercleugh*, on Scots-American cultural relations (Phantassie, 1999).

Christopher Whatley, *The Industrial Revolution in Scotland* (Edinburgh, 1999), and Roy Campbell, *The Rise and Fall of Scottish Industry* (Edinburgh, 1980) can be profitably compared with the regional treatments in Sidney Pollard, *The Economic Development of Modern Britain* (1974). H. W. Meikle, *Scotland and the French Revolution* (Glasgow, 1912) remains a good account, supplemented from the 'government' side by Michael Fry, *The Dundas Despotism* (1992) and *The Scottish Empire* (Phantassie, 2001).

CHAPTER 5

Smout's *A Century of the Scottish People* (1983) isn't infallible: sketchy on law, technology, and entrepreneurship, failings shared with Devine, but like him good on agriculture and urbanization, and exceptional on living standards and styles. Bill Knox, *Industrial Nation* (Edinburgh, 1999), updates Campbell, but is stronger on labour than on business. Tom Nairn, *The Break-up of Britain* (1978) and Lindsay Paterson, *The Autonomy of*

Modern Scotland (Edinburgh, 1994) examine the politics of the 'union state'. Ian Hutchison, *A Political History of Scotland, 1832–1924* (Edinburgh, 1885) creates a context for many detailed studies, and for nationalism see Richard Finlay, *Independent and Free* (Edinburgh, 1994).

G. E. Davie, *The Democratic Intellect* (Edinburgh, 1961) debates with Robert Anderson, *Education and Social Mobility in Victorian Scotland* (Oxford, 1983), both supplemented by Humes and Paterson, ed., *Scottish Culture and Scottish Education* (Edinburgh, 1983). Irene Maver, *Glasgow* (Edinburgh, 2000) deftly summarizes the three-volume history of *Glasgow* (Manchester, 1990–9) which is also excellent on the engineering economy. For the 'middling sort' see Olive Checkland, *Philanthropy in Victorian Scotland* (Edinburgh, 1980) and R. Q. Gray, *Labour Aristocrats in Victorian Edinburgh* (1980). On religion see Callum Brown, *The Social History of Religion in Scotland* (1987) and Jay Brown, *Thomas Chalmers and the Godly Commonwealth* (Oxford, 1982); Tom Gallagher, *Glasgow—The Uneasy Peace* (Manchester, 1987). Gallagher and Walker, eds., *Sermons and Battle Hymns* (Edinburgh, 1990) and Graham Walker, *Intimate Strangers: Scotland and Ulster in Modern Times* (Edinburgh, 1995) cover the fraught area of religious militancy.

CHAPTER 6

Recent Scottish history has had a volcanic output, besides the material which can be accessed on the Web—though few Scots books get noticed in England! Harvie, *No Gods and Precious Few Heroes* (1981 and later editions) is still the only general account of recent history. It has six pages of dense bibliography. Iain Hutchison, *A Political History of Twentieth Century Scotland* (2000) updates Fry until the 1970s while Neal Ascherson, *Games with Shadows* (1988) and Tom Nairn *After Britain* (2000), along with Gerry Hassan and Chris Warhurst, eds., *A Different Future* (Glasgow, 1999) survey ideas and policies since 1979.

Alexander Cairncross, ed., *The Scottish Economy* (Cambridge, 1950) surveyed an economy little changed since Edwardian times; Richard Saville, ed., *The Economic Development of Modern Scotland, 1950–80* (Edinburgh, 1985) shows where it went. Gordon Brown, ed., *The Red Paper on Scotland*

(Edinburgh, 1985) contains a lot about the oil-boom/nationalist years. A guide to the editor's future politics it is not. For narrative see Harvie, *Fool's Gold: The Story of North Sea Oil* (1994) and Harvie and Peter Jones, *The Road to Home Rule* (Edinburgh, 2000), while William Miller, *The End of British Politics* (Oxford, 1981) analyses a key shift in political behaviour, and David McCrone *Understanding Scotland* (1985) rounds up the sociologists.

G. E. Davie, *The Crisis of the Democratic Intellect* (Edinburgh, 1986) pursues his argument into the age of MacDiarmid. He figures along with Geddes and other savants in MacDiarmid, *The Company I've Kept* (1966). Craig Beveridge and Ronald Turnbull, *The Eclipse of Scottish Culture* (Edinburgh, 1989) and *Scotland after Enlightenment* (1996) carry on Davie's debate, and national ambiguity is displayed and worried over in Carl MacDougall, *Painting the Forth Bridge* (2001).

Rounding Up 2002–2014

. . . is best done across different modes as this shows a changing historical culture, summarised in the essays in Ted Cowan, ed., *Why Scottish History still Matters* (Edinburgh, 2013): a way into major projects such as the *New Edinburgh History* and on-line identification of centres and people.

This 'social impact' ranges from the late Colin Matthew's superb bequest of the *Oxford DNB* of 2004 (accessible online via your library card) to Alastair Moffat's publicising of recent archaeology and DNA research in *The Scots: A Genetic Journey* (Edinburgh, 2012), and his 'Tapestry of Scotland' project. The essays in Tom Devine and Jenny Wormald's *Oxford Handbook of Modern Scottish History* (Oxford, 2012) present much recent research. The tapestry (almost 100% woman-stitched) is male-dominated, the *Handbook*'s index disappointing, but Chris Smout's 'Land and Sea' essay (and his and Mairi Stewart's study of *The Forth*) are as much game-changers as his *Scottish People* was in 1969. New studies of the medieval/early modern period by Julian Goodare, Roger Mason, and Keith Brown have valuably reassessed the 'Great British' politics of 1485–1688 surveyed by Jenny Wormald in J. C. D. Clark's *A World by Itself* (London, 2010)—interpreting a confederal Britain that continued after 1707 on a civic scale, resumed by CTH's *Floating Commonwealth* (Oxford, 2008) on the Atlantic in the steam age, 1860–1930. Richard Finlay and Catriona MacDonald in *Modern Scotland* (London, 2004) and *Whaur Extremes Meet* (Edinburgh, 2009), broaden understanding of the reified nation of last century. For present discontents see Iain MacWhirter's *Road to Referendum* (Glasgow, 2013) and the year-by-year coverage of politics and society in Lindsay Paterson and Eberhard Bort's quarterly *Scottish Affairs*.

Online offerings are variable. Wikipedia's local entries range from good (Coatbridge, Kirkcaldy) to terrible (Motherwell, Airdrie). Websites like 'The Scottish Review' (see also Ken Roy's *Invisible Spirit*; Prestwick, 2013), 'Bella Caledonia', and *The Scottish Review of Books* repay visiting, but the economic collapse of 2008 has carried off the Scottish quality press— and investigative journalism. Numptocrats in financial services and 'arms-length' quangos are bearing up nevertheless.

Finally . . . Classic Films

Alfred Hitchcock's *The Thirty-Nine Steps* (1935) gets the spirit of John Buchan, while taking liberties with everything else. John Baxter's *The Ship-builders* (1942) is a decent adaptation of George Blake's novel of the Clyde in the slump, while Orson Welles's *Macbeth* (1948) and Vincente Minelli's *Brigadoon* (1954) convey Hollywood's Scotland at its most weird and wonderful. Sandy Mackendrick slipped a Mickey Finn into Ealing's lemonade: besides *Whisky Galore* (1949), *The Maggie* (1953), about a puffer-skipper, as decrepit as his boat, swindling credulous Yanks, is lyrical, witty, and pessimistic. Bill Forsyth's *Local Hero* (1983) is an affectionate variation on the same theme, spun off from the oil boom. Instead of the inevitable *Braveheart* and *Trainspotting* (both 1996), sample John Byrne's *Tutti-Frutti* (1987), its ageing rockers funny and tragic about Macho Mac. Michael Caton-Jones's *Rob Roy* (1995), with a script by Alan Sharp, is variable, but Tim Roth brilliantly suggests Scott's loathsome Francis Osbaldistone. Peter Watkins's *Culloden* (1963), Bill Douglas's *Trilogy* (1972–8), Bill Forsyth's adaptation of George Mackay Brown's *Orkney* (1981), and John McGrath's *The Long Roads* (1995) are all made-for-television masterpieces. The best? Harry Watt's *Night Mail* (1936), words by Auden, music by Britten: John Grierson's 'creative treatment of actuality' made celluloid.

PUBLISHER'S
ACKNOWLEDGEMENTS

We are grateful for permission to reprint extracts from the following
poems:

Hugh MacDiarmid: 'On a Raised Beach' and 'A Drunk Man Looks at
The Thistle', from *Complete Poems* in 2 Volumes (Carcanet, 1993/1994),
reprinted by permission of Carcanet Press Ltd

Edwin Muir: 'Scotland 1941' and 'The Horses', from *Complete Poems* (ASLS,
1991), copyright © the Estate of Edwin Muir, reprinted by permission of
Faber & Faber Ltd.

We have made every effort to trace and contact all copyright holders before
publication. If notified, the publisher will be pleased to rectify any errors or
omissions at the earliest opportunity.

INDEX

G

N